THE GIFT OF OUR WOUNDS

THE GIFT
OF OUR
WOUNDS

A Sikh and a Former White Supremacist
Find Forgiveness After Hate

ARNO MICHAELIS AND **PARDEEP SINGH KALEKA**

WITH **ROBIN GABY FISHER**

ST. MARTIN'S PRESS 🐾 NEW YORK

www.stmartins.com

Author's note: Some names and some identifying details have been changed.

Design by Kelly S. Too

The Library of Congress Cataloging-in-Publication Data is available upon request.

ISBN 978-1-250-10754-1 (hardcover)
ISBN 978-1-250-10755-8 (ebook)

First Edition: April 2018

10 9 8 7 6 5 4 3 2 1

This book is dedicated to the people who lost
their lives on August 5, 2012, and all of the victims,
past and future, of hatred and violence.

Forgiveness is a sublime example of humanity that I explore at every opportunity. Because it was the unconditional forgiveness I was given by the people I once claimed to hate that demonstrated the way from there to here.

—Arno Michaelis

Forgiveness is the ultimate vengeance against hatred. "Ek Onkar" means "Our Creator is One." It is in this Sikh foundation that we are being called upon to respond with healing the wounds of the past.

—Pardeep Singh Kaleka

CONTENTS

ACKNOWLEDGMENTS

PARDEEP

I would like to thank our entire communal family domestically and abroad who have fostered transformative healing in the aftermath of hate. Because of your love, our community was uplifted and continues to heal.

It is in the love of my mother, Satpal Kaleka, and father, Satwant Kaleka; and support of my brother, Amardeep, and the entire Kaleka and Nagra family that I have had the opportunity to find my purpose and strength. It is in my loving wife, Jaspreet Kaleka, that I have had the support needed to find my dreams. And it is in the eyes of my four beautiful children, Amaris, Jai, Rohan, and Taran, that I have been able to find vision.

This memoir is in deep gratitude for my homeland of Punjab, India, and my new homeland of America. As a first-generation immigrant raised in Milwaukee, I have truly been nurtured by countless family, friends, and communities who affirm that this country and this dream are worth fighting for.

Thanks to Jennifer Benjamin, who one day proposed the idea of writing a book because she believed in the mission of seeing humanity in one another. From that spark began a process. Thank you Elizabeth Evans, Jennifer Weltz, and Karen Wolny for the continuous support and guidance; none of this is possible without you. Robin Gaby Fisher, you have been our serenity, voice, and strength, and yes, we are connected for life, just as you told us the first time we met.

Arno, you have become my brother, confidant, teacher, and personal therapist. My strength when I felt weak, and a true ally to our small community. You exemplify both the excellence of Sikhism and the humanity. You model transformation, and remind us that forgiveness, courage, and compassion start the process of reclamation.

Our work could not be possible without genuine relationships of mutual love. Thank you to the entire team at Arts@ Large, who have helped Serve 2 Unite foster peace and empower students and communities to see solutions within themselves. Today as a therapist, my work could not be possible without the guidance of my colleagues at D&S Healing, Alma Center, and the *Milwaukee Independent*, who remind me that healing the wounds of the past is a gift to us all.

ARNO

Everything I do is for my daughter. For her, I strive to bring about a society where all are valued and included, as I want her to be. Everything I am wouldn't be possible without the eternal, undaunted love of my mom and dad, and my little brother. I know I put you all through hell. I can only hope that the work I'm doing today makes you proud and makes going through said hell at least somewhat worthwhile. Thank you for never giving up on me.

Massive thanks to Robin Gaby Fisher, for doing all the heavy lifting to make this book happen, and for the love you've given us. And I'll double down on thanking Jennifer Benjamin, Elizabeth Evans, Jennifer Weltz, and Karen Wolny for each having a crucial role in bringing our story to the world.

The entire Kaleka family, and the Sikh community around the world—I am such a lucky guy to count you all as kinfolk.

Pardeep, we've known each other a little over five years now and every day I find new reasons to be grateful for your friendship and inspired by our brotherhood. You have taught me so much about what it means to be a man and what it means to be a human being. At your side, I have realized my life's dream of waging peace professionally. Together we have reached so many young people that I can't help but feel great about the future they will create.

All of the wonderful students, educators, and Global Mentors who have made Serve 2 Unite the engine of peace that it is today. You all lift me up when I feel discouraged, and inspire me to be the best I can be.

Big ups to all of the peacebuilding orgs around the world that I've been so fortunate to collaborate with. Listing all of them and all of the brilliant individuals therein would be another book unto itself. Maybe the next one.

Finally, I must thank Chris and Melissa Buckley, and their lovely children, my nephew and niece, CJ and Miera. So proud of all of you!

What does hate look like?

Hate looks like the body of a devoted mother of two teen-age boys, crumpled inelegantly on a cold tile floor near the altar where she had been praying moments before her death. It looks like a young husband and father the way his little girl last saw him—his face ravaged by the fatal bullet that ripped through his eye and blew his head apart. And the kindly family man who lay in a vegetative state, with no hope of awakening, while his wife and children sat at his bedside praying for a miracle. And the tortured expression of a leader, mortally wounded, as he tried but failed to save his flock and himself.

Hate looks like the bullet hole in the doorframe leading into the prayer room at the Sikh Temple of Wisconsin—a vestige of the carnage that took place there on August 5, 2012, when a troubled man with a distorted view of what America should look like executed peaceful people inside.

Life goes on. Services still take place at the same time every Sunday. Congregants continue to worship in the prayer room. All people are welcome to the *langar* (kitchen) for the free communal meal. Families who lost loved ones persevere as they continue to pick up the pieces of their shattered lives.

The bullet hole remains, now enshrined with a tiny plaque inscribed with the message WE ARE ONE.

The victims were devout souls who strived to follow the tenets of their Sikh faith to live a meritorious life of honest hard work and service to others and God. Spiritual beings who graced this earth with love, inspiration, and *Chardi Kala*. Translated from Punjabi, the language of the Indian region where the Sikh religion was founded, Chardi Kala means "relentless optimism."

So why would anyone seek to harm these good people? Why would someone take the lives of his fellow human beings with such senseless cruelty?

Because hurt people hurt people. Because when suffering isn't treated with compassion, it seethes and spreads. Because when fear isn't met with courage, it deceives and disconnects humans from humanity. When ignorance isn't countered with wisdom, it festers and takes root in the hearts of the fearful. When hatred isn't cradled with kindness, it can corrupt the beauty of existence to the extreme that causing suffering is the only thing that makes sense anymore.

The killer, once as innocent and lovely a child as any other, became mired in a cycle of misery that ended in tragedy at the Sikh Temple of Wisconsin.

. . . And brought us together.

Rather than cultivate hatred with vengeance, we choose to commemorate our lost loved ones with the glory and grace of our common humanity. We choose to sow seeds of kindness and compassion.

Monsters are not created by God. They are shaped by the society we live in. By us. The ingredients that make monsters are hatred, suffering, isolation, and minimization. Seven people died that day, including the shooter, because one man's untreated suffering was inflamed by fear, ignorance, and rage. What if, instead, it had been met with compassion, courage, and wisdom?

If we can find the strength to forgive the one who took the others, we can answer the tragedy with unconditional love for the entire human race. We can address conflict with care and cooperation. We can meet fear, ignorance, and hatred by teaching truth. We can shape the reality we create collaboratively to be one of uplift and healing.

We can live in honor of Paramjit Kaur and Suveg Singh Khattra and Prakash Singh and Ranjit Singh and Sita Singh and Satwant Singh Kaleka; of the lives lost in Oklahoma City and at Columbine, Sandy Hook, the movie theater in Aurora, Colorado, the Boston Marathon, the Emanuel AME Church in Charleston, South Carolina, the Pulse nightclub in Orlando, Florida, the bicycle path in New York City; and of the people dying every day on the north side of Milwaukee, and on the South Side of Chicago, and in Syria, Afghanistan, the Holy Land, Mexico, Africa . . .

We can find the gift in the wound

. . . if we can forgive
. . . with vengeance
. . . with purpose
. . . with love.

ONE

A MEETING

Freedom is not an achievement but an opportunity.
Bhagat Puran Singh

October 2012

Pardeep

The shaggy block on Milwaukee's east side was dark, save for a single flickering streetlight and the neon glow coming from a string of ethnic restaurants. I arrived a few minutes early and parked my car at the curb, on the opposite side of the street from the Thai place. Arno recommended we meet there. It was his hangout, he said. I'd know it by the red vinyl awning and flashing CARRY OUT sign.

I left the car running while I waited. The rhythmic sound of the wiper blades scraping freezing drizzle from the windshield was almost hypnotic, though not enough to slow my racing thoughts. I wondered if maybe it had been a mistake to get there early. It gave me too much time to think. Too much time to back out.

More than once I shifted into gear, and then didn't leave.

Why did I stay? I've asked myself that a million times. I think it was that my need for answers outweighed the misgivings I had about being there. Still, sitting in my idling car, I wondered if I should have listened to my mother when she begged me not to go, lest I end up like my father, a victim of violence. She had asked why I was so blind to the dangers of the world, as he was, always seeking the good in everyone. Look where it had gotten him! Look where it had gotten us! We were a family without a husband or a father. Victims of the kind of senseless hate crime that most people only read about. A tragedy from which there would be no return to the good life we once knew.

————

A LITTLE OVER two months had passed since August 5, when my father and five other Sikhs were executed in our peaceful Wisconsin temple by a self-avowed white supremacist. Two of the victims were brothers, both with families and young children. The only woman killed left behind two teenage boys. Others had suffered grave injuries. Lt. Brian Murphy, the heroic police officer who was cornered by the killer and shot fifteen times at close range, survived by the grace of God. Baba Punjab Singh, a Sikh priest, a husband, and a father, was shot in the head and is still in a coma, likely never to regain consciousness.

From the start I'd been haunted by the question of "Why?" I wondered about it day and night. I couldn't ask the killer because he was dead. So who could tell me why he had chosen our place of worship? Why he'd gone after such peaceful people—men, women, and children whose religion was based on the practice of harmony and equality for all people? And yes, I'll admit it, I asked myself the question, "Why us?" Why had we been put through this hell? Because we had brown skin and wore turbans? Because we were mistaken for Muslims? The Taliban? ISIS? Because people were uninformed about who we were and where we came from? Although others ascribed to the theory that the shooter was targeting Islam, I thought it was as likely he chose our temple because it was open to everyone and secreted behind the crest of a hill. A soft target, if you will. But even if it were true that he mistook us for Muslims, how did that change the tragedy of innocent people murdered because they were different from the shooter's idea of what America should look like? Would such an act be somehow less horrifying, or more justifiable, if the victims read the Quran and worshipped Allah?

I remembered going to Dad's gas station after September 11 to support him in case of any misunderstandings. His English wasn't good enough to explain that we were not terrorists, or even Muslim. It felt strange having to differentiate ourselves back then, but ignorance about Islam and the backlash against Muslims after the terrorists identified as such made me feel as if I had to explain who we were. We were Sikhs who loved our adopted country and whose hearts were broken just like everyone else's by the attack. I discovered then that a little education went a long way to understanding. Our customers did ask questions about our faith and our homeland

and we answered all of them with the same respect with which they were asked. Luckily, we didn't need to defend ourselves. Dad had taught by example during his time here. His customers knew his heart. If only the shooter had been able to know my father, to know our people, he and the others might still be with us.

Was I angry? Hell yes. My anger was eating me alive. The head of our family had been violently taken and we were all struggling to find our places in this new and terrible reality. Everything was different now. My mother didn't want to live and my brother seethed with rage and bitterness. Time hadn't healed my grief or frustration either. I didn't know how much longer I could control the feelings I had locked inside, but I couldn't continue to wallow in cynicism and gloom. That would be a stain on my father's legacy. It went against everything he stood for, all that he was.

I was always surprised at how little people knew about the Sikh faith. Sikh means "learner," and our religion teaches us that teaching and learning, and learning and teaching, are the basis for our lives. We worship in the *Gurudwara*, "the door leading to God." Our theology is based on love, equality, and service to God and all others. Many Sikh men wear turbans and have beards in honor of our cultural and religious heritage. In India, the turban is a sign of valor. But, especially since Osama bin Laden, the turban has become an object of enmity in America. People see it and think *terrorist*, but that couldn't be further from the truth. Maintaining uncut hair is an expression of accepting God's will, and the turban is a symbol of our commitment to our faith. A man in America who is wearing a turban is almost without exception an Indian Sikh, and those bearded, brown-skinned men are less likely to commit violence than just about anyone on earth. They're much more apt to take in stray dogs or deliver meals to homeless people living on the streets.

Ours is a gentle, benevolent faith. We believe that everyone is equal before one Creator and that a good life is lived truthfully and in service to others. Our scriptures don't dwell on what happens after death but focus on our earthly duties. From an early age, we are encouraged to live as *sant-sipahi*, those who strike a balance of cultivating spirituality while also contributing socially to our communities. We are bound by the Golden Rules of our religion, as taught by Guru Nanak Dev, the first Sikh Guru: *Kirat Karo*—work hard and honestly; *Vand Chhako*—share what you have with those who are less fortunate; *Naam Jappo*—always remember God throughout the day.

Perhaps most importantly, our scriptures tell us that forgiveness is the only way to heal. My father was a student of the Guru Granth Sahib, our Holy Book, which we interpret as the living word of God. Dad strived every day to follow Sikh principles. I know he forgave his killer before he took his dying breath, but I needed answers to be able to get to that place.

WAITING FOR ARNO to arrive, I pictured my mother's face as she pleaded with me not to go. She had aged considerably in the short time since my father's murder. Grief had cut deep lines in her skin, and her once lustrous brown eyes were dull above moons of dusky shadows. Her suffering was so potent that sometimes it seemed to seep from her pores. She had lost the only man she ever loved, her husband of nearly forty years, the father of her two children. With him went her faith in the sanctity of our adopted country—a place she and my father loved so much that, as new immigrants, they'd erected a flagpole in our front yard and flew the red, white, and blue every day until my father's death. The irony was inescapable. My father, an American patriot, a proud immigrant who moved his young wife and two small boys from their poor farming town in India and assimilated into Midwestern culture through hard work and community service, murdered because his skin was brown and he wore a turban.

How could I not seek answers for that?

As my mother begged me to reconsider my meeting, my wife, Jaspreet, looked on, her brow creased with concern. "You have our children to think about, Pardeep," she said softly. Yes, two kids and a third on the way. Jaspreet was just weeks shy of her due date. I knew what she and Mom were thinking. I had never met this man with the violent racist past. How could I be sure he really had rehabilitated himself? Once a white supremacist, always a white supremacist, right? Yes, that was their fear, and maybe mine, too.

So what was I doing here? Jaspreet and Mom had been right to question my judgment. My introduction to Arno was through email. Anything I knew about him I'd learned second-

and thirdhand and from searching his name on the internet. How did I know I wasn't walking into an ambush? Arno was one of the founders of the same racist skinhead group that my father's killer belonged to. He had disavowed the group years earlier, but what was the point of taking the risk? What was I going to ask him? Mom had wondered, tears welling up in her eyes. What could he say that would matter? Dad was dead and nothing was going to bring him back.

What remained of my resolve was melting away with each swish of the wipers. How could I subject my family to more fear and uncertainty than they were already feeling? To what end? Mom and Jaspreet were right. This had been a crazy idea.

I threw the car into drive. Just as I did—as if on cue— a tall, lanky man dressed in dark clothing and a hoodie covering his head walked out of the mist. Holding my foot on the brake, I watched as he crossed the street. I didn't think he could see me, not in the dark and the rain. I figured it had to be Arno, and when he ducked into the Thai restaurant I was certain it was. Was it by chance that he appeared at the exact moment I was preparing to leave? My Sikh religion taught that all things happen according to the will of God. I remembered reading an analogy comparing the Sikh philosophy of fate to the orbiting of the earth. Although the earth revolves around and is influenced by the sun, it also has its own motion. So whatever it was that brought me here, I thought, the next move was mine.

I shifted back into park, turned off the engine, and stepped out into the street.

Arno

For once in my life, I was actually on time. I took my usual table by the window and ordered a pot of tea. I was nervous as shit. I could barely guide the tea from the pot into the cup without spilling it on the table. I didn't know exactly why Pardeep wanted to talk, except that it had to do with the Sikh temple shooting. What was I going to say? That I was sorry about his father and the others who were massacred by someone who, more than likely, had been influenced by me? I was drowning in sorrow, but what could that possibly mean to him? How would I explain the twisted ideology that led a member of my former racist skinhead crew to that sacred place in the quiet Milwaukee suburb of Oak Creek with the intention of such violence? Or the misplaced rage that drove him to fire at the innocent people inside? If that was what this grieving son was looking for, giving him answers was the least I could do.

I had been atoning for my history of hatred for almost two decades, and it never got easier to acknowledge the dreadful things I did in the name of saving my race. Speaking the truth about white supremacy and the people who adopted the hateful philosophy was part of my self-imposed penance for having drunk the Kool-Aid myself as a younger man. I didn't practice hate anymore. My heart was pure and my only intention was to promote the basic goodness of humanity and try to prevent other young people from making the same terrible mistakes I had.

I was certain Pardeep would question the genuineness of my transformation from violent racist to peace activist, an inevitability whenever I talked about my past. I always answered the same: "I've given the world a reason to mistrust me. I don't blame you for questioning my motives or my sincerity. By all means, scrutinize what I do." Answering for my past sins had become my mission, my full-time job, my whole life. I'd traveled around the country and the world talking about my life after hate in an effort to encourage harmony among all people.

But this was different. I was about to meet a man whose life had been tragically altered by someone with the belief system I once held. I was still plagued by nightmares about steel-toed boots and smashed skulls, and besieged by shame and guilt for the damage I did. Damage, I was sorry to say, that wouldn't die with me but would endure for as long as there were people willing to embrace the hateful rhetoric I once preached at rallies and bellowed in white power songs I wrote and performed. People like Wade Michael Page, the man who murdered Pardeep's father.

Waiting for Pardeep, I wondered if I should tell him that I'd doubled up on my sleeping pills after the temple attack because nighttime unleashed a lurking sense that I had a hand in causing it. Or that I lived in dread of the start of Racial Holy War because I was certain that was Wade Page's goal and his martyrdom would encourage others to follow in his footsteps?

As the moments ticked by, I wondered if Pardeep would show. I worried that he wouldn't, but I couldn't blame him if he didn't. I'm not sure that I would have the courage if I were in his shoes. Fucking hell, the guts it took for him just to reach out to me was awe-inspiring.

Keng, my favorite waitress, stopped by the table, breaking my train of thought. Was I waiting for someone? she asked, filling my cup with tea.

The bells on the restaurant door jangled. I looked up and saw a good-looking guy with brown skin, buzzed-off black hair, and tape over his left eye.

"Yeah," I said. "I think that's him now."

Pardeep

When I walked through the door I saw Arno in a friendly conversation with an Asian waitress and sighed with relief. I couldn't imagine the guy who killed my dad chatting with a "foreigner." I walked over to the table and extended my hand. "Arno? I'm Pardeep." Arno stood to greet me. He was much taller than he'd looked as I walked into the restaurant. His eyes twinkled with warmth, which surprised me. Somehow I expected empty or maybe even angry eyes. My mind raced with the things I wanted to ask him. *What do you know about the assault on the temple? Do you know the shooter? What would motivate Page to do what he did?*

I stood across from Arno, anxious to get the formalities out of the way and pursue what I was there for, but he spoke first. "Dude!" he cried. "What happened to your eye? Did you get into a brawl?" His voice sounded as if he chewed on gravel and his question caught me off guard. In my anxiety over our meeting, I'd completely forgotten about the tape over my left eye. Instinctively, I reached up and touched it. "Oh, this," I said, taking a moment to explain.

I had injured my eye while I was bathing my little girl. A hook on the end of a loofah brush somehow ended up in the white of my eyeball and through my eyelid. "Just like a hooked fish," I said. Arno cringed. "Fucking hell, man!" he said. "That's awful! I thought I was the only fool clumsy enough for that kind of shit to happen!"

I said the emergency room doctor told me I was lucky to have sight in that eye. Arno's concern seemed genuine. We sat down across from each other. He picked up the steaming pot from the table and poured me a cup of tea. I couldn't help but notice the sleeves of tattoos covering his arms. The image of this inked-up tough guy with the rasping voice looking sympathetic and pouring Thai tea into delicate little cups struck me as paradoxical and almost funny. It would have seemed more normal if he'd grunted and cracked open a bottle of Bud. But I was about to learn that many things about Arno weren't what they seemed.

Arno had this way about him that made me feel like I'd known him forever. We eased into a conversation about our backgrounds and our kids. We discovered that his teenage daughter, Autumn, and my eight-year-old girl, Amaris, were both a bit OCD and shared the quirky habit of having to have the toes of their socks line up perfectly straight. Arno was a little rough around the edges. He used the F bomb the way teenagers abuse the word "like," yet he oozed kindness and compassion. When he talked about Autumn, he turned to mush. It seemed inconceivable to me that this warm, personable guy—someone who seemed hurt that I was hurt, who teared up talking about his child—was once the image of the monster that murdered my father.

As one cup of tea turned into two and three, I told Arno about my experience as a poor kid coming from India to live in America and how I'd thrown myself into school and sports as a way to integrate into my new culture. He shared that, unlike me, he was given all the opportunities of growing up in a white, middle-class American family but, at an early age, had chosen to shun them in favor of wreaking havoc on the streets.

Two hours passed and we were getting on so well that I almost felt embarrassed to ask what I'd come for. But I had to ask.

Arno

We talked about a lot of shit. Pardeep was one of the coolest guys I'd ever met. He was funny and smart and engaging—and the eye I *could* see was warm. I was struck by what seemed like a contradiction that he could be so chill when just a couple of months earlier his father had been murdered. At times over the course of the evening I had to remind myself why we were meeting. After two or three hours of nonstop talking about everything except what we were there for, he finally asked if I'd known Wade Michael Page.

I said I didn't think I'd ever met Page, but I knew him intimately. Watching the news coverage, my heart sank, and I wondered if it was possible that I had recruited him into the racist skinhead movement. Photos showed him with the same steel-toed boots and racist tattoos that fed me when I lived in the white power world. I was certain he chose the temple because the people who worshipped there were a visual example of everything he believed was wrong with our country. When I discovered he was a "patched" member of Hammerskin Nation, the racist skinhead group I cofounded, I lay awake, asking myself, *Did I unleash this monster on the world?* But comparing the dates, I realized I left the movement long before he joined. That didn't excuse me from accepting responsibility for what he did. If nothing else, I helped to create the environment that created Wade Michael Page, a regret that will follow me to my grave.

Page became an official member of Hammerskin Nation ten months before he stalked into the Sikh temple and systematically executed Pardeep's father and the others. I knew the disdain that darkened Page's heart. No one's heart was darker than mine back when my life's goal was to kick off a Racial Holy War, which was the goal of all white supremacists. I was a teenager when I heeded the radical racist battle cry, "Fourteen Words," as composed by the late David Lane, one of the most ferocious racists in the history of the white power movement. "We must secure the existence of our people and a

THE GIFT OF OUR WOUNDS

future for white children." Those words had been my belief system, my religion, and my reason for being until I was in my mid-twenties.

I immersed myself in racist dogma beginning at the age of sixteen, and by the time I was eighteen I had bragging rights as a founding member of the largest white power skinhead organization in the world. During those years, I fought with my bare hands and steel-toed boots and thrashed strangers for the sole reason that their skin was darker than mine. The enemy was anyone who we decided threatened our people. Once, I pummeled a man because I suspected he was gay until he was limp and whimpering; then, as an encore, I fed him my boots while my crew whistled and cheered. The only difference between Wade Page and me was that I hadn't murdered anyone, at least not that I knew of.

I told Pardeep that, during my time in the trenches, I'd reeled in hundreds of street warriors by dangling the promise of "a whiter and brighter world." I'd influenced thousands more with racist lyrics I composed and performed as the frontman for a notorious white power band, Centurion. As ashamed as I was to admit it, back then it warmed my heart to stomp across a stage and see dozens of fellow skinheads gesturing at me with straight-armed Nazi salutes and shouting "Sieg Heil!" *Hail Victory!* My band's claim to fame was that our crowds were so violent that someone was always carried away in an ambulance. I fed my followers anti-foreigner, anti-black, anti-gay, anti-Semitic, anti-anyone-who-didn't-fit-into-our-crude-worldview propaganda with the same zeal as anyone fighting for a righteous cause. "Those people"—just like the people in the Sikh temple—were considered fair game in our war to save our endangered white race.

I explained to Pardeep that the only way out of the quagmire of racial prejudice was practice. We practice tennis, or piano, or writing to become familiar with it. The more we practice something, the more natural it becomes. It was no different with hate. Wade Page practiced it until he was so twisted and miserable that only homicide followed by suicide seemed to make sense. The antidote was getting people to practice loving kindness, I said. That had become my life's mission.

Page was an asshole, just like I had been. I was just sorry he didn't get to experience the acts of kindness and compassion that had helped me to turn my life around. It might have helped him to realize—as I did—before he resorted to killing others that his racist beliefs were bullshit and his hatred was killing him.

Pardeep listened intently. Our talk had helped him make sense of the senselessness of his father's death. "But how do I move forward from it?" he asked. I was afraid of the question. Afraid I might break down and cry.

I said I often raised the subject of "continuance" in my talks. I believed that all the actions we took in our lives had reactions—even after we were gone. Everything he'd described about his father—his love of family, the dedication to his community, his fierce determination to achieve the American dream—could be used for good. "Your father could live on through your work," I said.

Yes, Pardeep said. After the shooting he and his family had brainstormed ways they could refocus the tragedy for good. From those conversations had emerged an organization he named Serve 2 Unite, whose purpose it was, in the spirit of Sikhism, to promote understanding and peaceful coexistence for all people. That was a big task, I said, smiling, and it was the same message I had in mind when I founded my nonprofit, Life After Hate, three years earlier. I'd recruited a team of other former white supremacists to my board, and we could barely keep up with the demand for our services.

Maybe Pardeep and I could join together sometime to promote the message.

"Wouldn't that be something? A brown Sikh and a former racist skinhead, together, talking about unity and oneness."

Pardeep seemed to dig the idea.

TWO

EARLY LIVES

Every Gurudwara will have four doors, one to
the north, south, east, and west. All are welcome.
Martyr Guru Arjun Dev Ji

Arno

My mom called me "wild child." I was her firstborn, and she wasn't quite sure what to do with me. I kept her on her toes and often in the process of pulling her hair out because I was always moving, always doing something I wasn't supposed to. I was barely able to walk before I began toddling down the stairs from our apartment to my parents' tavern and climbing up on the bar for the bottle of grenadine. I loved the sweet, syrupy stuff, and as many times as my mother moved it, I could always find it and top it off with a blast from the soda gun. Mom didn't know how to discipline me, so she usually looked the other way and let me be me. I'm not sure it would have made much difference if she had been a strict disciplinarian, because I think I was born nuts.

We moved to our house in Mequon, a white, upper-middle-class town just north of Milwaukee, when I was eighteen months going on four or five years. It was a bland tract house with a striking two-story A-frame addition that Mom designed and Dad and his cousin built. As my dad was laying the last bundle of shingles on the peak of the roof, I watched from my swing set a short distance away. The way he tells it, out of the blue, I started screaming. I was a very loud kid who screamed all the time, mostly just for the hell of it, but apparently this was different. Convinced I was dying, Dad leapt off the roof to come to my rescue, badly spraining his ankle in the process. When he finally got to me, I pointed to the source of my terror: a ladybug had landed on my arm. Despite his throbbing ankle, Dad chuckled and gave me a hug. For him, it was just another day in the life of raising a quirky kid.

I could pretty much do anything I wanted, and that included things like raiding the medicine cabinet, which resulted in a frantic trip to the ER to have my stomach pumped, and climbing on top of the gas stove after lighting all of the burners. Once, I smeared my bedroom walls with Vaseline and shook baby powder all over them. Another time, I placed a raw egg on my sleeping mother's pillow and waited until she rolled over and broke it. I thought it was hilarious. She probably didn't, but lovingly took it in stride, just as my dad did.

My first real victim was my little brother, Zack. He was as quiet and sweet as I was loud and rambunctious. I would crash and bang my way into situations with no mind of the mess in my wake, while Zack was an unobtrusive observer of life. He would sit in relative silence for hours at a time, content with the elegant simplicity of his surroundings. My parents even became worried that he had a learning disability because his subdued behavior was so disparate from that of his hellion big brother. So while I threw my weight around and generally raised Hades and mayhem, Zack conducted himself with patience and grace. His first words were "Thank you." Mine was "No." His existence, along with everyone else's, was incidental to my thrill seeking. He was there for my amusement, which typically consisted of escalating forms of physical and psychological torture.

Zack was two years younger than me and a toddler when I began provoking him by taking away his toys and food, then pinching and slapping him when he cried. As we grew, so did the intensity and wickedness of my abuse. Like a lot of kids, Zack hated the pungent taste of mustard, so I would pin him down and squirt yellow French's from the squeeze bottle into his nose until it came out his mouth, then finish him off by dripping huge gobs of spit in his eyes. I initiated Mustard Torture at every opportunity, sometimes to the point that Zack would snap and chase me around the house with a kitchen knife, which I found all the more amusing.

Someone else might have called me a destructive little fucker. Mom chose to see me as "different" and "extremely precocious." She was stunned when, during her first preschool parent-teacher conference, the teacher said that I was a joy to have in class. She was so stunned, in fact, that she felt compelled to ask, "Are you talking about the little blond kid?"

Apparently I was a terror with a heart, though, because I took it upon myself to help the kids with special needs and protect them from rival bullies.

By kindergarten, I was an accomplished bully myself. Sometimes I wonder how many people mention the school bus bully when they're sitting in their therapist's office today. People like Timothy Bailey. I tormented that poor kid. We rode the kindergarten bus together. With his big Coke-bottle glasses and perpetual snotty nose, he was an obvious target. I punched him in the nose every time he got on the bus, and, every time, his mom showed up and yelled at me. I'd see her coming and hide in the back of the bus, and she'd point at me and shout, "I see you back there, Arnie Michaelis! You leave my son alone!" I got a big rush from all the chaos. So Timothy got on the bus the next day and the whole scene played out again. It was like *Groundhog Day*.

Until one day I took it up a notch, and the principal got involved. I held Timothy's head to the bus seat with my left hand on his throat, gave him a good slap across the face with my right, and sneered, "Hey, maybe I can slap that snot out of your nose for you, Tim?" Timothy had long since realized that putting up any sort of verbal or physical resistance would fuel the twisted fire that drove me to make his life hell, so, as usual, he responded to my slaps with grim silence, calculating that either the fire would burn itself out or the bus would get to school, ending the situation one way or another. That made me even madder and I influenced other kids to beat him up, too.

We were all called to the principal's office. Mrs. McCurdy was letting us have it and the other kids were shaking in their boots, but not me. I told the principal I wasn't afraid of getting in trouble. And I wasn't afraid of her, so there was nothing she could do to me that would make any kind of an impact. She was as stunned as my schoolmates were in awe. Apparently my dad was impressed as well. I heard him tell his best friend Roger during one of their marathon drunk-dialing sessions, "Arnie sure has old Shirley McCurdy up a tree!" They had a good chuckle over that.

It was no laughing matter, though, when the next time I headed to my throne at the back of the bus and the hairy fist of Frank the Bus Driver grabbed me by the collar and yanked me back. "Hold up there, Michaelis!" he said. "You got a new seat assignment." Frank proceeded to unceremoniously spin me around and plaster my butt into the front seat. "Didn't yer parents get the memo, kid?" he sneered. "Any more trouble from you and yer walkin' every day . . . heh!" That was the end of that, for a little while.

As strange as it may sound, I liked school, at least at first, because it gave me the chance to be around other children. Our neighborhood was made up of mostly childless couples or empty nesters. Even in places close by where kids lived, the houses were so far apart, with big yards separated by woods, that you wouldn't necessarily see them. I remember what a happy day it was when Mom announced that our new neighbors had a couple of boys about my age. They were in the process of moving in when I walked over, knocked on the door, and asked, "Hey, are there kids here?" Sure enough, two boys about my age came running. Chris was one year older; Phil, two years older. Their parents were happy to get rid of them while they moved things in, so the three of us went into the woods to play. We had wandered in pretty deep when we discovered the ruins of an old tree fort. The only way up was a rickety tree ladder, which consisted of a few boards nailed to the tree. Being the genius that I was, I convinced Chris that it was a good idea to climb it. Reluctantly, he went up. He was almost at the top when he stepped on a broken board and took a wicked fall. He hit the ground with a sickening thud and broke his arm. His parents, Ellen and Big Phil, blamed me, but good-naturedly. They nicknamed me "Arnohead," their code name for "Shithead." I thought it was pretty cool and the name stuck.

Mom talks about my idiosyncratic personality and how different I was from other youngsters. That's putting it kindly, I think. For as far back as I can remember, I wanted to be a warrior. I learned to read early and I chose stories with warriors both real and fantastical. In elementary school, when other kids were joining Little League, I preferred digging into Greek and Norse mythology. I devoured medieval folklore, tearing through tales about King Arthur laying waste with his magic sword, Excalibur, and Thor, the Nordic God of Thunder, crushing encroaching giants with his slayer hammer, Mjolnir, imagining myself wielding legendary weapons against hosts of foe.

I don't know which came first, my fascination with the

idea of waging war or the anger that drove it. It's not like I had much to be mad at back then. I came from a nice, middle-class family and I never went hungry or took a beating. Mom was an artist and Dad was an insurance salesman. Both were Milwaukee natives, but otherwise they were different as night and day, and that made life interesting—for a while anyway.

Mom came from a broken home and was raised, along with two siblings and two half-siblings, by her mother. They all lived with my grandma in Milwaukee. As the firstborn, and a bit spoiled, she was queen of the household, and she never let anyone forget it. She was beautiful, creative, and brilliantly artistic—and she had an ego to match; she was an "It girl" before the phrase was ever coined. She met my dad while she was waiting tables at a Milwaukee bar called the Safehouse. (It's still there, and customers are still required to give a password at the front door to get in. Don't ask.) The old "opposites attract" rule applied. She was as open and progressive as my father was old school, but she was taken by his sharp intellect and good looks. He liked her confident, sassy manner. She says her decision to marry him was made, first and foremost, because she wanted tall, smart sons. He saw her as the ultimate challenge: the girl he couldn't let get away.

Dad hails from a long line of Arnos, all of whom were charismatic, underachieving alcoholics with big intellects. His father, Arno II, had the intelligence and education to become a medical doctor, but he sold medical supplies instead. Dad inherited from my grandfather, as I did from him, what I have come to call the "Arno Curse" for booze, danger, and excitement. From what I can tell, my father's upbringing was similar to mine. His father could be disapproving and cruel when he was drunk, and his mother made up for it with saintlike behavior and unconditional love for all living things. Talk about confusion!

I'm not sure how much love entered the equation of my parents' marriage, and I don't know how much their precarious relationship affected me—or exactly how much it had to do with me acting out in destructive ways. I'm pretty sure it didn't help. Thinking about it, though, I wonder if my aggression wasn't more rooted in boredom than anything I was experiencing at home. Early IQ tests suggested that I was a genius, and those standard fill-in-the-ovals-with-a-#2-pencil exercises corroborated it. Schoolwork was less than challenging. I was borrowing my parents' *Time* magazines in the first grade, so reading a book in the fourth grade about the friendship between a pig and a spider didn't do it for me. Instead of paying attention in class, I drew battle scenes from medieval times and world wars and daydreamed about slaying dragons.

By the sixth grade, I had graduated from hard to handle to out of control. I ganged up with like-minded ruffians and terrorized the students and staff at Lake Shore Middle School. It was there that I started my first "radical group": the Kids Liberation Army, a takeoff of the Symbionese Liberation Army, the self-styled left-wing revolutionary group that had kidnapped heiress Patty Hearst a few years prior. I really had no idea what the SLA was all about, or what they did, but

"Liberation Army" sure sounded cool. Our mission was to free ourselves from teacher oppression. "Oppression" as in the teachers wouldn't let us run amok and victimize all the other kids. We littered the school with a series of drawings I did of teachers being beheaded. Needless to say, that didn't go over well. My punishment was a week's suspension in the principal's office, during which time my comrades stole the hubcaps off a Mercedes-Benz parked at the dentist's office next door and brought them to the playground in a show of solidarity. The message was clear: we were not to be fucked with.

Mom chalked my antics up to growing pains, but I was seething inside. Things at home were unraveling by then. My mother was constantly stressed out. Between her art and our need for a roof over our heads and food on the table, she worked all the time. Dad sold just enough insurance to coast on the premiums. He knew the insurance business like few others, and his clients loved him, but he didn't work up to his potential by any stretch. My father was (and is) a great guy. He was well liked, not just because he was the life of the party but because he was a good friend who cared about the people in his life. Still, there were times during my childhood when things he did while he was drinking scarred me, as I imagine he was scarred by Arno II, who was likely scarred by Arno I, and so on. Sometimes he'd come home after last call and hassle my sleeping mother to get up. The memory of being startled awake by the sound of Mom screaming at him to leave her alone and go to bed still haunts me.

Mom did her best to try to insulate my brother and me from the craziness. She would do cool things, like announce on a sunny spring morning that we were all playing hooky and going to ride roller coasters at the amusement park. For a few hours, the middle-of-the-night theater would be forgotten and we could pretend to be a normal family again.

If I had to sum up my relationship with my father back then, there are three directions I could take. My brother says he was the best dad anyone could ask for. Mom says he was supercritical when he drank, and I could never do anything right in his eyes. I'm going to take the middle road here and say that all of this is true, but we had fun. It wasn't the greatest relationship, but it wasn't the worst by any stretch.

My journey since then has taught me that those early memories must be met with compassion, and not just for me but for my dad, who was shaped by similar childhood trauma, as I suppose my grandpa also was. No matter what, I always knew my dad loved me, and today he is one of my biggest supporters. I've only heard him cry twice in my life: once when his beloved Corgi, Henry, died; the other when he told me how proud he is of the work I do. As we both have grown older and wiser, my relationship with my dad has turned into one of the most rewarding of my life.

I certainly can't say that my parents did anything to lead me into the life of extremism I chose as a teenager. I did that all myself. Yeah, there were issues at home. Their constant fighting certainly fueled my angst and added to my growing dissatisfaction with life. But our dysfunction paled in comparison to the billions of people on the planet with real problems who didn't turn out fucked up like me.

I was thirteen years old when I started my first gang. I did a lot of the things other boys my age did. I climbed trees and ran in the woods and swam and played tackle football to blow off steam—but none of it was stimulating enough to quiet my hyperactive brain. I thrived on chaos and destruction, hence my foray into wilding out. I recruited a bunch of kids from the block and we menaced the neighborhood like a pack of vicious dogs. Our headquarters was a tree fort we militarized with trenches and turrets. After dark, when most kids were doing homework, we went on raiding missions, desecrating other kids' tree forts, kicking off car mirrors (the more expensive the car, the better), and upending those big blue federal collection boxes and burning the mail inside (which, by the way, is a federal offense).

I was big for my age (I still am) with a foul mouth and an ominous stare, and after a while even adults began to steer clear of me. Looking back, of course, I understand that my hard shell covered up the insecurity and fear I felt inside. I think maybe somewhere in my subconscious I knew how vulnerable I was, so I terrorized others to be in control.

For the most part, my reputation as a badass protected me, but not always. I was shaken to the core when, during recess one day in seventh grade, a bunch of jocks jumped me. It was a premeditated attack, and I didn't see it coming. At the time, I was into breakdancing and Grand Master Flash. My group consisted of a couple of other white guys, a Filipino kid, and the handful of black kids who lived in my town. A kid named Jason had the richest parents of the bunch, and every weekend we'd watch VCR copies of *Beat Street* and *Breakin'* in his rec room and try to teach ourselves breakdancing moves. We got so good that my mom, who loved all kinds of culture expression, took us to a spot on the south side of Milwaukee where a group of kids gave breakdancing lessons behind a dilapidated storefront. She'd pay them twenty bucks and they would teach us complicated backspins and fancy floor moves. The lessons took us to a whole other level and we were really good.

So one day, my group and I were showing off during recess, practicing our six-step on the school playground when, with all of the teachers watching, the jocks ambushed me. There had to be twenty guys, and they came at me all at once. I was a rough kid, but I couldn't hold off a group of dudes that big. Some held me down while others beat me up. Then they pulled off my bandanna and cut off my prized rattail with a pair of scissors from the art room. I fought back like a cornered animal and it took some time for them to subdue me, but there were just too many of them.

When the jocks ran off, I stumbled around in a daze. That's when I realized my breakdancing homies were still there. They had all watched from the sidelines, and not one had jumped in to help me. Those guys were supposed to be my brothers. We had a promise to stick together, no matter what, and they let me down. I didn't snap at that point, but I was hurt and disappointed enough to hold a grudge. Not only was my pride badly bruised, but I had been betrayed by the very people I trusted to have my back, and that took my bitterness to another level.

That was pretty much the end of my breakdancing career. In the best of scenarios, the assault should have taught me empathy for the people I had persecuted over the years. But that's not what happened. It *was* a turning point, but I turned in the wrong direction. Suddenly it was "those black guys" who didn't come to my aid. It was the first time I remember cueing in on someone's race. Shortly after that, I dropped rap and breakdancing in favor of white friends and punk rock.

And my simmering anger turned to rage. Soon, Arno the class bully turned into Arno the racist street fighter.

Pardeep

My family story begins in the rural village of Dogal, about thirty miles southwest of the glittering city of Patiala in the Punjab region of India. Dogal was a poor farming community, but our family was better off than most of the people there because my grandfather owned twenty-seven acres of farmland and leased most of it to other farmers in the village.

My father was the seventh of nine children and the only one who didn't leave home to study in the city. He stayed on the farm with his parents. His siblings became doctors and professors but Dad, a deeply religious man, discovered that he could cultivate his spirituality by working the land, which made him a natural to take over the family operation after my grandfather retired.

Farming was in his blood. It was hard work, but working hard is one of the fundamental principles of Sikhism. The family grew fields of sugarcane, wheat, cotton, and mustard, depending on the season. Dad worked alongside the farmhands and led by example, working the hardest. The men did the heavy work, tilling the soil, planting the crops, and digging irrigation canals to bring water from the river. The women worked in the fields, harvesting the crops. "Work is worship" is a favorite saying my father used throughout his life.

My mother was also raised in a farming community, but many hours away from Dogal, in Uttar Pradesh, near the Nepal border. Her family started out with several acres of jungle that her father bought cheap, and they toiled for over two years to make it plantable. Once it was ready, they harvested sugarcane, wheat, and corn and used buffalo to plow the fields. With no irrigation system, getting water to the crops was left to "God's will." As the crops and the family flourished, they were able to move from a hay hut to a proper farmhouse built of brick and mortar.

Mom's role in the family was helping her mother with the household chores. She was ten years old and expected to cook, clean, and care for her younger siblings in addition to her studies. Whatever spare moments she could steal, she taught herself stitching, sewing, and knitting, and she was skilled enough to make clothes for the family. She got as far as the sixth grade when her mother became sick, and Mom had to leave school to take on more of the responsibilities at home.

Mom's was a cloistered world and one in which she lived until her parents arranged for her to marry. She had just turned twenty when she was shown a picture of my father and told that he had been chosen as her future husband. The arrangement was made by a *bachola*, someone who brought two people together based on the quality of their families. In their case, the bachola was a distant relative on Mom's side who was also familiar with Dad's family. By the time Mom knew anything about it, a dowry had been offered and accepted by Dad's family, and wedding arrangements were in the works. Asking questions would have been to go against custom, so there was no choice for Mom but to go along.

The wedding was set for December 30 of that year, 1974. My father and his family took the seventeen-hour train ride from Patalia to Uttar Pradesh to formalize the arrangements. A day of pre-wedding festivities followed, beginning with the offering of the ring, a traditional ceremony attended only by the groom and male relatives from both families at which gifts are also exchanged. While the men partied, Mom's family hosted a bridal ritual called a *Sangeet*, where the women gathered to sing and dance to traditional folk music and draw henna art, the symbol of a couple's love, on each other's hands. The bride and groom saw each other for the first time at their wedding ceremony.

It was only after my father's death, during late-night

conversations with Mom, that I learned the intimate details of my parents' early life together and the difficulties they faced coming to America. How could I tell the story of the man I am today without telling their story? I asked questions and Mom was generous with details. I think those talks helped us both: Mom, by sharing some of the most poignant moments of her life, and me, because it made me realize how much she and Dad endured together and how what began as an "arrangement" grew into a partnership based on mutual love and respect.

Mom said she had mixed feelings about the marriage because it meant leaving everything she had ever known. The actual term for the transition into an arranged marriage is *Dulli*, and Mom described it as a time of great anxiety. The only way she got through it was her faith in God and trust in the judgment of the bachola. Before she married my father, she had never been separated from her family or gone away from home. Yet three hours after the wedding ceremony, she was on a train, with a new family, headed to a faraway place she didn't know, with a husband who was a complete stranger. Indeed, the first conversation my parents ever had was on that train ride. Dad asked Mom if she was okay. She responded that she had a headache. It was a somber time in her life, but we both laughed at the memory. Dad got her an aspirin and a cup of tea. He seemed nice enough. But love? She had never loved. She was too young and too inexperienced to even know what love should feel like. People didn't "fall" in love, she always said. They grew to love each other.

The uneasy start got tougher when Mom was introduced to her new home.

Mom knew Dad was a farmer, but she didn't know anything about the farm or the village where she would be living. Her family had become quite successful over the years, and she was coming from a large farming homestead in the scenic foothills of the Himalayas.

The two-hour bus ride from the train station in Patalia to rural Dogal offered some clues about the life she was about to begin, and it didn't look anything like home. Unlike her hometown, with its wide vistas of snowcapped mountains and roaring rivers, the topography of this new place was flat and dusty. The farther away from the city they got, the more barren the land became. Looking out the bus window was like watching a monotonous slideshow of dull brown fields. The trip seemed never-ending.

Finally, the bus turned toward Dogal. The only access to the village was a narrow dirt road traversed mostly by bicycles, the main mode of transportation. The "town square" consisted of small houses, some brick, but most built of mud, as well as a few dilapidated shops, a school, a walk-in clinic, and a Gurudwara.

Dad's farm was a mile walk from the center of the village. The "farmhouse" that my mother would share with her new husband and in-laws turned out to be a tiny, rectangular brick structure consisting of three rooms. The apprehension she'd felt about leaving home turned into an acute case of homesickness.

Over time, my mother found her place within the family structure, but it was slow going. She had gone overnight from being a daughter to a married woman with no practice or instruction and no relatives nearby. Her role was that of a housewife. She spent her days with her in-laws, helping to cook and clean, and got to know Dad by listening to their stories.

Dad was rarely around. He worked in the fields from dusk to dawn, came back home to shower and eat, and left again to milk the cows. Evenings were spent in prayer, with each family member retreating into meditation by reading silently from the *Gutka*, a small book of sacred verses from the Sikh scriptures. Dad was already well versed in Sikh history and theology by then. The people in the village called him "Gaini," which means scholar or theologian.

My parents had been married for a year when Mom became pregnant with me. I was born on August 3, 1976. Dad's older brother, Jagjit, who immigrated to America and ran a successful veterinary practice, urged my father to follow him to Wisconsin. Dogal had nothing to offer a young family. The living conditions were poor, the medical care was subpar, and education was inferior. America, the Land of Opportunity, had everything we needed and more: high-paying jobs, exceptional schools, and doctors on every corner! Dad demurred. His place was on the farm.

After I was born, Mom joined Dad to work in the fields. She'd often take me when she picked cotton or delivered food to the workers. By the summer of 1978, when my brother Amardeep was born, she had become tired of the toll that farming had taken on her body. Tired of the 100-plus-degree days in the sun, the bloody cuts on her hands from harvesting cotton, the constant ache in her back from picking vegetables. She liked what she'd heard about America and made up her mind that she would convince my father to take us there.

Faced with an unhappy wife, Dad moved all of us to an apartment in Patalia. He bought an old motorcycle to commute between the farm and the city. Mom was happier with the easier lifestyle, but Dad missed having his family at home, and the constant back-and-forth between work and us was hard on him.

Still, I think we might have stayed in India had it not been for mounting communal tension between non-Sikhs and Sikhs that threatened our safety. Punjab was in turmoil in the early 1980s. The majority Sikh community was fighting for both political and religious independence from the Hindu nationalist government, and a movement by Sikh nationalists for a sovereign state within the region called Khalistan erupted in widespread violence. In Sikhism, violence is condoned only for the purposes of resisting tyranny and protecting human rights—and only after all peaceful means have been exhausted. This was *dharam yudh*, "war in the name of righteousness." The government intervened, and tens of thousands of Sikhs were arrested. No place in the region was safe, certainly not the city of Patalia, where curfews, gunfire, and exploding Molotov cocktails were a constant source of anxiety. The mounting danger, as well as continued pressure from my uncle, convinced Dad that a move to America was the right decision.

Two years after we left, the conflict boiled over with the infamous Operation Blue Star, a deadly military attack ordered by Prime Minister Indira Gandhi on the Harmandir Sahib of Amritsar (the Golden Temple), the holiest of Sikh shrines, where armed Sikh militants had taken refuge from the Indian Army. For many Sikhs, it is still seen as the darkest period in our faith. Hundreds of innocent men, women, and children were sacrificed in the bloodbath. Six months later, Gandhi was assassinated by her two Sikh bodyguards in retaliation, which led to anti-Sikh riots and thousands of Sikhs massacred. By then, we were safely ensconced in Milwaukee.

We'd arrived in America in the spring of 1982 as "resident aliens." I can't imagine how difficult it must have been for my parents to leave everything they'd worked for—everything they knew—to immigrate to a foreign land where their future was uncertain and they didn't know the language. They were poor farmers and their view of the world was Punjab. They had never even been on an airplane before they brought us here. As a parent myself now, I can't imagine uprooting my family and fleeing to a new country with a hundred dollars in my pocket and the clothes on our backs.

With no income and no place to live, we stayed with my father's brother in the Milwaukee suburb of Germantown (coincidentally, five minutes from Arno's house in Mequon) for the first few months. It was a tough adjustment. Everything in America was so big. The stores. The office buildings. The houses. Even the cars. My parents were overwhelmed. Coming from such humble backgrounds, they wondered how they would ever fit in.

Dad went to work pumping gas at a small station in Milwaukee's inner city, and, after three months, we moved into our first apartment. It didn't take long for him to realize that his earnings—even though he worked fifteen-hour shifts, seven days a week—didn't go far for a family of four. If they were to make it here, Mom would have to work as well.

My parents' solution was to send my brother and me back to India to live with an aunt until they could get on their feet. Mom was miserable without us, and, after six months, we returned to Milwaukee and a new home—a shabby low-income apartment with a tiny black-and-white TV and mattresses on the floor. We had some toys, but only a few, and Dad would fix them when they broke. We had homemade food, but never enough to overindulge. It was a far cry from the abundance of my uncle's house, but we were happy to be back together as a family.

I saw firsthand how hard my parents struggled to make a life for us. Dad had taken on extra hours at the gas station and Mom took English-language classes, then went to work for Dad afterward. When she got to the gas station, he ran home to check on my brother and me. Then he went back until closing, and Mom took the bus home, arriving in time to make us dinner. I was so young, but I understood the sacrifices of my parents and I was happy to do my part. It was my job to ensure Amardeep and I safely walked the mile to and from school.

America was a scary place for a young boy, especially a young boy who looked different than everyone else. The kids at school made fun of Amardeep and me and our long hair. In the Sikh religion, uncut hair, or *Kesh*, is a symbol of devotion to God. The Kesh is often concealed under a turban, which is considered a crown of spirituality. My dad was meticulous in wrapping his "just so." Younger males, like my brother and me, wore ours twisted into a tight bun at the back of our heads wrapped in a handkerchief. It's called a *patka*.

The man bun is trendy today, but for us it was a source of constant teasing and bullying. The boys at school called me a "girl" and laughed when I passed them in the hallway. It was worse for my little brother. After a few months of being relentlessly ridiculed, he broke down and told Dad what was happening. He didn't want to go back to school. The kids were pulling on his bun and it hurt. Dad went to the school administrators for help. But the school did nothing and the bullying escalated to the point where Amardeep was wetting the bed and refusing to eat. Our father was a tough man, but it was clear that my brother's tears hurt him. As difficult as it was for him to sacrifice a religious custom in which he deeply believed, he took us to a local barbershop for our first haircuts. Dad grimaced at each snip of the scissors. Afterward, we went to the gas station where Mom was working the cash register. I overheard him tell her, *"A din bhi dekhna pana se"* (This is a day that we knew we'd have to face).

Mom tried to comfort him with rationalizations. They were in a different country now. The culture was different. It was important for us, their children, to be accepted. As she spoke, I saw the anger on Dad's face fade into sadness and tears drop from his eyes.

I never really understood how much that chapter in our lives affected him until shortly after his death, when we discovered a box of his writings tucked away on a shelf in his closet. One of his missives was the story of those first haircuts and how painful it had been for him to see our shiny black locks shorn. As sad as it had made him to break with our culture, it was more important that we, his sons, not have to suffer the humiliation of having long hair in a society that didn't understand.

I read Dad's words with both sadness and gratitude. As his son, I felt a sense of sorrow for his pain on behalf of Amardeep and me. As a father now myself, I understood that this selfless act was driven by the deep love he felt for us—a love he found difficult to express in words.

I don't think I'd ever felt more connected to him.

THREE

TRANSITIONS

Before becoming a Sikh, Muslim, Hindu, or Christian,
let's become human first.
Guru Nanak Dev Ji

Pardeep

I was just getting accustomed to Milwaukee and Midwest culture when my father came home and announced we were
moving to the South. An acquaintance told him about job opportunities there and Dad had gone to scout it out. He'd
landed a job at a furniture factory in High Point, North Carolina, making double his gas station earnings. When he came
back to get us, we crammed everything we owned into our
beat-up Mazda hatchback and headed to our new home. The
car was so jam-packed that my brother and I had to lie on top
of suitcases for the entire fifteen-hour trip.

Dad found us an old two-bedroom house near his job, and
we settled in. The South was so different from Wisconsin in
so many ways, from the food to the weather to the religious
and political ideologies, and back then it was even more of a

culture shock than it would be today. We'd only been there a couple of weeks when, without any warning, Dad came home with his hair cut short. We were all gobsmacked. Mom thought it was a stranger at the door. When we asked why he'd cut it, his response was that the turban got in the way of his factory work. We knew better. Dad was a farmer! He'd spent most of his life laboring in the heat while wearing his turban, and he'd never complained about it getting in the way. We also knew not to question him further. Mom accepted his answer and we all carried on as if things were normal.

The biggest drawback of the move wasn't necessarily the lifestyle, though. It was feeling so isolated. We'd left everyone we knew in America back in Wisconsin. We missed our family, and even Dad felt the sting of separation from his brothers and our small, tight-knit Sikh community. Tensions in our house were mounting. So back we went after two months—this time for good—but with no jobs and no place to call home.

Without any income, we depended on relatives again to help us settle in. As was a tradition in our culture, family supported family until they could help themselves. We stayed with Dad's younger brother Gurwant, his wife Perminder, and their newborn son in a sparsely furnished ranch home they'd recently purchased in the suburbs. My brother and I were registered in our third school in less than a year, and Mom and Dad went to work for Gurwant at his gas station in a seedy section of the city.

As hard as everyone tried to acclimate to the arrangement,

it was doomed to fail. Too many people in too small a space only exacerbated existing familial tensions. The last time Dad and Gurwant worked together was on the farm in Punjab, and their roles were reversed. Dad had been Gurwant's teacher and Gurwant his disciple. Now Dad was working for minimum wage and his kid brother was his boss. At home, Mom went out of her way to share the household chores, but nothing she did was good enough in Perminder's eyes. The strained relations made for stressful living and, in just short of a year, with tears in our eyes, we moved out of their house and out of their lives.

One of the most important tenets of our Sikh faith is a practice we call *Chardi Kala*. Translated from Punjabi, it means living with "relentless optimism." We are taught that obstacles and hardships are not to be feared but embraced as stepping-stones toward the preordained plans God has for us. Chardi Kala is what Sikhs strive for, a blissful mental state, even under difficult circumstances—especially under difficult circumstances—as testimony to our unwavering belief in the will of God. It's a noble concept, but sometimes it's harder to put into practice than others, and this was one of those times.

It must have seemed to my parents that the American dream would never be ours. I secretly wished we could return to India and the farm, but that would have meant conceding failure, and my father was not about to do that. My parents took whatever work they could find to keep us fed, and we moved from one dingy apartment to the next in the worst neighborhoods in the city. A pall hung over the family. I saw Dad lose this temper, sometimes to the point of almost losing control. He was Sikh, but also human, and he sometimes took out his frustrations on my mother with harsh treatment, which made me angry. I hated hearing her cry behind closed doors. For many people, the situation might have seemed hopeless. But time and time again, my parents had risen from adversity through meditation and prayer, and this time would be no different.

Our divine spiritual messenger, Guru Nanak, the founder of Sikhism, wrote, "A God-directed person never faces defeat." My parents were nothing if not God-directed. So it was that when we were at our lowest, Dad saw an opportunity to lease a gas station with a partner, and Mom was offered full-time work sewing at a knitting factory. It looked as if our fortune was finally turning.

One constant principle stood the test of time: work hard and you can make it. My parents worked their hands to the bone. Mom put in long hours sewing infant and toddler clothing, while Dad ran the station. To save money, he became a jack-of-all-trades. He could take apart car motors, dive under a sink to repair a leak, or rebuild a refrigerator. Mom rode the bus across town to work, often leaving and returning home in the dark. Dad drove a beat-up pickup truck with an eight-foot flatbed for carrying the drywall, wood, sheet metal, and scrap he needed for odd jobs.

They scrimped and they saved, and, by the time I got to middle school, we were able to buy our first home. My parents' sacrifices suddenly seemed worth it. All of the time away from home and us, the blood, sweat, and tears—we finally had something to show for it. We moved from our tiny apartment with mattresses on the floor to a row house in a nice, blue-collar neighborhood across the street from a park. I still remember waking up on our first morning there and smelling the dew on the grass. It was the perfect metaphor for that time in our lives. That house symbolized the dawning of a new life. I was still the only Indian kid in my class at school, but the neighborhood was a melting pot of working-class white, black, and Latino families, and we were welcomed.

The park became my second home. Kids who were looking for someone to throw a ball with didn't discriminate, and I was a pretty good athlete, so I made friends quickly. Baseball was my sport, but I loved basketball and football, too. A group of eight of us kids bonded and called ourselves the Adams Park Posse, APP for short. We gave each other nicknames. My little brother was "Geeker"; I have no idea why. I was "Mama" because I was responsible and tended to watch out for everyone, the way I always had with my little brother. All of us came from different backgrounds, but at the park we were just a bunch of boys who loved playing ball.

Street gangs were endemic in the city, then and now, and our neighborhood was not exempt. The Latin Kings had a big presence in the park, and we interacted with them regularly on the basketball court. A group of them would roll up in one of their fancy cars (paid for with drug money, we suspected) and challenge us to a game. We were younger and, by far, the better players, but our choice was to either get our asses kicked or let them win. We chose the latter.

One of the regular Kings was a stocky brute of a kid named Bull. He was older, probably seventeen, and fierce. He liked to foul us on purpose and we always just took the hit and kept playing. Until, one day, our friend Jason decided not to take his guff. Jason came to the park that day in a foul mood. His father was abusive and I figured he'd probably just been beaten again that morning. We started a game and Bull fouled Jason, but rather than take it, Jason snapped. He went after Bull like a rabid dog. Both teams stood on the sidelines and watched the two of them slug it out. It was hard to know if we should jump in and help our teammate, except that we were no match for violent gangsters who, we knew, most likely had guns. I don't know why the Kings decided to stay put, but I'm grateful they did. Bull and Jason fought their fight and both came out pretty beat up. Afterward, we all went our separate ways. No hard feelings. Bull and his gang were back the following afternoon, as was Jason, ready to play ball. I think, in some weird way, the gang gained respect for us. Nevertheless, that was the closest I ever came to "gang involvement," and it was a little too close for comfort.

I couldn't have told my parents that we were playing against gang members or they would have forbidden me from going to the park, and I couldn't imagine anything worse. I decided what they didn't know wouldn't hurt them, and the games continued. It was one of the few times I took such a risk, keeping the truth from my parents. I was a pretty good kid, respectful and obedient, probably because my father's wrath was even scarier than Bull's. Looking back, I'm glad I was raised the way I was, and that my parents cared enough to make my brother and me toe the line. But back then their rules seemed draconian, at least by American standards.

I'm a quick study, and I'd learned early on that American kids were pretty individualistic, but Indian kids were raised to do what pleased their parents. My parents were strict, even by Indian standards. "Spare the rod, spoil the child" pretty much summed up Mom and Dad's philosophy on childrearing. Physical punishment as a means of discipline seemed counter to the teachings of our religion—especially when I was on the receiving end of it—but obedience to authority is highly valued in Punjabi society and if it took a swat to set us straight, Dad did. I wasn't allowed to do most of what my friends did. The kids in seventh and eighth grades were dating and going to movies and parties, but not me. I knew better than to even ask. If I wasn't in school or playing ball at the park, I had to be home. Eventually, my friends stopped inviting me places because I could never go. It hurt, but the thought of betraying my parents was worse. There were rare times that my resolve weakened. I could never have let on about my first kiss, in the eighth grade, which wouldn't have happened if the girl hadn't met me in the park. I felt the earth move when our lips touched, but I couldn't tell anyone, not even my little brother, for fear he might squeal.

My one little rebellion was listening to gangster rap music

on my cassette recorder. I always used headphones so my parents wouldn't hear. My idols were the Geto Boys, N.W.A, and DJ Quik, all pretty hardcore rappers. I even started copying their fashion, wearing hats with embroidery and Raiders gear. My buddies and I gave ourselves gangster aliases. Mine was P-Money. I don't know where that came from. That was the extent of my involvement in hip-hop culture, but I kept it from Mom and Dad because I knew they would disapprove.

I don't know what tipped Dad off, but one day I was in my room with my favorite song playing, the one with the most explicit lyrics in the genre, and he came in and asked what I was up to. I must have looked stricken. I was right in the middle of listening to DJ Quik's "Sweet Black Pussy": "Now I be knockin' bitches like it ain't shit . . . Yo, maybe it's the way I hold my dick." Dad held out his hand for me to give him the headphones. There was nothing I could do but obey. I literally shook as he put them over his ears, and I watched wide-eyed as his face went from curious to stoic to straight-up dumbfounded. If expressions translated into words, his said, "This is so bad I don't even know what to do." I sat on my bed, frozen, as he pulled off the headphones and called Mom into the room. I remember it like it was five minutes ago. "You love your son, right?" he asked in Punjabi. "Of course," she replied. He handed her the headphones. "This is what he is listening to," he said. I'm not sure my mother even understood the lyrics, but she followed Dad's lead and stormed out of my room. There was no talking about it, not with Mom or Dad. That

47

night, my father gave me the beating of my life. Maybe even worse, he took away my cassette player.

The summer before I entered high school, while other kids went to camp or swam in the community pool, I helped renovate Dad's new gas station. He'd sold the old one for a profit and bought a full-service station on Milwaukee's south side. The property was run-down but bigger and with more income potential. Dad, Mom, my brother, and I spent the hot summer months doing demolition and renovations. In addition to gas pumps, we had a mechanic's bay for car repairs and a small store where we sold coffee, newspapers, cigarettes, and sundries. It was quite a step up.

By then, Dad had grown his hair back and was wearing his turban again. The south side community was initially apprehensive about the new Indian-owned business, which was previously run by a white man from Kansas and his all-white crew. The neighborhood, once an Eastern European stronghold and predominantly Polish American, was in flux after a decade of white flight. As the old guard vacated homes and businesses to move to the suburbs, the city's exploding Latino population moved in, shaking up the status quo. Our business neighbors were a Polish bakery and a Spanish grocery. Then there was us, the only Indians on the block.

Over time, whatever preconceived notions people had about us were dispelled after they got to know Dad. He personified the Sikh values of "work, worship, and charity." He lived by example and his moral code was unbreakable.

"Never take what you can earn."

"Never borrow anything without paying it back."

"Be a person of your word."

"Always help others who are less fortunate."

Dad's heart was as big as the sun. He'd help anyone, sometimes with service, other times with money, and often by giving sage advice. When someone new came from India, he made sure they were fed and sheltered until they could get on their feet. When the temple was short of money and in need of repairs, he grabbed his tools, took out whatever he had left in his bank account, and went to work. His work was never done. In the evenings before bed, he cold-called parishioners encouraging them to come to Sunday services. Those calls were never short. People confided their troubles and Dad took as much time as they needed, which usually meant he was still talking well after our bedtime. The bigger the *Sangat* (Sikh for congregation) got, the longer he was on the phone. We often said that he belonged to everyone but us.

Dad's customers nicknamed him "Sam" because it was easier to remember than Satwant. Some called him "Uncle Sam" because he was tall and slender with a prominent nose and a beard. He formed deep bonds with his regulars. When one of them couldn't afford car repairs, Sam not only didn't charge for labor, he protected their pride by joking, "My labor is always free—so I can't give you a money-back guarantee." It was routine for him to buy meals for people who were hungry and pass out things from our store shelves, like chips and sodas and diapers for struggling moms. He never expected anything in return.

Not surprisingly, the "Mom and Pop" shop became a staple in the neighborhood. Business was so good that we were able to move from our house by the park to a bi-level in an all-white neighborhood in the suburbs. For Dad, it was the American dream realized. It meant that he had finally made it, and one of the first things he did was raise the American flag on a pole in the front yard. He said he'd noticed that none of the other homes had flags displayed and he wanted to honor this great land of opportunity. Most of the neighbors were welcoming, but apparently not everyone was happy having an Indian family on the street.

On our first morning there, I walked outside and discovered a pamphlet of Ku Klux Klan cartoons on the front lawn. It was remedial enough for anyone to understand, with crudely drawn pictures of men in white hoods and bubbles over their heads with racist rants written inside. I didn't know much about those kinds of things, but I knew what the Klan was and it scared me. I took the pamphlet inside and showed it to my father. If he had a reaction, I didn't see it. He glanced at the paper and coolly tossed it in the trash. Dad said there had been other times when he and Mom hadn't felt welcome here, but they didn't allow themselves to be bitter—they just continued to focus on keeping an optimistic view of life and being good citizens. I decided to follow his advice and get on with my life.

I had bigger worries anyway. I was trying to fit in at

another school. My new high school was ten miles from home, and, for the first time in my life, I had to take the school bus. It felt strange to be so far from home. The first days of being the new kid were the worst. I didn't have any friends, and I sat alone at the lunch table, feeling awkward but trying to look inconspicuous. Everyone knows that scary feeling. The school was diverse, mostly black, white, and Latino. But, once again, I was the only Indian kid. And once again, sports saved me.

Football season rolled around and I pulled out the pads. I got the attention of the coach, who was impressed by my athletic skills, and asked if I played other sports as well. I told him I played everything—basketball in the winter and baseball in the spring, which I really excelled at. With his encouragement, I joined every sport, which gave me "street cred" and an "in" with the girls who were attracted to athletes.

By then I'd discovered that sports was a universal language. I didn't have to say anything to be accepted, I just had to play. Mom and Dad could never come to my games because they were too busy working. But the other parents tried to make up for their absence by cheering me on. For all intents and purposes, I was torn between two cultures. At school I was an all-American kid, dressing and acting like everyone else. At home, I was an Indian boy living within the constrictions of a traditional Punjabi household. That made life confusing. I wasn't free to be myself in either place. I was muddled about who "myself" even was.

I know my parents would have liked for me to be more

involved in the temple, but my interest in our religion had waned during the time we'd lived in America. My parents, on the other hand, had only become more devout in the time we'd been here. When we first got to Wisconsin, there were only ten Sikh families, and we all worshipped together wherever we could find the space. Within a few years, the number doubled, and the parishioners pooled their money to purchase a small bank building on the north side of the city to hold services. We outgrew that building quickly, as more and more families migrated from Punjab to Milwaukee for the business opportunities and cheap property. When the congregation climbed to two hundred families, a decision was made to sell the bank building and build a new temple.

By then Dad was president, and he was deeply involved in a conflict over where to build. It came down to his idea of purchasing property on the south side, where most of the Sikh growth was happening, and a campaign by two wealthy Sikh businessmen who wanted to build in their affluent suburb. Dad wouldn't budge. He believed that many of the members would feel out of place in the tony suburban location and become disenfranchised from the temple. The congregation split, with the south side community choosing to worship in makeshift temples until they could raise enough money to build their own and the rich Sikhs constructing a new temple in their affluent part of town.

The temple became my parents' life, and, to their chagrin, I wasn't at all interested in the politics or Sunday services. I was too busy falling in love. During my senior year, I'd met a girl named Jenny. She was white—forbidden fruit—but I was drawn to her spirit. I knew my parents would disapprove of me dating someone outside of our religion, so I couldn't let on about her. The only date they wanted me to have was the one that would lead to an arranged marriage to a Punjabi Jatt Sikh woman of their choosing. Pursuing a relationship with Jenny was the first time I'd blatantly disregarded their wishes. I spent almost every day with her at school and at her house after school. Her family accepted me but they knew the rules. Our relationship had to stay secret. I couldn't risk my parents finding out.

Jenny was my first real love, and our relationship was in full bloom as we were applying to colleges. We wanted to go to the same place, so we'd both applied to the University of Wisconsin. Public school had done nothing to prepare me for the complicated college application process. My parents hadn't even been able to help me with my homework when I was younger, so I had to figure out everything on my own. I wrote a pretty decent admissions essay about the trials of trying to fit into American culture, and I was invited for an interview at UW. My acceptance letter came in early spring. I'd been accepted at both the Milwaukee and the Whitewater campuses. I didn't have to think twice about choosing Whitewater. Jenny was going there, and it was far enough from Milwaukee that I would have to live on campus. I was ready to get away from the restrictions of my parents to explore who I really was.

Mom and Dad sent me off with cautionary words about

abiding by the rules of the college and staying true to the tenets of our religion. My parents didn't know anything about
college life in America, but I could see their concern as I prepared to go off on my own. Mom broke down in tears when
she dropped me off and I promised I'd come home on weekends whenever I could. The thought of my new freedom was
both exhilarating and intimidating. I had never been away
from home before.

Whitewater was a town of thirteen thousand in the rural
southern part of the state, about ninety minutes from Milwaukee. The campus was set on four hundred green acres that
ended with Kettle Moraine State Forest, and the demographic
was 98 percent white. The only thing that was familiar was
Jenny. During the first few weeks of the fall semester, I found
my way from class to class, trying to learn the ropes and
the campus. Whitewater was a big party school, but I was
more interested in playing sports, and the gym was where I
made new friends. My new group consisted of guys I'd met
on the basketball court—all of them white, from rural towns
in Wisconsin. My routine became classwork, homework,
and playing ball every night until the gym closed. Any extra
time I had, I spent with Jenny.

Despite the radical change of lifestyle, I was able to maintain a solid GPA during my first year. Jenny and I were still
going strong at the start of our sophomore year, but having
to keep our relationship from my family created tension between us. We'd been together for two years. Jenny was tired
of being a secret, and I was tired of lying by omission. I went

home one weekend and started the conversation with Mom. It took all of the courage I had to tell her I was dating a white girl and had been for quite a while. Just as I'd expected, Mom burst into tears. "Are you going to marry her?" she asked. I tried to explain how dating worked in America, and that it didn't necessarily mean there would be a marriage, but my pitch fell on deaf ears. My mother was heartbroken.

My parents had always made it clear that they expected me to marry within our religion. It wasn't so much a conversation we'd ever had; it was understood. An arranged marriage was still the preferred way in my culture. The thinking was that you were not just marrying a person but each other's families, so the parents were the most logical judges of what constituted a good match.

I supposed I knew that telling my mother was a make-or-break situation for Jenny and me. I loved Jenny, but I think I knew all along that our relationship was impermanent because my family would never accept her. What really resonated with me, though, was how odd it felt to be on the other side of a bias and how difficult it would be to try to break through it. When push came to shove, my entrenched family values usurped the love I felt for Jenny. As much as I cared for her, I admitted to myself that we wouldn't have a future together because she was neither Indian nor Sikh. And that pretty much sealed our fate.

I promised Mom that I had no intention of marrying Jenny. At that point in my life, marriage was the last thing on my mind anyway. I returned to school with a different mindset.

Jenny wasn't a priority anymore, and she sensed it. The more she demanded of my time, the more I pulled away. At the end of the school year, she gave me an ultimatum. I had to choose what was more important: her or my family. After that, we decided to go our separate ways.

The fall semester of my sophomore year started off badly. Not only was I missing Jenny, but something else felt different. "Weird" is the only word I can think of to describe it. I felt like people were staring at me because, in my mind at least, I stuck out. I was suddenly hyperaware that I was a brown-skinned city kid in a school mostly made up of rural white kids. I even felt self-conscious around my white friends. When I tried talking to them about it, they told me a lot of what I was feeling was in my head. They didn't understand. How could they? As much as they cared about me, they couldn't know the isolation that someone of color felt when they were alone in an all-white world. I loved my friends, but I felt like a piece of me was missing when I was around them, and even sports couldn't bridge the gap. I was an Indian kid who'd been living a white kid's life, and it wasn't working for me anymore.

Depressed and confused, I retreated into the solitude of my dorm room. My grades plummeted and I was put on academic probation. I hated my classes. I'd known all along that I didn't want to be a business major. I wanted to be a police officer and be of service by working in an inner-city neighborhood. With so much time to think, I realized that if I was going to reclaim that missing piece of myself, the piece that was my heritage, which I could no longer ignore, I couldn't do it at Whitewater. I had to get out of there.

Amardeep was attending Marquette University in the city. I'd visited him often and liked the campus. But it was a Catholic and Jesuit college, and I certainly couldn't imagine finding myself there. Still, at least I would be near my brother, so I applied and got in. I changed my major from business and marketing to criminal justice and reluctantly began my junior year there.

I quickly realized that the experience would be life changing. Marquette's campus was a rainbow of colors and cultures, including students of Indian descent, which made me feel immediately at ease. I was back in the city, living off campus with my old buddies from the neighborhood. During the day, we went our separate ways. Some of them went to school and others worked. I had the best of both worlds. I had family and friends around and a whole new campus to explore.

The small, intimate atmosphere of Marquette motivated me. I still gravitated toward sports, but my social circle grew beyond the boundaries of athletics. I played ball and joined the Indian Students' Association. My classes were spiritual in nature but nondenominational and focused on religious philosophy and history and social justice, which I loved. I joined in conversations about important issues. I opened my mind to the views of some of my more white-collar, conservative-thinking classmates, but I found my voice speaking for blue-collar and marginalized communities.

Although it was a Jesuit college, we were encouraged to

question all religions, and I was a contentious student, constantly challenging details of the Bible, the Quran, the Torah and Talmud, and every other book of scripture. I asked things like "How could Methuselah have lived 969 years?" and "How could men be turned into monkeys and swine?" and "How could a river flow upstream?" Until one day, when a particularly patient professor challenged me to appreciate the scriptures for the lessons and guidance they offered rather than scrutinize every detail. His wise advice led me on the path back to my roots.

What I discovered in reading and rereading our scriptures was that the precepts of my religion really appealed to me. Our founder and prophet, Guru Nanak, was a really cool dude. Five hundred years ago, he traveled the world with his universal message of oneness and love—of a common brotherhood and absolute equality among all people, regardless of caste or creed or country. His religion was a way of life; one lived with peace and joy, honesty and optimism, and in service to others, especially those who were marginalized—in reverence to God. It became the basis of Sikhism.

The last line of the Sikh prayer called the *Ardaas* is *Nanak Naam Chardi Kala, teraa bhane sarbaht da bhala*. That line invokes the basic principles of the Sikh philosophy. Translated from Punjabi, it means, "In God's name, we shall be relentlessly optimistic because we want peace and prosperity for all people." I'd recited that line my whole life during daily prayers without ever really thinking much about the meaning. Now, as I continued on my journey to find myself, those prayerful words stirred deep within me. Why hadn't I seen it all along? My Sikh religion was the answer to a prayer. I wanted to live with hope and optimism for me and for all people.

What better way to live?

Arno

Busy Bob's Diner on the south side of Milwaukee is quiet, except for the faggot in the pink shirt crying into the pay phone. It's 2:30 in the morning and my crew and I are hammered and starving. We're about to dig into our burgers and this guy is such a mess that snot's dripping from his nose. Fucking hell. I should have knocked his teeth out on my way back from the bathroom, but I didn't want to catch AIDS.

"Hey, cocksucker!" I say, loud enough so everyone can hear. Eyes dart from me to him and then into space. "I said, 'Hey, cocksucker!' You don't know your name?"

The guy wipes his nose with the back of his hand, but doesn't respond. *I'm gonna kill this motherfucking degenerate.* He snivels some more. My heart beats with excitement. I can feel a confrontation coming on. We all watch as he pulls a cigarette from the pack in his breast pocket. It's one of those long, slim cigarettes; the kind girls smoke.

One of my buddies can't take anymore. He grabs the pickle from his plate and tosses it. The pickle sticks to the homo's cheek and we roll with laughter. That seems to get his attention. He stops his whining, wipes the pickle off his face, and glares at us. We watch with amusement as he reaches for a coffee can filled with sand and a couple of days' worth of cigarette butts. "Who threw the fucking pickle?" he asks, raising the can as if he's going to throw it. He can't be serious. Is he really challenging us?

I jump out of the booth and leap toward him, my steel-toed Doc Martens hitting the floor with a *thwack!* A chair goes flying. He looks stunned. No way am I going to hit him with my bare hands and get his blood on me, so I throw on my flight jacket, then wind up and slam the point of my elbow into his eye. I hear the snap and crack of his shattering eye socket. It sounds like a solid base hit. He cups his hand over his eye and drops to the floor, where he writhes a bit before losing consciousness. Almost like magic, the whole side of his face swells up and turns reddish purple. Right there in front of us! *A broken orbital. Nice!* I kick him in the side with my boot and spit on him. My crew follows suit, kicking and spitting, kicking and spitting. When everyone has taken a turn, we run out of the diner, laughing like hell.

Telling this story makes me feel like crying, but that is who I was for the seven years I called myself a white power skinhead. I hated anyone who wasn't white, straight, and on the same page as me. The page with "Fourteen Words," the slogan that sums up the white supremacist philosophy: "We must secure the existence of our people and a future for white children." Homosexuals were on our hit list. They were as loathsome as blacks, Jews, and race traitors. As much as it pains me to acknowledge who I was, I have come to live by the words of Ida B. Wells-Barnett, who so wisely said, "The way to right wrongs is to turn the light of truth upon them." Amen. The truth is my salvation.

By the time I left that gay man on the diner floor, I had stomped my way into the white power movement and was on my way to becoming a founder of the Northern Hammerskins.

Four years had passed since the jocks cut off my rattail on the eighth-grade playground. In the best of scenarios, that trauma should have taught me empathy for the people I'd bullied over the years. But that's not what happened. I had tasted victimhood and determined never to be someone's prey again.

Instead, I rode the river of violence and hate until I nearly drowned.

Punk

With my breakdancing days behind me, I went in search of something else to feed my adrenaline addiction. That's when I discovered the phenomenon of punk rock. My friend's older brother was blasting an album by FEAR, and the needle dropped on a song called "I Don't Care About You." *I don't care about you . . . Fuck you! . . . I don't care about you.* I'd never heard the word "fuck" used in a song before and I was awestruck.

By then, my contempt for propriety and mainstream culture was as obvious as the giant chip on my shoulder, and the hard-edged, anti-establishment, all-about-pissing-people-off punk subculture was right up my alley. Milwaukee had a strong punk scene, and I found my way to my first live show at a bowling alley between Mequon and downtown Milwaukee. Experiencing live punk was like nothing I'd ever seen. It was wonderfully chaotic. The music was so loud it stung your ears, and the crowd, a collection of the city's outcasts, had fucking *attitude*. The atmosphere was perfectly obnoxious, with everyone pushing and shoving each other and stomping the floor like jackhammers. A pastime that encouraged hitting and getting hit? I fit right in and made friends quickly.

My parents had lost all control of me. I was a freshman in high school and doing whatever I felt like doing. With a new crew and a new lease on life, my days became about finding the next DIY show, where fledgling local punk bands played in garages and basements and other small venues. Our idea of fun was getting wasted, beating each other up, and setting our armpit hair on fire. Bonus points if it was your own. In Mom's eyes, I could do no wrong, even when I was doing pretty much everything wrong. I was her firstborn. I couldn't be *that* fucked up! Dad tried to rein me in, but his attempt at heavy-handedness after a childhood of running wild made me even more determined to revolt. The truth is, I loved rebelling. For me, it felt like scratching poison ivy. When my father put his foot down and forbade me from leaving the house at night, my rote response was, "Try to fucking stop me." The one time he tried, I cursed him out, shoved him to the ground, and walked off. I didn't give a rat's ass what he or anyone else thought of me. My focus was satiating my thirst for thrills. And figuring out where my next buzz was coming from.

I was already in the honeymoon phase of my relationship with drinking by then. Beer was my go-to, but I'd gulp down whatever I could get my hands on, whenever I could get it. Dad had a liquor cabinet and I'd pour shots from every bottle into an empty gallon milk jug and mix it all together. When the jug was a third full, I'd drink half and ride my bicycle drunk to share what was left over with my friends, crashing all along the way.

Wouldn't you know it? My favorite local punk band, Stolen Youth, was straight edge, a wing of the punk community that rejected cigarettes, drugs, sex, and alcohol. I loved their music and went to every one of their shows. Their message was, "Don't go to college. College steals your youth." When the lead singer went off to college, the other members asked me to take his place. I was stoked, except that a condition of my joining was that I had to quit drinking.

I already had a reputation for rowdy drunkenness by then, and the band members said they couldn't afford to muddy their cred. They were willing to take a chance on me, *if* I promised to stop. I told them thanks, but no thanks. I wasn't giving up beer, not even to be in a punk band. I guess because they needed someone who knew the words to their songs, they decided to relax the rule. All I had to do was promise not to be drunk onstage. No deal, I said. I didn't make promises I couldn't keep. Finally, we struck a compromise. I agreed I wouldn't bring beer onstage while I was performing. So I drank myself stupid before and after every show.

The band rocked on until the rest of them left for college; everyone but me. I got in tight with a crew of hardcore punks I knew and their band from West Bend, a city just north of Milwaukee. Their only rule was that fighting and getting fucked up were required. I hitched rides to all of their shows and after-parties that summer. My connections led me to the punk scenes in the cities of Racine and Kenosha, the heart and soul of Wisconsin punk. The Kenosha punk world was especially decadent and dysfunctional. It was like one big maladapted family gone berserk. We ranged in age from thirteen to thirties and had more in common than we should have, namely booze, drugs, and a thirst for mayhem. Our basic existence was getting wasted and going to punk shows, where we'd pummel each other in the name of having fun.

When fall rolled around, my parents dragged me, kicking and screaming, back to Homestead High for the start of my sophomore year. That's when everything really started going to hell. I had always gotten straight A's, because A's were pretty easy for me. But school had come to seem so banal compared to my crazy punk life that, even when I did go to class, I used the time to disrupt the lessons and taunt my teachers. My aim was to provoke them into physical fights. "C'mon! Take a swing!" I'd say, getting up in their faces and challenging them. I didn't get any takers, which only gassed up my general frustration. It was inevitable that my grades would eventually tank, and, when my A's dove to C's and then D's and F's, I just stopped going to school. My parents were at a loss for what to do. Mom and Dad appealed to me to get my shit together. I had too much potential to let it all slip away.

Not one to be idle, I spent the rest of the school year immersed in the punk world. I managed bands and promoted local punk shows, with some success. I was a juvenile delinquent with visions of grandeur. I was a bona fide fucking genius! There was nothing I couldn't do. The first show I planned was at a VFW hall on the south side of Milwaukee. I lied and said it was for a birthday party. The crusty old guys at the bar looked pretty freaked out when a couple of hundred punk rockers with spiked hair, bullet belts, and combat boots showed up on the appointed night to rock out to the band. For four straight hours, the frenzied music and screamed lyrics reverberated off the hall walls. It was pandemonium, with people slam dancing and throwing shit and punching each other, all for kicks. People got hurt, a bunch of shit got broken, and we left the place in shambles, which meant the show was a rousing success. The VFW made enough from the bar to cover the damage and then some. My take was a pile of cash that I spent on a weeklong party with my friends.

Where were my parents? Between a rock and a hard place, to use an old cliché. No matter what they tried, the outcome was the same. I stayed away for days at a time and went home when I needed to eat or sleep. Neither physical nor emotional restraints could hold me back from my perpetual quest for chaos. I was unmanageable and no one could figure out how to contain me, much less control the spiral I was in.

Whatever little was left of my relationship with my family went to shit that summer. I'd organized a tour for a band I "managed" called Nuclear Overdose, NOD for short, and really fucked it up. Every show fell through because we were drunk most of the time and I hadn't confirmed the gigs with the promoters. We packed up two vans and went on the tour anyway. By the time we reached Indianapolis, our traveling money had dried up. We'd spent everything we had on gas and beer and we'd eaten our way through the two flats of generic cream of mushroom soup we brought for the road. Broke and stranded, all fourteen of us crashed at the home of a Mexican girl I was sleeping with until, one day, her mother got fed up with our drunken nonsense and screamed at us to *"Sal de aquí! Sal de aquí!"* (Get out of here!) All that was left to do was panhandle, and we learned really fast that none of us were very good at it. Finally, one of the guys got up the courage to call his parents and convince them to wire enough money to get us back home.

We made our way back to Milwaukee, arriving shortly after my parents and brother had left on a two-week vacation to drive across country to my grandpa's place in Washington State. I'd forgotten they were going. Hallelujah! I had the run of the house! I sent the call out to the entire Wisco punk scene.

So began a huge punk rager in our pretty suburban home in the nothing-ever-happens-here town of Mequon. It was ten straight days of drunkenness and debauchery. Bands from Kenosha came to play in the basement and we all got fucked up in whatever way we could. We started by chugging bottles of Mad Dog 20/20, a cheap, high-octane wine that tasted like cough syrup mixed with aftershave. When that was depleted, we huffed rubber cement out of an empty bread bag until I felt like my lungs were cemented together. We smoked pot from a bong my friend Chad made from a mayonnaise jar and, when the weed ran out, I smoked cat shit from the litter box, just to see what would happen. Wasted out of our minds, we broke dishes, threw food on the walls, and crushed lit cigarettes on the floor. People came and went at all hours. One night, someone took Dad's riding lawnmower for a joy ride and carved a swath through my mother's prized vegetable garden. This was my parents' home, my brother's home, my home, but nothing was sacred to me. I was such a degenerate that I rented out my parents' bedroom for anyone who wanted to hook up. I shudder to think about what happened in their bed, and what condition they found it in.

With all of the laws we broke and damage we caused, I'm surprised we weren't arrested. The cops dropped by a couple of times, but never came in (thank God), and the mom of another girl I was dating came beating at the door, threatening to call the cops until I sent her daughter out. Other than that, we were pretty much left alone to wreak havoc, and wreak havoc we did.

On day ten of Arno's Great Adventure, Mom's friend Cindy dropped by to check on the place. What she found was like a scene from the movie *Animal House*. Cindy stood there with her mouth agape. She couldn't find words. If I could feel feelings back then, I would have felt sorry for her. But all I could think of was getting out of there, and fast.

Rather than face my parents, I took off to Racine and squatted in the basement of a run-down house where Chad's mom was shacked up with a biker dude. Chad had a home-made tattoo gun, and I began my love affair with ink there. I began identifying myself as a skinhead, a tougher, slicker off-shoot of the punk subculture, and one of my first tattoos was an eight-point chaos symbol with the word "Skins" scrawled across the bottom. The two S's were in the form of SS bolts, the symbol of Hitler's paramilitary organization, not because it meant anything to me at that point but just because it looked cool. Another was an upside-down cross with the word "Amen" inked above it, because somewhere along my path of destruction, I'd decided I hated Christianity.

After three or four weeks, my heartbroken mother tracked me down and brought me home. I went willingly, on the condition that I would not have to return to school. I was dead to my father and brother, but Mom would have agreed to anything to get me back. "If you're not going back to high school, I'll get you a job," she said. And she did, printing t-shirts for a Jewish friend of hers who sold bootleg rock shirts.

I kept the job, but soon left the tensions of home to live in the city with a group of hardcore punks and skins who were renting a house in Riverwest, a mixed neighborhood that buffered the posh east side from the inner city. It was a party place and where I wanted to be. The address was 700 E. Wright

Street, and we took to calling ourselves "The 700 Club," a mocking play on the Christian television program hosted by evangelist Pat Robertson. When I should have been attending my junior year of high school, I was working the third shift printing t-shirts and partying with my five roommates at our little den of iniquity. My life consisted of working, drinking, street fighting, and crashing around the local punk scene. But that wasn't enough excitement to keep me satisfied for very long.

Traditional punk was a rejection of mainstream values. It was anti-establishment and pro–working class. That was okay for a while, but I was growing tired of it. Sometimes it seemed like there were more subgenres than followers. Anarcho punk. Death rock. Emo punk. Hardcore. Cow punk. Even Christian punk. I despised the emergence of "peace punks." They annoyed the shit out of me, with their snooty high-mindedness and starry-eyed rhetoric about peace, love, and justice for all. Their mere existence kindled my rebellious gene, and their whiny, self-righteous rants made me want to do wrong. True to my antagonistic nature, I did everything I could think of to incite them. They launched a protest against Coors beer because Coors didn't "hire black people," so Coors was the only beer I would drink. And, just to be a dick, I wore a Coors baseball cap when I was around them. That's how I rolled.

The way I saw it, if the movement was going the drastically leftist way of the peace punks, I was taking my act to the right. I wanted to fight and break shit and beat people up, not rock against racism, and even the skinhead subculture wasn't tough enough to accommodate my simmering hostility toward the world. At that point, I hated everything. I hated rules and conformity. I hated the idea of religion. I hated government. I hated my former friends. I hated home because it was in a fucking mundane suburb and I thrived in the grit of city life. I was a drunken street thug, full of vim and venom, looking for a place to land.

Skrewdriver

I was standing outside of a hardcore punk show on an Indian summer night in 1987 when I found what I thought I was looking for. I was outside smoking cigarettes and drinking Coors when my skinhead buddy Pat's girlfriend called out to me. "Hey, Arno! Listen to this!" she said, handing me her headphones. Jane had just returned to Milwaukee from driving a tour van to New York for an Italian hardcore punk group called the Cheetah Chrome Motherfuckers. She'd bailed after a week on the tour, apparently because the group held a grudge against personal hygiene and the stench in the van was untenable. On her way back, she'd stopped over in Chicago to see some punk friends and ended up hanging out with members of the Chicago Area Skinheads.

CASH, as they were known, were not your ordinary apolitical skinheads. They were a bloodthirsty racist gang from the south suburbs of Chicago with a reputation for violence and depravity, but at least they brushed their teeth, shined their boots, and washed their clothes. Their leader was an ex-con named Clark Martell, a pioneer in the fledgling American racist skinhead movement. He was Mansonesque: super smart, charismatic, manipulative, and batshit crazy. Like Manson's, his followers were lost teenagers who worshipped him, and he had an affinity for surrounding himself with young females. He'd dialed in on Jane, and she came home with a bootleg cassette of the British skinhead group Skrewdriver, the standard bearers of white power music.

I took the headphones from her Walkman and cranked up the volume.

. . . The streets are still, the final battle has ended
Flushed with the fight, we proudly hail the dawn
See over the streets, the White man's emblem is waving
Triumphant standards of a race reborn.

The song was "Hail the New Dawn," and the first time I heard those seething lyrics, I was swept away. The simple, chugging bar chords and chants of "HAIL! HAIL!" in the front man's gravelly voice sent chills through me. It was so passionate. So angry! Glorious!

I was smitten, just as German teenagers were a half century earlier when Hitler used music as a recruiting tool. The racist lyrics spoke to me.

Are we gonna sit and let them come?
Have they got the white man on the run?

71

Multi-racial society is a mess.

We ain't gonna take much more of this.

What do we need? White power!

Was I still holding a grudge against my old homies from the eighth grade, my breakdancing buddies who hadn't come to my defense when the jocks chopped off my rattail? Probably, because I would have bled for them if they had been the victims. But this sensation was much deeper and more dangerous than any teenage grudge. It was almost like I'd been possessed.

Skrewdriver was in constant rotation after that. The more I listened, the deeper and faster I fell under its spell. I embraced its anti-Semitic, anti-foreigner, anti-black, anti-gay, anti-anyone-who-didn't-support-white-power ideals. It made me feel part of something greater than myself. I had finally found an intention that matched my craving for violence. After all, like Jane had said, what more righteous fight was there than the one to save our race?

Milwaukee seemed as good a place as any to launch my new mission, considering its reputation as a hotbed of racial tension. The city always made the list of the most physically and socially segregated cities in the country, thus the nickname "the Selma of the North." That kind of divide makes for endemic ignorance and friction among the races, and we had plenty of both. Old-timers still openly repeated the joke about the 16th Street Viaduct, the span that connects the black side of the city to the white side. The joke goes that it links

Africa to Europe, which makes it the longest bridge in the world.

I was somewhat aware of the racial divide growing up, but there was nothing in my background that would have foretold the path I was on. Dad was politically conservative (how many times had I heard him say that Reagan was "the best thing since sliced bread"?), but I don't recall him ever saying anything particularly racist, and Mom was a downright bleeding-heart liberal. She would have died if she'd known what I was getting myself into.

With Jane's encouragement, Pat and I gravitated toward the white power world. We weeded out the punks from our house and named ourselves the Skinhead Army of Milwaukee (SHAM). Mom embroidered the acronym on my flight jacket, with no idea what it meant. We stole a copy of Hitler's autobiographical manifesto, *Mein Kampf*, from the local library, thinking it could be a primer for our gang, but the writing was so bad I couldn't get more than a few pages in. Instead, white power songs guided us. Pat, our friend Clayton, and I formed our own skinhead band called One Way. We titled a song "One Way" and used it in our recruiting efforts. "One way, the right way, the white way!" Music was always the best way to attract other disaffected teenagers who could easily be swayed to our way of thinking. A typical recruit was a poor white kid from a blue-collar family who was either outnumbered by minorities at his school or rejected by his richer, more popular white peers. We offered them the opportunity to provide us with a continuous supply of beer in exchange for a place to fit in. It was us against the world. We shaved our heads and wore t-shirts with swastikas and the words "White Power!" proudly. Jews and mud races (anyone who wasn't white) were the butt of our jokes.

On most days, our tribe got all tanked up, tied up the red laces on our steel-toed Doc Marten boots, the symbol of all good racist skinheads, and wreaked havoc on our city streets. A good day consisted of manhunts along Downer Avenue, with a lot of fag bashing and at least one good racially charged street brawl. The truth is, we were just a bunch of Milwaukee street thugs who gave ourselves a title and adopted a cause that legitimized our drunken violence. It felt hollow to me. Empty. Same old. I needed something bigger to identify with. Something with more excitement. More passion!

My continuing quest for fucked-upness soon led me to the place where real haters played. And it was there I found my new niche.

Hammerskins

The letter arrived at our post office box in May 1988. Anonymous PO boxes were how groups in the fledgling racist skinhead network connected. "Sieg Heil, Comrade!" it began. "I am from the Confederate Hammerskins of Dallas. We are hearing about your brave fight for our race and we would like to come and visit." Fucking right they wanted to come and visit! Our crew was the scourge of the North! I didn't care that the letter was sloppily written on a lined sheet of paper torn from a notebook. What mattered was what it meant. We had made a name for ourselves. We were King Shit and we'd let everyone know it. Now our skinhead counterparts were looking to us for leadership. Pat and I responded immediately. "Sieg Heil, Comrade!" we wrote. "Yes! Come!"

Our group, which included me, Pat, and Jane the Alpha Bitch, had recently moved from the 700 Club in Riverwest—which we'd trashed to the tune of uninhabitable—to a house on Amy Place on the south side of Milwaukee. Angus Porter arrived on a Greyhound bus. His reputation as a ruthless street soldier preceded him, and he didn't disappoint. He presented like a pit bull, short and solidly built with a menacing stare that said, "Don't even think about it, motherfucker." With the word SKINHEAD tattooed across his forehead and white power icons inked on his biceps, he looked really legit—the way a real racist skinhead was supposed to look. He had our attention before he ever spoke.

Angus and his brother were pioneers in the racist skinhead movement in the US, which had only really surfaced a few years earlier. They'd founded the notorious Confederate Hammerskins less than a year before and had earned the hard-fought honor of a mention in the Anti-Defamation League's special report entitled "Young and Violent: The Growing Menace of America's Neo-Nazi Skinheads." Now that was worth its weight in gold in street cred. They'd recruited dozens of troops in the south and shaken up Dallas with bold attacks on blacks, Hispanics, and Jews. They were flourishing in Texas and making headlines with their violent exploits, and they were looking to expand. Angus explained that their plan was to set the standard for skinheads across the United States by bringing together the toughest of us under one umbrella. We told him we were interested in hearing more.

On his first night in Milwaukee, we all went drinking at a section of the lake where the metalheads hung out. The evening was going swimmingly. We got blind, rip-roaring drunk and even recruited a couple of metalheads while we were there. It was late when we headed home. The streets were dark and no one was around. We were traveling in a deserted area, under an overpass, when what sounded like a gunshot or a rock hit our car. Our friend Will slammed on the brakes and we all jumped out. A couple of kids who were dressed like punks took off and we went in pursuit of them. We caught them before they could climb the embankment and pulled them back down to where the car was parked. Pat beat one kid while I took on the other. They were crying and screaming like babies when Angus joined in.

We thrashed those little punks into bloody unconsciousness then jumped back in the car and went home to continue our night of partying. Angus won mega points with us for his performance. He was as ferocious as we were. The way we fought also convinced him that we were the perfect crew for his master plan.

With that settled, Angus decided to hang around for a while. We had plenty of beer and plenty of fights to pick in our "diverse" neighborhood to keep him busy. After the bloodbath under the overpass, we started keeping count of our altercations. One weekend we counted twenty-five. We fought hard and we fought dirty, with our bare hands, with baseball bats, with knives and razors and bricks and anything else that could win the war. If there were ten of us and we came upon one unlucky black guy who just happened to be in the wrong place at the wrong time, he felt the fury of ten pairs of boots stomping on his back.

Our skinhead girls were as tough as we were. We got our crew together for a picnic by the lake one day and the girls left to fetch more beer. While they were out, some middle-aged white guy commented that they looked like a bunch of dykes. Wrong thing to say to a crew of skinhead girls, asshole! Skinhead girls fight dirty. They jumped him and beat him to the ground. When he cried for mercy, they all took turns kicking him in the head. They came back to the picnic with ear-to-ear grins, and we all celebrated with beer and songs.

In war, there is no such thing as a fair fight. We won some and we lost some, and each one was a measure of our worth. It was easy to win a ten-on-one beatdown, and we always did, but when you're hopelessly outnumbered, that's what separates the men from the boys. At least that's what we told ourselves when we lost one.

That's what happened one night that summer of 1988 when our crew went looking for trouble at a festival on Downer Avenue. Downer was where our nemeses, the anti-racist skinhead group we called Baldies, hung out. We existed to fight each other. I thought they were a bunch of wusses. Every time we tangled, they called the cops. It had gotten to the point where all we had to do was set foot on Downer and the cops would arrive and shoo us away. It was infuriating. Our way of life depended on conflict. Without a good fight to be had, what was the point?

We went to the festival looking for the Baldies but discovered that we had many more enemies than we knew. It wasn't just the Baldies who were tired of our bullshit. People from all over the festival ganged up on us. Some were students from Marquette. Some were our neighbors. Blacks. Jews. Gays. It must have been a hundred to our thirty. A magnificent melee ensued. I squared off with a black dude who whipped my ass. He was blasting me in the face and I couldn't even get close to him. It was rare when I got knocked down or out, but I saw stars that night. The cops finally swarmed in and we made news. Sometimes getting publicity was better than winning. We couldn't buy the kind of attention we got from a headline. Our numbers always increased afterward.

Angus was really enjoying his time with us, but, sadly, his stay was cut short when he and Pat got into a gunfight with a carload of kids who attempted a drive-by shooting at our house.

I was working my shift at the t-shirt place that night, but I heard all about what went down from Jane when I got home. A week or so earlier, a bunch of us were sitting on the porch, drinking of course. It was one of our favorite pastimes, and we did it so often that we called ourselves "porch honkies," a play on the racial slur "porch monkeys." People in the neighborhood hated us, and for good reason. We commented out loud about everyone who passed, and never was it neighborly. On that day, we were doing our thing, drinking and carrying on, when someone took a shot at us from the alley. Most of the blast hit the side of the house. You could see the pellets of birdshot in the aluminum siding. The rest of it was embedded in Angus's face. The Milwaukee gang squad was there before the smoke cleared. Squads were always cruising nearby. We only found out later that the Milwaukee PD had us under constant surveillance. It was clear they had no intention of helping us that day, but they issued a warning: We were in gangbanger territory and on the radar of the Latin Kings, they said. Word on the street was that there were going to be some dead skinheads in the neighborhood. We'd better watch it, "because those guys don't fuck around."

We didn't either. We armed ourselves with rifles a friend "obtained" for us and started a round-the-clock watch. There wasn't a moment that one of us wasn't stationed at a window with a rifle pointing outside. Pat and Angus had been holding down the fort, and a carload of high school kids drove past, they said later to get a glimpse of the neo-Nazis they'd heard about on the news. Our guys watched as the car slowed down and the kids threw bottles at the house. The kid in the front passenger seat leaned out the window holding a handgun. Pat fired at the car from an upstairs window. Angus followed up with a couple of shots that shattered the car windows. The kids raced off, but the cops were able to track them to a nearby emergency room across the city where the one kid was being treated for a gunshot and the others for shrapnel wounds from flying glass. A search of their car turned up knives, bats, and sticks, but no gun, which was bad news for our guys.

At trial, Angus was repentant and was sentenced to eighteen months in a detention facility. Pat was unapologetic, even defiant, and got ten years in state prison.

That left me to move things forward. I had always acted in tandem with Pat, but now I was on my own. Everything that happened to him affirmed the white supremacist narrative: the law and the Constitution were meaningless under the Jewish master plan to bury white people under a tide of mud races. I was more determined than ever to do my part to stop that from happening.

More and more tattoos of white power ideology found their way onto my skin: swastikas on the middle finger of my right hand and on the side of my right calf; the bust of an SS soldier with the words "White Power" on my right forearm. I vowed to uphold the white supremacist code 14/88: fourteen for the number of words in the movement's core belief that "we must secure the existence of our people and a future for white children"; eighty-eight for "Heil Hitler," as H is the eighth letter of the alphabet.

I met with racist skinheads from Chicago, St. Paul, and Detroit and invited them to join us under the Northern Hammerskins flag, just as we had envisioned during our talks with Angus. Our political agenda was inspired by the doctrine of the Führer himself: preserve and promote the white race by any means necessary, even if it meant killing our enemies.

We wore the Northern Hammers emblem proudly on our jackets: a circle of thirteen white stars on a field of colonial blue, emboldened with twin clawed hammers, crossed. Ironically, it was the hijacked symbol used for a fictitious neo-Nazi group in the film *Pink Floyd: The Wall*. The fact that we copied a contradictory symbol to represent our movement and made it our own was poetic in a way. Hitler had appropriated the swastika, after all. It wasn't his idea. He stole an ancient religious icon that had been synonymous with positivity and good fortune and made it the symbol of Nazism. If it was good enough for Hitler . . .

The Northern Hammerskins were smarter, more so phisticated street fighters. We strategized and recruited susceptible white kids by going into neighborhoods that were already simmering with racial tension and posting flyers—which were shipped to us by Tom Metzger, the notorious white supremacist "celebrity" from California who founded the revolutionary organization White Aryan Resistance (WAR)—with swastikas and crude warnings to Jews, blacks, and gay people. Our new recruits were assigned white power readings and encouraged to educate themselves on our ideals.

We were still urban warriors who preyed violently on blacks, Jews, and homosexuals and launched attacks on our race traitor counterparts, but I told myself that being part of the movement was no longer just a reason to brawl.

It was who I had become: a white man willing to sacrifice everything to save his race.

David Duke

The 1988 presidential election was a boon for white supremacy—at least that's the way we saw it in our cloistered culture. David Duke, a right-wing extremist whose résumé included a stint as grand wizard of the Ku Klux Klan, was running as a third-party candidate. Even though he didn't have a snowball's chance in hell, he was on the ballot with George H. W. Bush and Michael Dukakis, which gave him a platform for his pro-white agenda.

I wasn't a Duke guy. I thought he was too soft to represent our movement, a "politically correct" white nationalist, if you will. My comrade Will, on the other hand, was head-over-heels enamored with him. Will begged me to go when Duke rented out a conference room at the local Howard Johnson's for a "town hall"–style campaign appearance. My preference was to stay home and drink copious amounts of beer, but I finally agreed.

The dingy conference room had stained carpeting and smelled like cigarettes, which was fine by me. It held around a hundred people, but it was less than half full, mostly skinheads and old, white racists who called themselves Populists. Duke was, as I'd expected, too tame for me. In his soft Louisiana drawl, he talked about wanting equal rights for whites, rather than the real issue of expelling the mud races from our land. He wasn't anti-black, he said, rather "pro-white" and "pro-Christian." His rote campaign rhetoric struck me as weak and disingenuous, hardly the kind of blatantly racist stuff he spewed during his tenure as the exalted leader of the Knights of the Ku Klux Klan. That guy, I might have voted for.

As disenchanted as I was, Will was fucking besotted. When the gig was over and he walked up to introduce himself to the candidate, he was giggling and sputtering like a teenage girl with a crush. I was caught off guard when he invited Duke back to our house, and even more surprised when Duke accepted the invitation.

The minute we got home we started scrambling to get people there. It was important to Will to show Duke that we had a big crew. We made a bunch of calls and, within the hour, had thirty people in our living room. I don't know whether it was Duke or the promise of free beer that persuaded them to come.

Duke arrived right on time, accompanied by two of his cronies. By then we had worn out our welcome on Amy Place and were living between Marquette University and the worst ghetto in the city, on Milwaukee's north side. The house was made of rotting wood, peeling paint, and a roof that looked like it might collapse with the first fist to the wall (it didn't), but it had two stories and was big enough to accommodate our growing crew. We'd furnished it with a couple of beat-up couches we found in an alleyway, a half-decent recliner someone had brought from somewhere, and empty cases of returnable beer bottles that doubled as seats.

Duke took a seat in the good chair.

I asked if he wanted a beer and he accepted.

It was Red, White, and Blue in a bottle, a shit beer; the only kind we could afford and the epitome of quantity over quality. I was impressed when he drank and didn't grimace.

Duke was a good-looking guy; almost too good looking. His face was different than the pictures I'd seen of him when he was leading the Klan. His features were more chiseled and his hair was bleached blond. I was certain he'd had cosmetic surgery, perhaps to match the newer, softer image he was going for to try to get elected.

In the privacy of our home, Duke sounded much more militant than he did in public, talking openly about the great Jewish conspiracy to rule the world and the obvious superiority of whites over blacks. I'd heard he was a ladies' man, and, sure enough, he hit on every skinhead girl there, telling them they were "awfully cute," and "another reason we have to save the white race!" Because no white guy worth his weight was going to be caught fucking a Negress. That got the skinhead girls all atwitter and elicited a question from one of the guys in the room.

His name was Rich, a huge muscle dude who lived with his thirteen-year-old female cousin in an obscure house at the end of an alleyway. Rich was super shady and a lot scary. Even Will, who was a badass, was afraid of him. Rich was known for being crass and saying whatever came to his mind. When he raised his hand, grunting like the dorky "Sweathog" Arnold Horshack from the TV comedy *Welcome Back, Kotter*, I saw Will cringe.

"Mr. Duke! Oh! Oh! Mr. Duke! What about Whitney Houston? Tell me you wouldn't eat the peanuts out of her shit!"

The room fell silent. I suffocated a cackle and looked over at Will, who was as white as a sheet and looked like he was about to keel over.

Duke looked dumbfounded. It took everything I had not to collapse with raucous laughter. A full twenty or thirty seconds passed before he finally stammered out an answer.

"Well, um, there are some negresses with enough white blood to be attractive, but that's beside the point," he said.

Way to ruin a perfectly nice evening! Rich was oblivious. I asked Duke if he wanted another beer, but he declined.

Duke lost the presidential election, needless to say. He managed to get forty-seven thousand votes, but that was less than one half of one percent of the vote. Will was inconsolable, but I was happy about the outcome.

I thought he was a pussy.

Martyr's Day

We stood in a ring around the blazing bonfire, my crew of Northern Hammer skinheads and our Confederate Hammer comrades, arms raised in crisp Nazi salutes.

December 8, 1988: Martyr's Day. Six of us had jammed into my recently purchased used Mercury Monarch and

driven twelve hours from Milwaukee to a forest on the out-
skirts of Tulsa, Oklahoma, to pay tribute to Robert Jay
Mathews, who'd martyred himself for the white power movement four years earlier.

Our master of ceremonies was a guy named Jim Denko,
a super-militant exalted cyclops of the Oklahoma Klan and
White Aryan Resistance organizer. I wasn't a fan of the Klan
because of its Christian bent, but Denko leaned more toward
Odinism—a belief system based in Nordic mythology—and
that gave him cred in my book.

Denko knew how to stir up a crowd.

Pacing around the fire, he told with determined fury the
story of Mathews's heroism and fiery demise. In 1983,
Mathews founded the Bruders Schweigen (Silent Brotherhood), a cadre of hardened men also known as "the Order,"
who declared war against the "Zionist Occupied Government"
in the name of the white race. Their plan was to establish a
war chest by robbing banks and bringing enough attention
to the movement to start an armed white revolution. In their
short existence, the Order had made a name for themselves
with daring armored car heists, the bombing of a Jewish
synagogue, and the murder of a Jewish radio personality before the government finally caught up with them.

In the eyes of his white power comrades, Mathews was a
hero to the end. He was hiding out on an island in Puget
Sound, Washington, when dozens of federal agents descended
on his cabin. Cornered, Mathews refused to surrender. He
held the agents off for thirty-six hours before burning to death

when they shot flares into his retreat, setting off a fiery blaze. Legend had it that his body was found charred but he was still clutching a rifle in each hand. How noble he was! Denko cried. How brave!

"Hail Robert Mathews!" fifty-some voices shouted in unison, the glowing orange light of the fire reflected in our eyes. "Hail the Order!"

Denko gestured dramatically as he described the day in 1983 when the Order was born. At Mathews's invitation, eight men stood over one of their infant daughters in a barn at Mathews's Washington State compound and took an oath to do whatever was necessary to protect all white children from the Jews and mud races "and bring total victory to the Aryan race."

In their Declaration of War, they wrote, "It is a dark and dismal time in the history of our race. . . . Evidence abounds that a certain vile, alien people have taken control of our country. How is it that a parasite has gained dominion over its host? Instead of being vigilant, our fathers have slept. What are we to do? How bleak these aliens have made our children's future."

The words sounded like poetry to me.

Standing before the fire, I thought about how much I'd changed in a short time. A year earlier, I was a street hoodlum, in it for the drinking and the fighting, pretending to be something I wasn't: someone with an intention for a noble cause. I had talked the white power talk and butted heads with my anti-racist skinhead counterparts, but to what end? What had I really accomplished? What made me worthy of putting myself in the same category as a Robert Jay Mathews, who'd given his life for the fight?

Listening to Denko talk about the heroic acts of the brave warriors of the Order seared a deep love for my race on my soul.

Hearing about Mathews being burned alive, his charred hands still on the triggers of his assault rifles, I knew I had to avenge him by fighting to the death myself. For my people. For our people.

Denko roared: "We must secure the existence of our people, and a future for white children!" *Fourteen words.*

The familiar feeling of hatred surged through my body like a strong electric current, and the image of that symbolic white baby fueled my thirst for violence. I wanted to tear our enemies limb from limb, and I would die doing it. For the future of white children!

"Whether you were an instigator of the treason or whether you just went along for the ride will make little difference to us," Mathews wrote in a letter to Congress before he was killed.

We will not listen to your explanation that you were really on our side all the time. We will only remember that you could have stopped what has happened to America, and, for whatever reason, you did not.

No, when the day comes, we will not ask whether you swung to the right or whether you swung to the left; we will simply swing you by the neck.

With those things said, let the battle begin.

The fire burned ever brighter, driving back the cold and damp of the night.

Denko read another passage from the Order's Declaration of War:

A long forgotten wind is starting to blow. Do you hear the approaching thunder? It is that of the awakened Aryan. War is upon the land. The tyrant's blood will flow.

"Hail Robert Mathews!" I shouted, thrusting my right arm in the air. "Hail the Order!"

Thanksgiving 1989

The always-eventful Michaelis family Thanksgiving was in full swing and I was finishing the last of a twelve-pack of Huber when someone brought up the name Michael McGee. McGee was a bombastic black Milwaukee alderman and former Black Panther who was always blasting off about evil white people and how he was going to take us out using violence. "Fucking nigger!" I said, shoving another forkful of Grandma Gerry's cream cheese mashed potatoes into my mouth. "The guy's talking about picking us off from the freeway overpass! He needs to stay on the north side where he belongs."

Mom's face went gray. I'm sure she'd never used the N-word in her life and she was horrified to hear it spoken at Grandma Gerry's Thanksgiving table.

I was going off about how superior white people were to blacks and how Jews were out to get us and that McGee was the best thing that ever happened for our white power recruitment program when Dad cut me off. Drinks all around, he said, hoping to distract me from my continuing racist rant.

Michaelis Thanksgivings were always at Grandma Gerry's and always turned into drunken shitstorms. This one was different only because I'd been radicalized since the last holiday gathering and my parents couldn't make excuses for me anymore. I was eighteen and too old to be the impressionable young man whose behavior Mom had always excused as "going through a stage." Mom and Dad were as ashamed as I was proud of the person I'd become: a militant racist who was willing to die and kill for a righteous cause.

I took another swig of beer and, stabbing my finger in the air, continued to make my point. "Look at the north side!" I said. "It used to be a nice neighborhood. Now it's a hellhole!" My racist skinhead girlfriend, Gina, shook her head in agreement. "Blacks! They're savages! They destroy everything. They're going to come and get us if we don't do something."

My sweet mother had had enough. She put her fork down and looked me dead in the eyes. "Well, Mr. Nazi, do you know you are one-sixteenth Indian?" she asked.

The statement stopped me dead in my tracks. What was she talking about? "How could you say that?" I asked, clenching my teeth in rage. "That's *bullshit*! You're lying!"

"No," Mom said. "I'm not." My great-grandfather—her grandpa—was French Canadian, and we had some Indian blood from his side, she explained.

"You're making that up!" I shouted, pounding my fist on the table.

Grandma Gerry chimed in. "No, it's true, Arno," she said.

Everyone sitting around the table was laughing—everyone except Gina and me. "You're an Indian!" my brother said, cackling. "You think it's fun being a Nazi, but you're an Indian!"

My stomach churned. Could it be true? Was I . . . *mixed*? Was it possible that the identity I had embraced, a racially pure white American male, was a lie? I felt as if my entire world had been yanked out from under me.

Grabbing Gina's hand, I stomped off, shouting at everyone to "Fuck off!" before I left.

I went home and pulled a beer from the refrigerator. I wanted to be alone, I told Gina. Closing the bedroom door behind me, I chugged down the beer without taking a breath. It tasted bitter, to match my mood. *I have fucking Indian blood*, I thought. Why the fuck did my mother tell me? Everything I stood for was fucked. Everything that meant anything was ruined.

I smashed the empty bottle on the floor, picked up the jagged neck, and, with one brisk movement, sliced open my wrist. At first it just stung. My heart raced, followed by a feeling of release, as if all of the pressure that was building inside was draining away. Drops of blood hit the bedroom floor. Indian blood? I recoiled. The stinging changed to a searing, throbbing kind of pain that I welcomed. I deserved to suffer for my Indian blood.

Gina burst through the bedroom door. "What the fuck did you do?" she cried, running out to grab towels from the bathroom. "You drunken idiot!" she shouted as she rushed back in and wrapped my bleeding wrist. "I guess I didn't do a good enough job," I said before passing out.

"Fuck you!" Gina replied.

I awoke the next morning with my wrist wrapped in gauze and began planning the next time. The next time I would be successful. I had to be. There was nothing left for me in this life. My purpose was gone. My self-esteem was shattered. I was a dirty mongrel, not the white warrior I had been so proud to be. That guy was a fraud and didn't know it. Now I knew it. Now what?

Wallowing in the worst depression I'd ever felt, I sat down and wrote a letter to Tom Metzger at his WAR PO box.

> Tom,
>
> I'm a white power skinhead from Milwaukee. We started the Northern Hammers here, and I sing in a white power band "One Way." I've been racially conscious for about two years now and I'm committed to kill and to die for our great white race.
>
> Last night my traitorous mother told me that I'm 1/16 Indian.

I don't know what to do. My race is everything to me. It's everything I am. Last night I tried to kill myself by slitting my wrist. I passed out and my girlfriend stopped the bleeding. I wish she didn't. I still want to kill myself. I don't know what to do.

How can I be a warrior for my people when there is mud race in my veins?

I don't know what to do.

Arno

I couldn't imagine that the leader of one of the most prestigious white power organizations in existence—one of the most revered white supremacists in the world—would respond. But a few days later, a letter from Metzger came to my PO box.

Metzger wrote that he knew about the good work my crew and my band were doing for the movement. Music, after all, was the most effective way we had to awaken white youth to what was happening to our race. As for my supposed Indian blood, I had so little I would lose it in a nosebleed. I'd already spilled much more than that in the war to save our race. Rather than be so hard on myself, I needed to get myself back out there and spill the blood of our enemies.

The letter was like a shot of adrenaline. Metzger had restored my confidence in my whiteness and my will to fight. I vowed that I wouldn't stop until victory was ours.

Racist Summer Camp

The following summer I was invited to attend the inaugural session of Ben Klassen's School for Gifted Boys. Klassen was the founder and self-proscribed Pontifex Maximus of the Church of the Creator (COTC). He was an icon in the white power movement, and his book *The White Man's Bible* was on the bed stand of every serious white supremacist. The School for Gifted Boys wasn't so much a school for intellectually superior adolescents as it was a two-week summer camp for promising young racists to learn leadership and paramilitary survivalist skills. And the Church of the Creator wasn't a typical church where people went to worship, either, but rather what Klassen called "a new religious movement for the survival of the white race exclusively." Its crest was a "W" capped with a crown and a halo: the "W" stood for the white race, the crown symbolized the superiority or aristocracy of whites, and the halo represented the sanctity of the white gene pool.

It sounded like an adventure to me.

I took a road trip to Klassen's compound in the Blue Ridge Mountains of North Carolina with two friends from the Milwaukee white power movement; the three of us *were* the inaugural class. The school had classrooms and living barracks and was still so new you could smell the wood. Behind it, sitting majestically at the crest of a hill, was Klassen's sprawling home. He'd obviously made a shitload of money from the Can-O-Matic electric can opener he'd patented as a younger man. I was impressed with his stature and his success. I didn't know anyone that rich and celebrated, and I was excited to meet him.

On our first full day there, Klassen came doddering down the hill from his house to the school. He saluted us with the Nazi salute when he entered the classroom and took his place behind a table draped with the COTC flag. I don't know what I was expecting but he wasn't it. Klassen was ancient. His pants were hiked up well above his waist, and he was wearing white shoes. He looked like he belonged on a Florida golf course, not the head of a radical racist school where young recruits were taught how to implement and fight a Racial Holy War. And he talked like the 1960s cartoon character Deputy Dawg!

His fifteen-minute welcome speech felt like half the afternoon. He was deadly dull and a terrible speaker. As uninteresting as he was to listen to, what he said inspired me. Pointing to the portrait of Adolf Hitler ("the greatest leader who ever lived") on the wall behind him, next to a portrait of himself, Klassen said the mission of the school was about training young recruits for war. His vision was to build an army big enough and mighty enough to accomplish what the Führer had in Germany, except that our task was even more significant because we weren't just fighting for a country. We were going to save the entire white race.

"We have the start of something that is as big as anything that has happened in history and we need leaders," he said in his plodding, distracted way. "We want to put you through some rigorous training, and education, and discipline." There-fore, absolutely no cigarettes, drugs, or alcohol were to be brought onto the property. Fucking hell! *Good luck with all that, Pontifex*, I thought.

I liked the physical activities at the camp. That's probably what kept me there for the first couple of days. Our survival lessons were taught by a former Green Beret named Pete and his sidekick, Ben. Pete was a short, solidly built guy with a leathery tan and a handlebar mustache. Ben was probably twenty years younger, with a mop of wavy auburn hair and long, strong limbs honed through his work as a tree surgeon. Both were authentic Appalachian hillbillies, and they knew the mountains the way most people knew their neighbor-hood. They taught us how to make mantraps and car bombs and took us on "night ops," where we did things like hike some of the roughest mountain terrain in the pitch dark and rappel down an abandoned mine shaft that was three hundred feet deep with a thirty-foot mouth. It felt like descending into hell.

Mornings were class time with Klassen, or what he called "Bible Study." With a huge swastika as a backdrop, he lectured about "Jews, niggers, and the other mud races," and read pas-sages from *The White Man's Bible*, a six-hundred-page tome that set forth the church's guidelines for achieving "a whiter and brighter world"—the holy book for white supremacists.

"Just as in our early school days we were repeatedly drilled first in the alphabet, then in words and spelling and in the multiplication tables, as well as other key tools of learning, so too have I repeatedly hammered away from different angles at the key ideas, key issues, the natural laws that must become part of us if the White Race is to survive," Klassen wrote in *The White Man's Bible*. "This book is meant to awaken, to clarify, to give direction and to arouse men to action. Our goal, I repeat, is the survival, expansion and advancement of the great White Race, in short, the resurrection and redemption of our people."

The idea was to get us "racially oriented and racially aware." The classes were mind-numbing until I got used to his humdrum delivery and started really listening to his words.

Our homework consisted of reading assignments from the *Bible*, from which we chose our own passages to share in class. Klassen was a prolific writer and I found myself really getting into the readings.

> We must then expel these parasites from our shores. It is our program to ship the niggers back to Africa, and the Mexicans and other mud races back to wherever they came from.

His prophecies lit a fire under me.

> We must fully realize that as goes America, so goes the White Race. . . . It is our objective to make this country a rich prosperous and beautiful land for the White Race and the White Race alone, to convert and educate the White

THE GIFT OF OUR WOUNDS

Man back to the fundamental truths of race, to accept a
racial religion and build a finer better race and finally a
Brighter and Whiter World.

After a week or so, I forgave Klassen his dreary affect and
begrudgingly came to respect him for his keen intellect and
cogent arguments. I tried not to notice his Western bolo ties
and accepted his word that his belt buckle with the Texas
Ranger straddling his horse was historically significant
because it symbolized what we were about: "The only good
Indian was a dead Indian, and the rangers cleansed Texas of
Indians and Mexicans," he said. "We adopt the same view. We
want to cleanse the mud races and make [the world] a beautiful home for the white race."

Klassen's personality sucked, but the guy was fucking
brilliant. He unabashedly compared himself to such revolutionary thinkers as Darwin and Nietzsche and I had to
agree. Anyone who could write a six-hundred-plus-page *Bible*
that kept my attention had to be saying something worth my
time.

I liked that Klassen was vehemently anti-Christian. I had
been put off by the emphasis that the Klan was always placing on Christian values. "We all know what happened to the
Romans shortly after they were 'converted' to Christianity,"
he wrote in the *Bible*. "With their instincts deadened and their
thinking perverted into worrying about the spooks in the sky
instead of struggling for their own survival and advancement,
they soon shrank into oblivion. . . . They paid the penalty of

allowing themselves to be mongrelized and not recognizing their eternal enemy, the Jew. . . . Let us again make this clear: our every position is and must be from the White Man's point of view. From the White Man's point of view the Jews, the niggers, and the mud races are his eternal natural enemies. . . . At this crucial stage of world history, either the White Race will survive, or the Jews and their enslaved mud races will. It will be one or the other."

He knew his stuff about Darwin's evolutionary theory of natural selection and survival of the species, and he'd spent years studying ways we could contribute to the proliferation of our race. Our race was our religion, he said. "It is the supreme purpose of the Church of the Creator to see to it that it will be the White Race that shall survive," the *Bible* said.

That worked for me.

The "Commandments of Creativity" became my spiritual guide:

It is the avowed duty and holy responsibility of each generation to assure and secure for all time the existence of the White Race upon the face of this planet. . . . Be fruitful and multiply. Do your part in helping to populate the world with your own kind. It is our sacred goal to populate the lands of this earth with White people exclusively. . . . Remember that the inferior colored races are our deadly enemies, and the most dangerous of all is the Jewish race. It is our immediate objective to relentlessly expand the White Race, and keep shrinking our enemies.

These were words to live by.

The church's blueprint for achieving white domination was as ruthless and malevolent as any radical group out there. It was almost hard to imagine this meek-looking guy developing such a heinous plan. His pro-white agenda advocated genocide against all non-whites and white race traitors, but the way to a "whiter and brighter world" had to be fought militantly, politically, financially, and morally.

By the end of my stay at camp, I felt like I'd learned valuable lessons from Klassen—first and foremost that we couldn't win the war by just spilling blood. We had to be smarter and shrewder if we were to build the kind of support we'd need to win the race war.

I went home to Milwaukee with *The White Man's Bible* under my arm and new marching orders for our troops. I realized that if my crew was going to help save our race, we needed to change our way of doing things. We had to get smart. Regroup. Grow up.

I copied a passage from Klassen's book of daily affirmations as inspiration for me and my guys.

A RACIAL HOLY WAR. RAHOWA! IS INEVITABLE. It is the ULTIMATE and ONLY solution. No longer can the mud races and the White Race live on the same planet and survive. It is now either them or us. We want to make damn sure it is we who survive. This Planet is from now on all ours, and will be the one and only habitat for our future progeny for all time to come.

We were about to become more savvy warriors—no less vicious when we had to fight, but more thoughtful about the best way to reach our goal.

We held weekly strategy meetings and recruited susceptible white kids by going into neighborhoods that were already simmering with racial tension and posting flyers with swastikas and crude warnings to Jews, blacks, and gay people to "beware." Our new recruits were assigned white power readings and encouraged to educate themselves on the ideology of the movement. We needed to know our stuff if we expected to attract intelligent people with money and power. It was time to get earnest about our mission, and to do what was needed to get the attention of influential people who could give us the credibility we needed to make a real impact.

We had a Racial Holy War to start. Or, as Klassen liked to call it, RaHoWa.

Propagandizing and Proselytizing

The smarter, softer strategy our crew had adopted after Klassen's summer school had begun to manifest results. We were still fighting, but less, and mostly as a show of strength to the kids we were most interested in having. We were still drowning in beer, but we were more informed and actually articulate sounding when peddling white power propaganda. Our new level of sophistication aimed for entrée into more mainstream white society, not just the radical fringe, which is what we needed if we had any hope of saving our great race.

By the summer of 1991 we had enough followers to open the doors to the Milwaukee chapter of the Church of the Creator. The church was a building we rented in a diverse section of downtown. The neighborhood was predominantly Latino, with a gang problem. We prepared for conflict by arming ourselves to the teeth, and I was often stationed as a lookout with a Ruger Mini-14 Ranch Rifle at my side. I don't remember ever using it, but paranoia was endemic in the movement. The sense of importance that came with thinking there was always someone out to get us fostered our egos and gave us a sense of value.

Church meetings were held on Sundays. The "sermons" were led by our crew's elder statesmen and built around readings from *The White Man's Bible*. Afterward, the leaders went around the room asking everyone what he or she had done for their race since the last meeting. We weren't looking for the stock answers that racist skinheads were accustomed to giving, such as "I beat the shit out of someone." We wanted to hear that someone had recruited a new member, or spent an afternoon rolling up and putting rubber bands around the church's latest *Racial Loyalty* newspapers, or that a group had gotten together and distributed thousands of the newspapers in white neighborhoods. We were smarter, more sophisticated racists, and our numbers told us we were doing something right. The church was about propagandizing, proselytizing, and getting as many people as we could out on the streets to recruit. We regularly got anywhere from eighty to a hundred people at a service, but attendance could get as high as 150.

We came out after every service, armed and bristling with animosity, but no one wanted to fuck with us.

I thought I should feel good about what we were accomplishing. But a funny thing happened. As the adrenaline rush I got from daily street brawling began to wane, I found myself fighting off troubling questions—questions I had been suppressing for years. What did the way to Klassen's "whiter and brighter world" really look like? Were we fighting now so we could kill later? Kill people by the billions? Would we— would I—really have the stomach to pull the trigger on a genocidal scale?

Each time those questions invaded my brain, I fought them off by reciting the Fourteen Words. *We must secure the existence of our people and a future for white children.* But with the passage of time, the words began sounding just a little hollower, my recitation just a little less impassioned.

Looking back, I realize that my passion had just begun to wane at that point. The fire within me had turned from white hot to a yellow glow. I blamed it on boredom.

FOUR

FORKS IN THE ROAD

I set out to find flawed men but when I finally peered into myself,
there was no man more flawed than me.
Kabir

Arno

I'd known Alicia for six months when she suggested we have
a kid. She said it was our responsibility as racially conscious
people to bring a white child into the world. The mud races
and blacks were pushing out kids at a rate that would shame
rats. We were being outbred by non-whites at imposing odds.
The world was growing darker, and if we didn't do something,
there would be none of us left. We had to do our part to try
to get things back on the white track.

Who was I to argue?

I'd met Alicia during services at the Church of the Creator
in Milwaukee in late summer of 1991. Word had spread about
our church, and racist skinheads from around the world were
coming to Milwaukee to see what it was all about. Alicia came
with two of her fellow skinheads from the old Chicago gang,

CASH, the one led by Clark Martell. I was part of our paramilitary security unit, the White Berets, and I was on lookout duty when I first saw her. Even from my post, in a window five stories up from the entrance, I could see that she was smoking hot. I was smitten before I ever talked to her. When I finally got the chance, the chemistry between us was off the charts. She stayed for the after-party, and we made arrangements to meet up the following weekend at a Bound for Glory concert in Muskegon. She was different than the butch skingirls I was used to. She was drop-dead gorgeous, with a rockin' body, pretty little laugh, and only a bit of an edge. We spent the next couple of weekends partying together, and from that point forward we were magically involved.

Alicia's name was well known in racist skinhead circles. Three years earlier, she had made headlines as the witness who helped put Clark Martell in prison. She'd been one of Martell's minions and was with him when he carried out a brutal attack on a girl who'd quit the Chicago gang. What had sent him over the edge, apparently, was that she'd befriended people from different races after she went AWOL. To punish her, Martell rounded up Alicia and four other followers, and they broke into her apartment, beat and pistol-whipped her, then painted a swastika in her blood on the wall. He and the others were charged with felonies and later indicted. Alicia was eight months pregnant when it came time for trial. The district attorney gave her the choice of either testifying against Martell or having her baby in prison. She'd wisely decided to be a witness for the state. Martell was sent away for eleven years, which had effectively gutted the Chicago gang. Afterward, Alicia married the father of her child and they'd had another daughter before separating.

Ours would be her third child.

Alicia rented an apartment in Milwaukee, and within two weeks I moved in with her. She got pregnant right away. Her other two kids, who were two and four years old, bounced back and forth between our house and their father's. With the baby coming, we moved to a bigger place in a borderline neighborhood in west Milwaukee. We were there for just a couple of months when we decided it wasn't white enough to raise kids and moved again, this time to a townhouse an hour north of the city in one of the whitest suburbs in the state.

Just before the move, I'd gotten my racist skinhead band, Centurion, up and running. I wrote most of the lyrics to our songs.

> Nigger! Prepare to burn!
> You've attacked our people—but now it's your turn,
> you act so bold—but we'll slap you down,
> the Legions of Hate will put you underground! . . .
> Jew boy! Tremble in fear!
> Your days are numbered: Centurion's here.
> We'll leave your kind to wither on the vine.
> We've made up our minds to be rid of Jew swine!

Our CD, *14 Words*, sold twenty thousand copies, a smashing success by hatecore music standards but hardly enough to support a family. We scraped by on the meager salary I earned at my job at another screen-printing factory and contributions from Alicia's family. Even with a baby to look forward to, it wasn't a happy union from the start. We fought constantly over money, my drinking, and the time I spent with the band.

Alicia went into labor on November 7, 1992. I was in the delivery room when she gave birth. The labor went quickly; before I knew it, a nurse was whisking our daughter away to a baby warmer, but not before I had the chance to look into her magnificent blue eyes. To say it was love at first sight doesn't begin to describe what I felt. I adored that little being. I had never felt such true, pure love before that moment. This was my little girl! I was a dad! I celebrated by getting wasted at a bar down the street from the hospital. Everyone wanted to buy the new dad a round and I accepted until they threw me out of the place.

We named our baby Autumn. She was a week old when, after a night of drinking and fighting at a local bar, I came home stinking drunk and covered in someone else's blood. Alicia let me have it. She tore into me, telling me what a pathetic man and shit father I was, and how I'd let both her and our baby down. My response was the same as it had been when my mother told me I had Indian blood. I drew my combat dagger from the bed stand—a seven-inch knife that was sharp enough to shave with—and nearly took off my left hand. Lucky for me, Alicia, like Gina on that Thanksgiving night, was versed in first aid. She wrapped a bedsheet around my wrist and knelt on it while she dialed 911. The paramedics were there straightaway and I took a swing at one of them before losing consciousness.

I woke up in the ICU a couple of days later with a stitched wrist and a resolve to quit drinking. A thirty-day attempt at sobriety after that went out the window in December on my twenty-second birthday. Alicia threw a surprise party, and the booze flowed. "I'll just have one" turned into the inevitable case-plus of beer, and I was back on the drunk train, speeding further out of control. Once the drinking took over again, so went the shitshow that my life had been since I chugged my first beer at age fourteen. My first priority, I'm ashamed to say, even over my precious child, was getting shitfaced. Alicia berated me constantly. I was a loser. An alcoholic. A no-good, good-for-nothing waste of a human being. As our relationship deteriorated, I spent less time at home and even more with my band. There I was, composing and singing hateful lyrics about killing and dying to protect precious white babies, yet I was shirking my responsibilities for my own infant daughter.

After a few months of staying home, Alicia took a job as a cocktail waitress in the city, which forced me to be with Autumn more. By then, the baby was crawling and making sweet sounds. She wasn't the tiny infant I was kind of freaked out by, but this amazing little being who was developing a real personality. As she and I bonded, Alicia and I grew more distant. I suspected she was having an affair. Predictably, our relationship wobbled into a flat spin and crashed nearly as quickly as it had taken off.

Alicia came home one day when Autumn was around

eighteen months old and announced she was moving to Key West to be near her two older daughters, who lived with her estranged husband. I couldn't bear the thought of losing Autumn. "Fuck that," I said. "She's my kid and she's not going with you." Alicia put up some resistance, and we finally settled on joint custody. Autumn would spend six months with me in our townhouse in Wisconsin and the rest of the year with Alicia in Florida. When it came time for her to go to Key West, I protested and Alicia didn't push back.

Then it was Autumn and me.

I was twenty-three and an out-of-control, alcoholic single parent. But I loved my kid. I lived for her, because without her I didn't care what happened to me. She was my little buddy, vocal and sweet. Before I knew it, she was walking and talking. A genius, just like me! While I put in my time printing t-shirts, Mom watched over her. Otherwise she went everywhere with me. That's not to say I was Father of the Year. Hardly. I didn't even know what that meant. I continued to live in a haze of alcohol-fueled instability and irresponsibility. I worshipped my child, but not as much as the high I was constantly chasing. At home in the evenings, I'd play Legos with her, then plop her down in front of the TV to watch *Scooby-Doo* while I listened to white power music and swilled every last bottle of cheap beer in my twelve-pack. I hosted wild parties at our house where everyone got wasted and crazy. Autumn was super social and my crew looked after her, as if they were any more capable than me. I shudder to think of what could have happened while I was living so recklessly.

Maybe it was a blessing when I got evicted after noise complaint number thirty-two. I had nowhere to go but home and, once again, my mother saved my ass. What would I have done without her support? I'm certain I wouldn't have made it to the age of twenty-four. No matter how selfish and destructive I was or how many bad choices I made or the damage I'd done to people I supposedly loved, and who loved me, my mother never turned her back on me, and this time was no exception. She took us in without hesitation.

During some of my more sober moments with my daughter, I thought back to the times that others had shown me kindness; often when I least deserved it, usually from the people I professed to hate. Kindnesses I'd made myself overlook when they happened, because how could I hate people who were being so nice to me? My Jewish boss had always been fair even though I wore swastikas on my clothes. My Latino coworkers always tried to engage me in friendly conversations. A black colleague once offered me his sandwich when I was so broke I couldn't afford lunch—even though he knew I was a racist skinhead.

A person I could never forget was an older black lady behind the counter at McDonald's. As much as I tried to get her out of my head, she slipped from my subconscious into my thoughts at the most random times. It had been years since our encounter, yet I could still see her warm smile as clearly as if she were standing opposite me again.

It was during my early racist skinhead days that we crossed paths. I was working in the t-shirt factory, and on paydays I would treat myself to a Big Mac. One night I was at a party and they had a homemade tattoo machine. I got a swastika tattooed on my middle finger. The next time I went to McDonald's, the old black lady was there. It had been easy enough to hide the sleeves of white power ink I had, but not the one on my finger. "What'll you have today, honey?" she asked, her eyes literally shimmering with humanity. Placing my order, I found myself shoving my hands in my pockets so she wouldn't see the tattoo. When it came time to pay, I fiddled every which way with my wallet in an attempt to hide it, but her eyes went right to my guilty hand. She looked up and our eyes met. I don't know why I cared about what she thought of me, but I was ashamed she'd seen the swastika. I expected the cold shoulder or a lecture. Instead, the kindly woman looked at me with compassion. "That's not who you are. You're better than that," she said softly, in the way that a doting grandmother might. I grabbed my burger and fled.

By the time I got to the bus stop, I had talked myself into remembering what it was I stood for and why. *The conspiracy to wipe out the white race is real. It's them or us. The future of our white children is at stake.*

I never went back.

As the months passed and my daughter grew into an active toddler, I spent less time thinking about a Racial Holy War and more about her and the world the way I wanted her to see it. She was bright eyed and innocent, not cynical and angry the way I was. She didn't see race. She saw people. She had an open heart and offered unconditional love to everyone. Everywhere we went, people were taken with her. How could I ignore the kindheartedness she brought out in others with her pure intentions and inviting smile? How could I ignore the way people of every race and creed reciprocated her goodwill?

I began having serious doubts about "my way" when my little girl's way looked and felt so much better. At the same time, I was haunted by the idea that if I continued on the path I was on, as a racial holy warrior, I was bound for either prison or death. Most of my crew had self-destructed by then. Comrades had been murdered. I lost count of how many were incarcerated, but there were probably only ten or fifteen of us who were still active. I wondered, how did that help secure the future for all white children? How would being locked up or dead help my white child? I was all she had. We were all each other had.

Through my daughter, I was forced to have more contact with the world outside of my white power bubble. At the park. At the grocery store. On the playground. The more people I interacted with—people of all kinds—the harder it was to deny a truth I faced daily: people could be good and kind, regardless of their race or religion. I had witnessed it with my own eyes, over and over again. I wasn't ready to turn my back on the movement—it was all I had known for my entire adult life—but I was having serious doubts about it.

Then, a defining moment: it happened after a racist skinhead concert in Racine. I'd left Autumn at home with Mom that night. The concert was a tribute to Ian Stuart of

Skrewdriver, who'd died in a car crash in England the year before. My band was on the program along with four or five others. Several hundred skinheads attended. When it was over, my buddy Joe Rowan, the lead singer of the group Nordic Thunder, left for an after-party. He stopped to pick up beer at a local convenience store and got into a war of words with a black gangbanger inside. Joe's skinhead group and the black guy's crew all joined in the pissing match. It escalated, and Joe was shot and killed.

Word filtered back to us quickly: the enemy killed our brother. We needed to call the troops into action. If not a Racial Holy War now, then when? *Not me*, I thought. *I have to have a future for the sake of my child.*

I went home and watched Autumn sleep. She looked angelic, lying there under her soft, pink covers. I don't know if the tears running down my cheeks were for Joe or for us, but I silently vowed to my sleeping child that I was going to leave the movement. Lately, I'd felt as if I were just going through the motions anyway. I didn't have the fiery passion to match the white power rhetoric anymore. I had already known, somewhere deep in my psyche, that I had to leave, if for no other reason than my daughter. I just hadn't known when or how or why it was going to happen. Joe was the excuse I'd been waiting for. He was the second friend I'd lost in the so-called race war.

The first was four years earlier. I'd recruited a kid named Chuck Miller from a poor neighborhood in Kenosha, and we'd become good friends. Like all of us, he'd been looking for a place to belong and we'd indoctrinated him into our crew. He reminded me a lot of myself, and I sort of looked after him. One night, he and a few of his buddies went to a bar where Latino gang members hung out. I don't know which side started it, but there had been a brawl. The Latino guys took off, but they drove back to the bar just as Chuck was leaving to walk to his buddy's house. One of them popped off a shot that slammed through Chuck's back and pierced his heart. He died right there on the street. Now Joe was gone, too, and what the fuck for?

I had had enough. What had their deaths proven? What had they accomplished by dying for "the cause"? What *was* the cause? Was it real or something cooked up by a group of angry losers? In the months since I'd started doubting, I'd opened myself up to the people from every group I'd professed to hate. Jews. Gays. Blacks. People I'd once called Muds. I guess that made me a race traitor, but I had begun to discover that I liked not hating people. It was a lot less exhausting. And guess what? The exposure led me to the discovery that "the enemy" wasn't planning and perpetrating the extermination of the white race. He was busy making a living and raising a family; struggling through life, just like me. The white power ideology was starting to smell a lot like bullshit.

I confessed my doubts to my longtime friend Will from my Church of the Creator crew. I didn't believe in what we were doing anymore. It was unnecessary. For seven years I hadn't had a conversation with anyone who wasn't white, and the only interaction I'd had with white people outside of the movement was to proselytize to them. I'd been so deep into the movement that I hadn't been able to see anything outside of it. I wasn't even sure that my thoughts were my own anymore, but even if they were, they had changed. I'd met the enemy, spent time with him, gotten to know him, and he wasn't what we had been taught to believe. People were people. There were good and bad in every ethnic group. I was tired of hating. Tired of hurting people. Tired of watching friends die. For what?

Will gave me the same worn-out talking points. White people were superior, so it was our responsibility to take charge and save our race. The Jews had a grand plan to extinguish whites so they could take control of the inferior races and ultimately the world. As the superior race, it was our responsibility to stop what was happening or our children would be forced to face the dire consequences of living in a muddy society. I had my doubts. Nevertheless, the movement had wiped me out and I needed to be there for my daughter. "I'm in the real world now and I'm not going back," I said. Will shook his head. I thought he looked sad. I wondered if he had his own doubts, his own regrets about the path we'd been on. I turned and walked away.

I began easing out. I left Centurion and spent less time with my racist skinhead friends. I had a daughter I had to focus on; that was my excuse. I didn't have time to attend Sunday meetings or hatecore concerts.

The rave culture was taking shape at about that time, and one of my friends from the old days convinced me to give it a try. The culture was the polar opposite of white power. One of its founding philosophies was called P.L.U.R.: Peace, Love, Unity, and Respect. Think modern-day hippies fucked up on ecstasy. Peace, love, and more love. Please leave all of your prejudice and hatred at the door. Talk about culture shock! I thought I'd hate it, the way I'd once loathed the peace punks, but I went to my first party and got hooked. I loved the house music, the beautiful, friendly girls, and the free-flowing supply of molly. It was romantic. Very Hunter Thompson–esque.

Neo-hippies were much nicer to hang out with than neo-Nazis. For the first time in years, I began to feel optimistic about life. I hadn't lost my appetite for drugs and alcohol, but I had lost my taste for fighting and ugly racial slurs. It was much nicer to be with a blend of people than the same small clutch of white people. Sometimes I felt as if I'd broken out of prison. I felt free, like I was discovering the world all over again.

Did I ever really believe in the "new dawn" that Skrewdriver sang about? Or Ben Klassen's grand plan for a whiter and brighter world? I wasn't so sure. I thought I was a believer when I was in the throes of the movement, pursuing the twisted goal of an all-white world that had consumed me for so long. But I'd never really questioned the white power rhetoric. I'd never stopped hating long enough to step back and analyze what I was doing or why because, had I done that, I would have realized the answers didn't make sense.

Now I questioned everything. Who decided who was white and who wasn't? Who said white was the superior race? Ben Klassen? Tom Metzger? What made them authorities?

Metzger repaired TVs for a living. Klassen invented a fuck-ing can opener. In just a few months, I'd met plenty of people who were brighter and far more successful than those guys, who didn't subscribe to their racial or political beliefs. I won-dered how Klassen and Metzger would answer, who was going to fight the billions of non-whites in the Racial Holy War they promised? The white power army of a few thousand street fighters? Why were a relative few white power believ-ers right and the rest of the world wrong?

When had hate ever trumped love?

With new friends and my eyes beginning to open, I be-gan to see the futility, the absolute madness, of hating based on someone's race or religion or sexual orientation. I thought about how many of my former friends were lost to death and prison because of an ideology based on fear and lies. I won-dered, had it not been for my child and being able to see the world through her eyes, even just a glimpse, would I have succumbed to the same pointless fate of many of my former comrades? I was certain I would have.

Autumn was headed for her third birthday when I left the white power movement for good. As old friends had dropped away, new opportunities presented themselves. Once blinded by bigotry but now with eyes wide open, I sought out experi-ences involving people for whom I had once harbored a vi-cious hatred.

People of all stripes and colors populated the rave scene. I began to appreciate the beauty of a slanted eye. An aquiline nose. Full lips. By living in an opposing universe, one in which

I felt safe to explore different ideas and beliefs, I discovered the fear that had motivated me to hurt innocent people was based on desperate propaganda and not reality. I was learning that the world was filled with good people, some of whom I once would have attacked because of my warped views of humanity. Oftentimes they were the same people who now forgave and accepted me.

I loved the rave scene, but, ultimately, it was living in my daughter's world that showed me how terribly wrong I had been for the past seven years of my life. One particular occasion really drove the epiphany home.

Autumn was in daycare, and I'd arrived early one day to pick her up. Watching her with the other kids, I got a hitch in my throat. What struck me was how they played together. They were children. Not black children or white children but kids who were romping and giggling and enjoying each other's company. As I sat there waiting, a young black man around my age came in to pick up his daughter. He called to her, and she leapt into his arms and hugged him, the same way my little girl hugged me. I watched his smile grow bigger and wider as he listened to his daughter gleefully recount her day. It was the same kind of loving smile I got when I was with my daughter.

Watching that dad and his little girl made me think about all of the people I'd hurt. Moms and dads and brothers and sisters. Good people I'd battered and broken for no reason other than the color of their skin. It could have been the father of the little girl sitting next to me I'd left for dead. And for what? What would that have done to her? To him? To experience such hatred in their loving existence? My eyes filled with tears. The man swooped his daughter up and away, I imagined to their happy home.

As tears spilled down my cheeks, I mourned all of the time I'd lost hating others when what I'd really felt was hatred for myself. I looked over at Autumn saying goodbye to her friends and was overcome with love. The depth of feeling I had for my child had awakened in me the dormant empathy I didn't remember I had—not since grade school when I took kids with disabilities under my wing. My daughter had given me the gift of a second chance.

If only I could learn to forgive myself.

Pardeep

When the first images of the terrorist attack on the World Trade Center flashed on the TV screen, I feared we would have to reintroduce ourselves to the community. As American as we felt, people were sure to have questions because of the way we looked. I was working at Dad's gas station, having graduated from Marquette but before I started training at the Milwaukee police academy. I was fortunate I could be at the station to help my parents with whatever situation arose after the attacks. Indian Sikhs were often mistaken for Middle Easterners because their skin was brown and they wore turbans. After 9/11, the comparison became dangerous. That's when I learned that no matter how accepted we felt in our new culture, a single incident could spark tension and create division.

Four days after the towers fell, a Sikh gas station owner in Arizona was murdered in retaliation for the attacks because his killer thought he looked like a terrorist. We were warned about people who wanted to kill "towel heads." Some of our customers were curious about our background and our beliefs, and I always took time to explain. It surprised me how little people knew about our religion, that it is the gentlest of all faiths and based on tenets of equality, brotherhood, and working for the well-being of all people. Sikhs are probably the last people on earth to resort to unjustified violence.

I think the reason our community supported us so roundly when so many others around the country were blindly rejected because of how they looked is because of Dad's deep belief in the Sikh spirit of *Seva*, which means service to others without consideration of personal benefit. I remember after the attacks, gas stations around the city jacked up their prices, sometimes doubling the cost of a gallon of gas because the world financial market was in chaos and no one knew when their next delivery would be. We kept our price the same. If we ran out, so be it, Dad said, and I agreed. It was our community and our neighbors. We were all Americans and we all suffered that day. For years afterward, our customers thanked us for not taking advantage of that terrible tragedy for monetary gain.

Our Sikh scriptures say, "One who performs selfless service, without thought of reward, shall attain his Lord and

Master. You shall find peace doing Seva." My father was always doing something for someone, and he never expected anything in return. I think his example is what led me to pursue policing as a career. I really believed I could make a difference in people's lives.

I was humbled and more than a little bit disappointed when, after college, I couldn't get a job in law enforcement. Here I was with an education from one of the top universities, having majored in criminal justice and sociology, and I couldn't get my foot in the door. I couldn't even get a callback. I think a lot of it was that many of the places I applied to didn't see a "Pardeep Kaleka" fitting into their police culture. I must have tried twenty or thirty municipalities before I finally landed a job with the Milwaukee PD. Milwaukee had a diverse police force—white, black, Latino, and a smattering of Asian— but even in Wisconsin's largest city I was the first Punjabi Sikh.

Before I could get out on the street, I had to spend nine months in training at the police academy. It was like boot camp, very regimented and militaristic. One minute you were being screamed at to shine your shoes, the next, ordered down to the floor for pushups. *Kaleka! Drop and give me twenty! Kaleka! You didn't call me "Sir." Kaleka! Tuck in your uniform! Salute with a proper snap! Come to attention! Let's move! Push yourself. One more!* Seven recruits dropped out the first week. It was survival of the fittest, and the most determined. They broke us down to build us up—but what had they created?

After graduating from the academy, my probationary beat

THE GIFT OF OUR WOUNDS

was in the worst part of the city, in a neighborhood with abandoned houses, boarded-up businesses, and an epic crack epidemic. A community made famous by a documentary, *Milwaukee 53206*, that was named for its zip code, notorious for having the highest incarceration rate of black men in the entire country. Shootings and homicides were a regular occurrence there. We called the place Little Beirut. The residents called it "The Zoo." The area was so crime ridden that it was crawling with cops, and backups were always just around the corner. My shift was 4:00 to midnight, the time when all of the action happened. I quickly learned community policing wasn't part of the job. There was no time to walk the beat and get to know who lived there. My partner and I rushed from one assignment to the next with no break in between. Shootings, knifings, drug wars, gang fights, and domestic-violence calls were the norm. My partner was the driver and I was the runner. Every shift meant at least one foot chase and I always had to be ready to run.

When my probation period ended, I was assigned a new beat and a new partner. John Delaney's reputation as a tough, no-nonsense city cop preceded him. He was highly respected on the street, and the people in our jurisdiction knew better than to pull any BS on his watch. It didn't take me long to understand why. On my third day with him, Delaney and I left our godforsaken territory to get lunch at a pizza place in a better part of town. As we walked into the restaurant, a guy sprinted past us and out the door while a lady inside screamed that he had her purse. Delaney and I took off after the purse-snatcher. This time, Delaney was on foot and I was driving the squad car. I caught up with them in an alleyway where Delaney had the purse-snatcher hemmed in. He proceeded to beat him stupid. *Okay, we're not in Kansas anymore,* I thought as I watched him pummel the perp. I stepped in to cuff the guy, who, I was pretty sure, was never going to steal another purse. Delaney explained that that was how we subdued criminals in the city. We roughed them up until they knew enough not to do that kind of shit again. It wasn't what we were taught in the academy. It was just the way it was done.

Got it, I said.

I was a year into the job when I married a Punjabi Sikh woman I'd met during my last year at Marquette. I'd seen Jaspreet around but never introduced myself, until one night I went to a concert on campus where she was performing an Indian dance. She was dressed in a white Punjabi suit and I thought she looked beautiful. After the show, I got up the nerve to introduce myself. A group of us were going to an after-party. She and her friends were welcome to come. In our culture, girls usually didn't go to parties unattended, so I was surprised when she showed up.

The party was on the rooftop of an apartment building with a stunning view of the city. My buddies and I were doing shots and I saw Jaspreet, standing in a corner. I was in the midst of my wild days after breaking up with Jenny. It was a period when I was a dog with girls and drinking far too much. Emboldened by the whiskey shots, I went over to her and we

made small talk. I was already half in the bag, but I continued drinking. The next thing I knew, I was waking up in my
apartment the next morning.

I called my friend Harpreet to ask what happened between
the party and my place. Apparently he had driven me home,
and Jaspreet still had my jacket. I'd offered it to her when she
had gotten cold. He passed on her phone number and I called.
"I'm sorry if I made a fool of myself," I said. Jaspreet was kind
enough to say that I hadn't. She and Harpreet found me
laid out in the bathtub with all of my clothes on. The two of
them walked me outside, got me into a car, and Harpreet
had taken me home. I felt so embarrassed by my behavior.
"Was I nice to you?" I asked. "I hope I was because I intended
to be." I was relieved when she said I'd been a perfect gentle-
man. We made plans to meet for dinner that night, ostensibly
so I could retrieve my jacket.

So began our courtship. After three years of dating, we
were married in a traditional Sikh ceremony at the temple.
My parents were thrilled that I'd married within my faith.
They admired Jaspreet for her kindness and her strength. I'd
always said I would only marry for love, and I had.

I GAVE POLICING my best shot, but it wasn't for me. One of my
last assignments was a shooting involving a young boy. He'd
been on the streets, selling fake drugs, and someone paid him
back with a .22. The kid was "motherfucking" me all the way
to the hospital. *Motherfucking pig. Dirty motherfucker. You ain't*

shit. I ain't saying shit. I took his feistiness as a sign he was going to survive and told his mother as much when she arrived at his bedside, but I was wrong. He died that night. The kid was probably twelve or thirteen years old.

Every one of those kinds of incidents brought me closer to the realization that I had gone into police work with naive expectations. I'd started out with such a simplistic mindset: the good guys protected law-abiding citizens from the bad guys. Of course, it was so much more complex. Sometimes I'd see kids whose lives were so chaotic that they were actually relieved to be arrested and locked up. They'd fall asleep in the back of the squad car because they felt safe there. It was as if they were thinking, *Thank God I was caught and this is over. I don't have to do this anymore.* My heart hurt for those kids. My background, my interest, was studying human behavior and using whatever knowledge I gained to work for the betterment of the community. But it wasn't as easy as the good guys locking up the bad guys. Humankind just wasn't that simple. Yet in order to survive the trauma of policing you almost have to maintain that simplistic worldview because to lose it, as I was beginning to do, made you vulnerable in an unforgiving profession. Cops have a saying: "I'd rather be tried by twelve than carried by six," meaning going home alive after every shift justified whatever it took to survive the job. Better to be brought up on charges for excessive force— or worse—than give someone the benefit of the doubt and be carried out in a coffin. I began waking up in the middle of the night, second-guessing everything I did on the job. *Had I*

*been too easy during that stop? . . . Was I careless? . . . He could
have killed me . . . If she had pulled a gun, would I have been able to
shoot her?* I didn't want to be the cop who pulled the trigger too
fast. I didn't want the job to make me hard and cynical. And
the cop I wanted to be was beginning to seem impracticable
and naive. Sometimes I'd be awake all night and go to work
feeling sick in the morning. I suffered from asthma and anxiety. Jaspreet tried to help, but there was no comforting me.
One night she asked me about work and I snapped. I told her I
didn't want to talk about it—not ever—because it meant reliv-
ing the shit I had just been through. People always said it was
the badge that took law enforcement officers on a power trip.
That wasn't true. It was the gun and bulletproof vest that in-
flated your sense of importance and invincibility. Badges didn't
do damage. Guns did. I wanted to help people, not kill them.

I was four years on the job when I responded to the call
that gave me absolute clarity about what I needed to do. It was
late at night and the dispatcher had gotten a report of "shots
fired," a routine call for my partner and me. We arrived in the
area to find a young woman slumped over the steering wheel
of her car. I slipped into the passenger seat beside her. She was
probably nineteen or twenty, and she had a bullet hole in
her head. I looked up and saw a man walking toward me. He
was hysterical and crying, "I killed her! I killed her!" Choking out his words, he said he had shot his girlfriend during an
argument. *I didn't mean to do it. I was just so fucking angry!
I'm so sorry. So sorry!* He handed me his gun and I cuffed him
and put him in the back of the squad car. Returning to the

young woman, I felt a deep sense of grief. She was so young. I wondered what her life had been about. Had she finished high school? Gone to college? Did she have friends? Have big plans for her future? Was she loved?

It was my job to notify the next of kin. As it turned out, she lived nearby with her parents. It was around 1:00 A.M. when I knocked on their front door. A man answered and the look on his face told me he knew what was coming. I asked after the girl and he said he was her father. "I'm so sorry, sir," I said, explaining that his daughter had been killed. The man struggled to hold it together while I told him what I knew. His wife stood behind him, clutching his shoulder. When she heard that her daughter was dead she fell to her knees, wailing. Her name was Rose, the mother said. She was a good daughter, but she'd been involved with the wrong man. They fought constantly and he abused her. Her mother had tried to warn her, but she never listened. "My daughter had a baby!" the mother sobbed. A two-year-old who was asleep upstairs. What were they to tell their granddaughter? Her daughter loved that little girl so much. They were everything to each other. What would happen to the child now?

I saw the agony on the woman's face and choked back my sadness. Jaspreet was pregnant with the first of our four children, and I couldn't imagine our child growing up without her. My stomach churned. Most of the homicides I'd handled involved scumbag dope dealers, never the young mother of a small child, who physically resembled my wife.

I told the parents I would stay in touch and gave them my

card. "Call me anytime, day or night," I said. Walking back to my squad car, I pictured their daughter, so young, her whole life ahead of her, slumped over the steering wheel of her car. Feelings of sadness and frustration bubbled to a boil of helplessness and anger. I wanted to be able to do something. *But I can't do shit about this.* I couldn't save her from her abuser. I couldn't save her for her little girl. I couldn't make it better for anyone. All I could do was notify her heartbroken parents. *This is not where I belong.*

That night I knew I could not do the job for another year, much less twenty—not without turning into someone I didn't want to be. If I were going to make a difference, it wasn't going to be wearing a badge and carrying a gun. I needed to try to reach people before they needed the cops.

A month later, I handed in my resignation.

———

JASPREET DELIVERED OUR first child soon after, a daughter we named Amaris. I went back to work at Dad's gas station and decided to return to school for my teaching certificate. Two weeks after the start of the semester, Scott Campbell, the principal of an alternative school in the same dicey part of the city I'd once patrolled, contacted me to say he'd heard I'd left the department and was working toward becoming a teacher. One of his teachers had just walked off the job and he was looking for a replacement. With my experience with at-risk kids and my familiarity with the neighborhood, I would be a perfect fit for the job. I could teach there while I was pursuing my official teaching certificate. Was I interested?

When could I start?

How about tomorrow?

The Northwest Opportunities Vocational Academy (NOVA) was a last-chance school for at-risk seventh through twelfth graders living on the northwest side of Milwaukee. They were tough, troubled kids who came from poor, single-parent households and had been labeled incorrigible and unfit for public school. Most were mixed up with gangs and drugs and all of the other evils of the mean streets of the city. Some had criminal records; some were on probation.

Because I had just come from policing in the same neighborhoods where these students lived, I felt competent to deal with whatever I was confronted with. I knew the population well. I had seen where these kids came from and what they went home to. They lived in barren apartments with dark, makeshift curtains covering the windows and stained mattresses on the floor. Their cupboards were bare and their refrigerators were empty. As a cop, I had always made it a rule never to sit down when I went to a call because I didn't know if there were rats or cockroaches crawling around. It was common to go into an apartment and find a parent and four or five other adults inebriated or strung out on drugs while children roamed around unsupervised. Those kinds of conditions passed as normal for these kids. I called it *normalized misery*. There was a code switch between their home lives and the expectations of school. They came to class on Mondays agitated from the weekend and ready to fight, calmed down during the week, and left in survival mode on Fridays.

My strategy for helping my students was to first make an initial investment in them by getting to know their stories. During my first week there, I met a sixteen-year-old kid named Devante who was always in trouble. I saw him sitting outside the principal's office and introduced myself. "Hey, man, how you doing?" I said, taking the chair next to him. "Why are you here?"

Devante looked at me quizzically and explained that he'd had an argument with his teacher. I listened patiently as he talked about how unfair the teacher was and that she had it out for him. He gave me a bunch of half-assed reasons for why he was justified in his behavior. After about fifteen minutes, I said, "Let's go to the classroom. I'll have the teacher come outside and you can apologize to her." Devante shook his head and groused that that wasn't going to happen. "Look, Devante," I said. "The teacher is having a hard time. She has twenty other students. She wants to be able to help you, but think about how difficult it must be for her with so many others who also need her help. Have empathy for her."

Invoking empathy and developing a connection resonated with wounded kids. I'd seen it over and over when I was policing. Devante finally softened and agreed to hear the teacher out and apologize to her. We walked to the classroom and they talked outside in the hallway. When they were finished, I suggested Devante also ask for forgiveness from his classmates for disrupting the class. He hemmed and hawed, but conceded. "Okay," he said. "Okay, I'll do it."

Teaching empathy and empowerment was almost like a magic pill. I'd seen many a student do an about-face when they were put in a position of helping others. An incident that exemplified the point was when Scott was robbed at gunpoint after school one day. We were the last two to leave when, in my rearview mirror, I saw a young black teen holding a gun to his head. Instinctively, I threw my car into reverse in an attempt to run the kid over before he shot Scott. That had managed to scare him away. When our students heard about what happened, they took it upon themselves to help secure the school and keep everyone safe. For us, NOVA became a sanctuary from the madness of our Milwaukee environment.

We had a hundred really troubled kids in our school that the system had given up on, throwaways that no one else was willing to take on, and every one of them was capable of growing into a good, productive adult. We made a difference there. More than teaching, our job was to help the students discover that they were not the worthless human beings that society had labeled them as. They were valuable young people with plenty to offer their communities and the world.

Watching the students find themselves, that was where my heart lay. I had found my niche. During my seven-year tenure teaching at NOVA, I'd experienced deep heartache and witnessed countless success stories. I thought I would never leave.

If the temple shooting hadn't happened, I'm certain I'd still be there.

FIVE

A CALLING

Truth is high, but higher yet is truthful living.
Guru Nanak Dev Ji

Arno

After years of alcohol abuse, drunk-driving charges, jail time, and being buried beneath a mountain of regret over being intoxicated for the first eleven years of my daughter's life that will haunt me to my grave, I decided to quit drinking. With my daughter tucked safely away in bed, I spent the last hours of 2003 in my parents' garage, with rave music blasting and a case of Bud Light on ice beside my chair. Chugging bottle after bottle toward sobriety, I had to choke down the final few. *This is your last case of beer, motherfucker*, I told myself. *Make it count.*

After draining my last brew, I wrote a drunken email to my buddy Dave, a recovering alcoholic I knew from work. I knew about his sobriety because he told me about it in granular detail every fucking day we worked together. "I want to quit drinking and go to AA and I want you to be my sponsor," I wrote him. Dave responded right back. *WTF is a sober guy doing up at three in the morning,* I wondered. His response was melodramatic, I thought, about how I needed to check into a hospital because I could die from the DTs if I wasn't properly supervised during my withdrawal. I didn't really know anything about AA except that it involved going to a few meetings and having a sponsor. Dave wrote that I would have to attend meetings every night for the first three months. *Wait. What?*

I read his response, passed out, and woke up sometime on New Year's Day 2004 with an epic hangover. In the midst of my suffering, I contemplated my next step. I made a deal with myself: rather than spending every night for three months— and surely beyond—in a church basement with chain-smoking, black-coffee-swilling dry drunks, I would quit cold turkey on my own. And that's what I did. I haven't tasted alcohol since. The very few times I've been tempted, I've only had to recall my then eleven-year-old daughter's response when, a few days after my decision, I told her I'd stopped drinking. "I'm so glad, Dad," she said. "I always hated it when you were drunk."

My daughter had shown me the way from hate to acceptance, which made me a better man. After I abandoned the white power movement, I'd built a successful IT consulting business, made new and wonderful friends of all stripes, and traveled to places I had never been. That same love had led me, finally, mercifully, to quit drinking and begin to be the father I always wanted to be. Looking at myself in the mirror, I'd been forced to examine how I could have put my beloved little girl through the heartbreak of having an alcoholic parent when I knew how angst-provoking and scary that was from my own experience of growing up in an alcoholic home. As the product of that environment, I was angry and insecure. I had trouble trusting and feeling and talking about important stuff. Was that what I wanted for Autumn? Had I been so narcissistic—or just plain fucking addicted—that I had put her happiness and her precious future at risk because of my own selfish craving for something—anything—to sedate my fearful, restless spirit?

My daughter, the person I loved most in the world, the little girl who gave me breath when I couldn't find my own, was my savior. Searching my soul, I realized that my whole life until then had been about myself—what I wanted, how I felt—without a thought about how I was affecting anyone else, even the people I loved, who loved me.

Thinking about it, I recognized that the parallels between alcoholism and extremism were striking. Both were consequences of a victim mentality, or persecution mindset, and resulted in detachment from reality and emotional numbness. It was always someone else's fault, something someone had done to you, everyone else who was screwed up. I knew what it was like to get fucked up with my buddies and how the group mentality and booze desensitized me and made me into the shit person I was. I'd put my dependence on hate behind me. Now it was time to make up for the damage I'd done with my addiction to booze.

The only way I could live with who I'd been to that point was to change it, to lay myself bare, to confess my weaknesses and regrets, wholly and without reservation or restriction. I would make my apology to my daughter and the world by devoting whatever time I had left on this earth to being a good father and an honorable citizen, one who was committed to righting social wrongs and forging acts of loving kindness. Someone Autumn could be proud of.

Life After Hate

Once the fog of alcoholism cleared from my head, I started writing the next chapter of my life. As a member of a white power band, I had made some of the most violent, hateful records ever recorded—records that were still galvanizing racists years later. There was no way I could undo that damage. My words and songs lived on the internet for anyone to access. I could, however, speak in a new voice, a voice that railed against violence and hatred with even greater volume than my racist songs had.

Deliberating ways to do that, I came up with an idea to start an online magazine as a platform for both perpetrators and victims of hate. I envisioned publishing stories from other former racist skinheads and street gang members, and maybe even former jihadists, as well as survivors of violence. I'd call it *Life After Hate*. The more I thought about it, the better I liked the idea, and I began hitting up people I knew who'd left the movement to ask them to be part of it. Between my IT consulting and working toward a bachelor's degree at the University of Wisconsin, I laid the groundwork for the magazine. When it became evident that I needed help with the new venture, I reached out to my friend Angie Aker.

Angie and I had met a few years earlier through a dating site. We hadn't worked out romantically, but we stayed in touch over social media. Angie was a social activist and prolific writer. With that in mind, I approached her and gave her the rundown on my idea for a new venture, then asked if she might be interested in being the cofounder of Life After Hate. Angie loved the idea and jumped right in.

With Angie on board, I decided it would make sense to add another former white power skinhead into the mix. The name Christian Picciolini came to mind. Christian was a former member of CASH, the Chicago Area Skinheads, and he had briefly managed my old band. I knew he'd published a couple of essays denouncing the white power movement. I looked him up on Facebook and explained what we were doing. He was involved in another endeavor that took up most of his time, but he agreed to lend his name and support us with a couple of articles. That was cool with me.

After that it was full steam ahead. We decided to launch the magazine on the holiday honoring Dr. Martin Luther King Jr. What could be more fitting? I worked on early versions of the launch webpage and sent out a proposed mockup that included articles by Christian and Angie, as well as pieces by Tamara Westfall, an old raver friend, and Dimitry Anselme, a teacher I'd befriended. By design, my name was nowhere on the site. As things were shaping up, I had become concerned about being the face of Life After Hate. Ideally, I wished to build a platform where I could use my story to promote a message of peaceful coexistence for all people, but I didn't want my identity to become that of "a former white supremacist." I preferred a behind-the-scenes role that would help forge my positive agenda.

The others saw it differently and insisted my name be featured prominently as the creator and founder of Life After Hate. Christian was particularly adamant: "Give credit to yourself for an amazing idea."

Grudgingly, I agreed. Angie, Tamara, and our web consultant, Dan Knauss, worked ourselves silly preparing for the launch. After months of building and testing and planning and designing and writing and promoting, LifeAfterHate.org went live, as scheduled, on the Martin Luther King Jr. holiday in 2010.

LAH was well received from the onset. We received thousands of views and instant feedback from both people who were affected by violence and others who were desperate to change the path they were on. We decided to change our idea from a quarterly to a monthly publication. Opportunities flooded in from people and organizations wanting to collaborate. A local newspaper published a story about us that caught the attention of Tanya Cromartie, a peace activist with a program for inner-city youth called Summer of Peace. She asked me to speak to her group and I accepted. It was my first time speaking publicly about peace, the first of many.

I could barely keep up with the demands of my new role. The country was in the midst of an era in which domestic terror attacks and mass shootings had become the norm. The demand for information and answers was mind-bending. I was pushing out too many stories and fielding too many speaking invitations to count. We'd gained so much momentum so quickly that I took a hiatus from my studies at UWM to free up more of my time for my peace advocacy work.

In June 2011, I was invited to attend the Summit Against Violent Extremism (SAVE) in Dublin. My name had been thrown in the hat by another former white supremacist and accepted by the sponsor, Google Ideas, after a lengthy phone interview. The event was life-changing. The discussions centered on finding the most effective ways to address radicalization. A dozen countries and forty groups were represented. I met other former violent extremists from around the world, from former jihadists to former leftist militants and militant Israeli settlers to former IRA and loyalist fighters. We were a gnarly-looking bunch, tattooed and battle scarred and some with missing limbs. The bond we shared was nothing short of profound. No matter where in the world we came from or what form of extremism we had fallen prey to, our stories were essentially the same. We were hurt people who had hurt people and were now dedicated to healing ourselves and others.

At the other end of the spectrum, I met mothers who lost children to terror attacks; a woman who lost both legs below the knee in the London Tube bombing; a woman who reconciled with the IRA bomber who killed her father; people who survived kidnapping, rape, and every imaginable horror that a human being could endure. I was in awe of all of them and inspired to push forward with an idea to grow Life After Hate into a proper nonprofit organization.

Two months later, it became a reality. In August 2011 Life After Hate was official. We had a board made up of former white power skinheads, an executive director—me—and a mission "to inspire compassion and forgiveness for all people" through education, guidance, and counseling. It couldn't have been more prescient.

One year later, a gunman walked into the Sikh Temple of Wisconsin and murdered six people. The killer was a white supremacist named Wade Michael Page.

SIX

THE SHOOTING

Give up your head, but don't forsake those needing protection.
Martyr Guru Teg Bahadur

Pardeep

Sunday, August 5, 2012, began as a beautiful sunny day. Jaspreet awoke early and headed into work to finish up reports that were due the next day. She was gone by the time the kids and I got up. "Where's Mom?" my daughter Amaris asked. I explained to her and her younger brother, Jai, that Mom had to go to the office for a while, but she'd be home in time for our regular Sunday family dinner.

The day promised to be a busy one. My plan was to drop off the kids at the Gurudwara before 11:00 so that Amaris could attend Punjabi class and Jai could play with his cousins. While they were occupied, I would run the household errands that had been stacking up all week.

The Gurudwara, or "door leading to God," our Sikh house of worship, was a network of family and friends who were always looking out for each other and each other's kids. Dad was president of the temple and Mom was there more than she was home. I respected our faith but never completely grasped it, probably because I wasn't as practiced in the Punjabi language as I should have been. That's why it was so important to me that Amaris attend Sunday school, so she could learn our native tongue and develop an understanding and appreciation of Sikhism.

Amaris was having a hard time getting started. She was moving like a turtle and complaining about everything. She didn't want to go to Sunday school. She couldn't find anything suitable to wear. Her hair didn't look right. Worst of all, her socks weren't cooperating. The crease had to form a perfect line across her toes before she put on her shoes. I thought to myself that she was either a perfectionist or suffered from a mild case of OCD. Jai, on the other hand, didn't care if he wore socks, much less that they fit perfectly. It took five minutes for him to brush his teeth, wash, and dress. I was discovering that boys were easier to raise than girls.

The morning was getting away from us. The Gurudwara was only ten or fifteen minutes from our house, but I needed extra time to be able to greet everyone there and say a small prayer in the prayer hall before I ran errands. Precious minutes came and went as Amaris lollygagged and carried on about the condition of her clothes. "Amaris! Let's go!" I said.

Finally, I got both kids in the car and buckled up, and off we went. Despite the late start, we still had enough time to get everything done we needed to, and I was feeling good. I had played in a basketball tournament the day before and, although our team didn't win, we did well. I was in my mid-thirties and appreciated still being able to compete without breaking a bone. I was reflecting on the final game when I heard Amaris cry out. "Dad! We need to go back! I forgot my notebook for class."

We were only five minutes from home but behind schedule nevertheless, thanks to my fussy eight-year-old. I started going through options in my head. Should I turn around and risk being later than we already were? Or proceed to the Gurudwara with a daughter who was unprepared for class? I weighed the pros and cons of each. I was leaning toward staying on course when Amaris reminded me that she had forgotten her notebook the Sunday before. I couldn't let that happen again and have my parenting called into question.

All the way home I let Amaris have it, about her forgetfulness, about dawdling, and, because I'm a cheapskate, about how I was wasting gas. But I could never stay mad at her for long. All she had to do was flash her sweet smile and all was forgiven. Thankfully, we got home quickly. Amaris ran inside as fast as her little legs would take her. She returned with her notebook and we headed to the temple again.

I quickly fell back into the spectacular mood that the picture-perfect Sunday brought. The kids were giggling in the backseat, and I jammed out to the music playing on my Bluetooth. The windows and sunroof were wide open and the wind felt warm on my face.

Coming up on our exit, I glanced in my rearview mirror

and saw a riot of flashing lights. There had to be a dozen police cruisers racing up behind us. I'd responded to my share of emergencies when I was a cop, but I found it alarming that they were weaving through traffic at such a dangerously high rate of speed.

I pulled over to the shoulder to allow them to pass. As they did, I noticed squads from several different jurisdictions. I thought to myself that whatever the emergency, the response seemed a bit dramatic. The posse of police cars exited the highway ahead of us and quickly sped out of sight. I drove on, hoping that whatever occurred wasn't too serious.

When I reached my intersection, I saw a large, black police SUV barricading the road leading to the Gurudwara and an officer redirecting traffic away from it. I explained that I was taking my kids to the temple for Sunday school. "Can I pass through?" I asked. The officer shook his head stubbornly. There was a shooting nearby and the scene was not yet secure, he said. No one was getting through. My first thought was that a cop had been shot. I asked if he knew an alternate route to the temple. I didn't know another way there. "No one is allowed near it," he said. "There's been a shooting. The scene is not secure."

The officer's words were crystal clear, but I asked him to repeat what he said. I told him that both of my parents were at the temple. Dad was president and Mom always arrived early on Sundays to help prepare food for the Langar, our communal meal. He seemed sympathetic, but he had concerns of his own, such as keeping people away. People like me.

"Was the shooting at the temple?" I asked. "Like ten minutes ago. I'm sorry," he said, returning to his work.

I understood his reluctance to engage in more conversation, but questions were pounding in my head like a bad migraine and I needed answers. I pulled into a grassy area off the intersection and parked the car. Feeing panicky, I told myself I had to stay calm for the sake of my kids.

I was only parked for a minute or two when a friend called and confirmed my fear. He said he had just heard there was a shooting at the temple. The temple was in lockdown. Were my parents there? Had I spoken to them? Yes, they were there, I said, feeling nauseous. No, I hadn't spoken to them.

The phone didn't stop ringing after that.

The next call was from Jaspreet. Trying to stay calm, she told me she had just spoken to my mother. Mom was whispering. She said she was hiding in the pantry in the kitchen of the Gurudwara with about a dozen other women. They had been cooking when they heard what sounded like gunshots in the distance, but they'd dismissed it, thinking it had to be something else. A moment later, two kids who had been playing outside the temple ran into the kitchen crying that there was a man outside with a gun. Mom grabbed the kids, and everyone who'd been in the kitchen pushed into the tiny pantry, the only place to hide. Just as they were about to close the door, a woman ran in, bleeding, saying she had just been shot inside the main entrance. Mom told Jaspreet she had tried calling me but couldn't get through. She would try me again, but I shouldn't call her number because any sound could tip the shooter or shooters to their hiding spot. "They are out there," she had said ominously before hanging up.

I took as many calls as I could answer, hoping to get more information. When the number on the caller ID was my father's, I quickly switched on my Bluetooth. "Dad?" I cried. My heart dropped when the voice on the other end was not that of my father but of the head priest, Gurmail Singh. His first language was Punjabi, but I understood enough to know that he was saying my father had been shot. It was serious and he needed help right away. "Please put my father on the phone," I said. "He can't talk now," the priest replied before the line went dead.

My heart hammered with anxiety. I cupped my face in my hands. My father had been shot and my mother was in imminent danger. I felt completely helpless and didn't know what to do. Just then, I heard whimpering in the backseat and remembered my kids were there. They had heard everything over the Bluetooth speaker. Amaris was crying and Jai was mad. "Dad," he said. "I will get the bad guys." Suddenly it occurred to me: if Amaris hadn't forgotten her notebook, we would have been in the temple. I switched the speaker off and turned to comfort my children.

In all the confusion, I hadn't noticed that others were gathering on the grass. I was grateful to see the familiar faces of some of our family members and friends. I spotted my cousin Kanwar, who taught Sunday school at the temple. "Watch the kids, please," I said to friends. I told Kanwar I thought we could make it to the temple through the woods. It would be quite a distance, with no set path, I suspected, but it was worth a try. He agreed; we couldn't just stand by idly.

We set out into the woods but were quickly thwarted by thick brush, making the way forward impossible. Turning back, we were spotted by the officer at the intersection. "What are you doing?" he shouted. "Get out of there or I'll arrest you!"

Feeling completely defeated, I walked back to the car. Jaspreet was there by then, and soon my brother, his wife, and her parents arrived. They didn't know anything more than the bits and pieces they caught on the news, which was very little.

Minutes dragged by like hours when, finally, mercifully, my mother called. Her voice was shaky, but at least she was alive. She whispered that she was still hiding in the tiny, sweltering kitchen pantry with the others. They had been in there a long time with no water. The woman who'd been shot was bleeding and all they had to treat her were kitchen napkins. I asked if she heard gunshots. Mom said the shots had stopped a while ago, but she believed the bad people were still inside the Gurudwara.

Choking back sobs, my mother asked if I'd heard from Dad. I told her about the call from the priest. "Please tell someone to help us," she whispered before hanging up.

Where the hell were the police? I wondered. They were obviously aware of what was happening. Had they even tried to enter the Gurudwara to help the people inside? Was it still an active shooting? How long would they allow this to go on?

Desperate, I called my former partner from the Milwaukee PD, Mark Harms. He said he knew about the shooting but had not yet been to the scene to know exactly what was going on. I told him about my conversation with Mom and with the priest. He was asking questions and taking notes. I appreciated that this was his job, but my parents' lives were in limbo. I didn't have the time or the patience to stay on the phone. "Listen, Mark," I said. "I need to get to the command post. I can help if they'll let me in. I can translate and make introductions. I can help them with the layout of the Gurudwara." I would have promised anything to get beyond the police barricade that was keeping me from my parents.

Mark asked a few more questions and finally gave me the name of the person in charge. Within minutes, I was allowed to pass through the barricade, leaving my brother, my wife, and everyone else behind.

———

THE MOBILE COMMAND center was located in the parking lot of the bowling alley across the street from the temple. It was parked alongside armored SWAT vehicles, police cars, ambulances, and the Red Cross. Swarms of people wearing badges and FBI jackets rushed around frantically. I saw people in riot gear. I asked an officer if anyone from the temple was there. I didn't know how many were inside the Gurudwara when the shooting started. Services usually attracted in the neighborhood of 150 worshippers, but it had been early, so I figured probably forty or fifty were there. He pointed to the bowling alley. There were some people inside, he said.

I was stopped again when I tried to enter the front door. Security was tight. Explaining my situation, the official at the door contacted the head guy and I was finally allowed inside. Distraught people milled around aimlessly. Walking through the crowd, I heard bits of conversation that did nothing to quell my fears. *My husband is still in there. She was lying on the ground in a pool of blood. Are we still in danger? Are they still inside?* So many questions, but no one in authority seemed to have answers—or they just weren't willing to share them.

I moved about, searching for my parents. Faces seemed to melt together. *Stay calm*, I told myself. *This is no time to panic.* I looked from person to person, finally spotting my mother at the end of a long hallway. She was sitting against a wall, looking like a lost child. Flooded with relief, I ran to her, dropped down, and lifted her up off the floor. She said that she and the others who'd been in the pantry were rushed out of the temple and into an armored police vehicle. They had seen people lying on the floor. We hugged for a long time. "Find out what is going on with Dad," she said, tears filling her eyes.

I didn't get the chance. Mom was summoned into a large conference room to be interviewed. I wasn't about to leave her alone. While she told her story to a pair of investigators, I did my best to translate for others who were questioning victims who spoke little or no English. I picked up whatever information I could. *We were going about our morning routines . . . preparing for services . . . waiting for classes to begin . . . cooking in the kitchen . . . praying in the main hall . . . We heard shots outside . . . At first we thought it was in the neighborhood . . . He came in through the front doors . . . He was white . . . I don't know if there was one shooter or more.*

When Mom was excused, I left her with friends from the temple and went in search of Dad. By then, the crowd inside had swelled with more victims and family members, many of whom I knew. One of the first people I saw was Gurmail Singh, the head priest who'd called me from Dad's cell phone. I watched as he steadied himself against a wall, and then I approached him to ask what he knew.

He said that the priests had gathered in the lobby of the temple, preparing to welcome the congregants who would soon be arriving for services, when a gunman walked through the door and started firing. Everyone scattered, he said. He found shelter in a bathroom at the far end of the temple and barricaded himself inside. My father was shot in the adjoining room. "I heard him praying and calling out for help," the priest said. "Do you know what happened after that?" I asked. Gurmail said he'd been rescued by a SWAT team and brought to the bowling alley moments earlier. He thought the police were still searching for gunmen inside the temple. They had made him come out of the bathroom with his hands held high in the air. He hadn't seen Dad again, but he thought he was transported to a hospital. His answer allowed me to hold out hope that my father was still alive.

I thanked Gurmail and moved on. Talking to everyone I

could, I learned about a family who survived the shooting and witnessed a lot. They were there, somewhere in the bowling alley. I asked around until someone pointed to a woman and two young children huddled together in a corner, looking lost and afraid.

Taking a deep breath, I walked over and introduced myself.

I CAN SEE in their eyes they have witnessed something terrible, something so traumatic that their warm brown skin has turned a drab shade of gray. They are staring ahead, saying nothing. I don't recognize them. Normally I wouldn't dare to approach them at what is obviously so painful a time, but I am fraught with worry about my own family, so I muster the courage to introduce myself. They look at me uncertainly. What do I want from them? Am I there to help?

I ask if they need anything, and they politely decline. They speak Punjabi. I can't bear to ask them what I want so desperately to know. What happened inside? Are people dead? Do you know my father? Please, what did you see? I start to walk away and see the little girl is looking up at me with pleading eyes, as if she wants to tell me something. I ask the mom if I may speak to the girl. Hesitantly, she agrees.

"What is your name?" I ask the girl.

"Palmeet," she says.

"How long ago did you come from India?"

She tells me they arrived in Wisconsin a few weeks earlier. Her dark eyes dart back and forth, up and down. I think about my own daughter, who is about the same age, and I want to wrap my arms around the little girl, to comfort her and tell her that everything will be okay.

"My father is dead," she says, so suddenly that my head jerks back. "My mom and my brother and me have seen it with our own eyes."

"Do you want to tell me about it?" I ask.

Just as I suspected, Palmeet speaks very little English. This is one of those times that I deeply regret I'm not fluent in Punjabi. I struggle to understand, and she is patient with me, often repeating things I don't grasp until I am finally able to piece together her story.

Palmeet says that she and her brother were in the Gurudwara, in a room next to the kitchen watching the Indian version of an American crime drama on TV, when they heard a series of pops. At first they thought it was the show, but a moment later her father rushed into the room, frantic. He threw her the keys to the basement and ordered her to take her brother down there to hide, then he ran back toward the danger. She knew from the tone of her father's voice that something bad was happening. He is usually so soft-spoken. I ask her father's name. "Prakash Singh," she says. I know him. He is a young temple priest my dad sponsored to come to America from India seven years ago. He must have finally gotten clearance to bring his family here after all that time.

By the grace of God, Palmeet says, just as she and her brother headed toward the basement door, her mother found them and they all rushed downstairs. There were already a dozen or so people down there, adults and other children. They could hear gunshots upstairs. *Pop-pop-pop-pop-pop!* Everyone was panicked and crying.

When the shooting stopped, Palmeet, her mom, and her brother waited awhile and then crept upstairs to find her father. They got as far as the prayer hall when they saw the bloodied body of a woman lying by the doorway. They were horrified, she says, but the woman was beyond help. Cautiously, they moved past the dead woman and walked on. They came upon a second body, an old man lying outside of the library. He, too, was dead.

After that, they went room to room, not knowing if they would run into a killer. When they reached the room at the far end of the temple, they discovered her father's body. He was covered in blood, but even worse, one of his eyes was missing. He had been shot in the face. Her mother became hysterical, draping herself over the body and crying for her husband to wake up, but Palmeet knew he was dead. She touched her father's face around his missing eye and got blood on her hand. That really frightened her.

"Did you see anything else?" I ask gently.

Yes, Palmeet says. She saw another man in the room. He was bloody and lying in a fetal position with his back to the door. She could barely get a look at him when, suddenly, the bathroom door swung open and a priest motioned her and her family inside. The priest locked the door behind them and told them to be very, very quiet. It was then she heard the cries of the injured man, she says. "And what was he saying?" I ask. The man was saying *Waheguru, Waheguru,* Palmeet says. Waheguru is the Sikh call to God. *Wondrous Enlightener who eliminates the darkness of our mind with the light of divinity.* After a few minutes, she says, the chanting stopped.

Palmeet says they stayed in the bathroom for an hour or so when the police came knocking. They were ordered out of the bathroom with their hands held in the air. By then, the room outside was empty. Neither the body of her father nor the other man was there, she says. She is sorry for not having any more information.

I am sorry for what her innocent mind has had to endure.

BY TWO O'CLOCK, we still didn't know anything definitive about my father. My brother, who had by then made it into the staging area outside where the reporters were, said some of the networks were reporting that several people from the temple were being treated in local hospitals. All were men and all were in critical condition. Family members had scoured all of the area hospitals with no luck. Someone suggested that maybe our father had been released and went home to rest. As ridiculous as the idea sounded, he had sent a relative to check the house, but Dad wasn't there.

The authorities continued to be tight-lipped. All we had to go on were conflicting news reports and social media feeds. There was one gunman . . . There were two or more shooters . . . Three people were in critical condition . . . Several people died . . . Hostages were being held in the temple . . . The shooting was an act of domestic terror . . . White supremacists were responsible . . . The shooter was a racist skinhead. "What is that?" my mother asked.

The sun fell in the sky. I begged Mom to go home and get some rest. She was coming apart. At one point she had become hysterical, screaming, "Where is Satwant? Where is Satwant?" Finally, she agreed to leave with Jaspreet and wait at home.

I walked out of the bowling alley and into the night air. Nearly ten hours had passed since the shooting. The parking lot was brightly lit. The crowd had dispersed, except for official types, members of the media, and the few of us who still didn't know the fate of our loved ones. My heart broke for two teenage boys who had been there almost as long as I had and begged for any news of their mother. They had repeatedly called the police hotline and even posted inquiries on Facebook, trying to find out something, to no avail.

Looking out over the Gurudwara, I saw my father's pickup truck parked in the same spot it had been that morning. Amardeep walked up behind me. He looked tired. I had watched with awe as he met with reporters, exchanging information and carrying what he'd learned back to us. I was proud he was able to put on a strong front when I knew his heart was breaking. He was the embodiment of Chardi Kala, maintaining relentless optimism in the will of God, even in this time of adversity.

We stood there in silence for quite a while, two brothers

alone with their thoughts, when Amardeep finally spoke. "Are you thinking what I'm thinking?" he asked. I nodded slowly. "Yes," I said. "Dad is still in that building and he isn't coming home."

SEVEN

HATE CRIME

The tongue is like a sharp knife; it kills without drawing blood.
Guru Nanak Dev Ji

Pardeep

On a different night, I might have taken time to appreciate
the majesty of the stars shimmering against the black sky, but
now everything looked ominous. With every moment that
passed, my heart plunged deeper into darkness. Joyful imag-
inings of seeing my father walk out of the temple were fad-
ing into despairing thoughts about what was to come.

My brother and I continued to watch the Gurudwara in
silence when we spotted a familiar face walking toward us
from the police staging area. Harpreet Dulai and I grew up
together. Our families were friends. Our fathers were founding members of the temple. They pooled their money to help
with a down payment on the land and oversaw construction
of the building, pitching in wherever they could be useful.
Mom had photographs of them digging trenches and lugging

concrete blocks for a retaining wall they helped build together. Our parents were all still deeply involved in the running of the temple. Harpreet and I lost contact when he moved out of town to work for the FBI, but we'd kept in touch through our parents. The last I'd heard, he had been transferred back to the Midwest. Seeing him gave me a sense of relief. Finally, we would get answers.

"Harpreet!" I cried.

We greeted each other warmly. Harpreet said he came to the scene initially because his mother called him from the pantry to tell him that the temple was under attack. A bullet grazed her foot as she ran for cover in the pantry, but she wasn't seriously injured. He and his father spent the afternoon triaging some of the survivors until he was called upon to serve as the FBI liaison between investigators and the Sikh community.

I told Harpreet that we still didn't know about our dad, only what we'd heard secondhand and on the news, and so much of it was in conflict. We heard reports that seven people died but, if that was the case, why hadn't their names been released to their families? Every official I'd asked about it gave me the official "I can't tell you much" response. When I was a cop I'd made dozens of notifications and I couldn't imagine allowing loved ones to dangle as long as we had. A badge didn't mean you couldn't have a heart. With nothing to encourage us, my brother and I were left with a sinking feeling our father wasn't coming home with us. If I had to, I would stay all night, and the next, and the next, until I knew something. "Please, man," I said, "you need to find out what's going on with our dad."

Harpreet seemed sympathetic. He said he was making his way to the Gurudwara for the first time that day and as soon as he knew anything about Dad he would come back and tell us. As he walked away, I noticed he was wearing a bulletproof vest. Why? Was there still some threat in the temple? Was there even a slight chance Dad was alive in there? Did he know more than he was telling us?

The mind is a funny thing. Mine wouldn't allow me to wholly accept the only explanation for my father's absence that made sense: that Dad was among the seven who didn't make it. Denial was my armor. I couldn't bear the thought that my father, a man I always saw as invincible, could be gone.

Only a day earlier, we'd been together at a family party, drinking Patiala Pegs, a whiskey drink that is legendary in northern India. It was my thirty-sixth birthday and we'd all gathered at my cousin Gary's house for a family get-together. For us, that meant anywhere from twenty to fifty people, and the house was full that day. Jaspreet, the kids, and I had arrived a bit late, which was customary. In fact, we called it "Indian people time." We were never on schedule. That day, at least we had a valid excuse. Jaspreet was seven months pregnant and we had two little ones to dress for the party. Even so, we got there before my parents, which was also typical. Mom liked to get all dolled up for family functions, and getting ready took her forever. Dad, on the other hand, was never one to worry much about what he wore. He would have arrived home from work with just enough time for a short shower and a change of clothes. Most of his time was spent tying his turban. It had to be meticulous. Just so.

I had just poured my first Peg when Dad came in. His turban, as always, was perfect. He had this way of tying it that made him look regal and even taller than he was. He had turbans in different colors, but that day he chose his favorite: gray. When we complimented him on it, he answered the way he always did. *"Ko budhi gul ne hai,"* which literally translates to, "It's not a big deal." Everyone greeted him, which in our family we did by closing our palms together, pointing our fingers to the sky, and saying, *"Sat sri akal"* (God is the ultimate truth). Dad took a seat across from me while my uncle poured him a drink. I lifted a toast to our family and everyone clinked glasses.

It said something that we had gotten to the point of having a drink together, especially that drink, which Punjabi tradition held was a measure of a man's masculinity.

It hadn't been all that long ago that my father still treated me like a kid. I had spent my early life trying to earn his praise, but he was tough to please. His measure of character was how hard someone worked, and I knew of no one who worked harder than he did. Up until just a few years ago, he constantly challenged my work ethic by outworking me, which made me feel inferior. I had finally moved out of his shadow with my own family and career—first as a police officer, now as a teacher at a high school for at-risk kids. Over the last few years, we had reconciled our father-son tug-of-war and come to a place of peace. Now, when Dad showed up at my house to pick weeds or shovel snow while I went off to my job, I knew it wasn't to show me up but a token of his love. He was proud of the man I had become. We respected each other. We were finally able to be openly affectionate with each other. My mind flashed back to the last time we were together and Dad allowed Amaris and Jai to ride on his back. He was glowing, as were they. He couldn't be taken from us!

Ten or fifteen minutes went by and Amardeep and I were still reflecting when we saw Harpreet sprinting toward us from the temple. I held my breath. *He's running!* I thought. *Is that a good sign? Would he be running to give us bad news?* To our disbelief, he raced right past us without even making eye contact. When he passed, I noticed his bulletproof vest was unfastened. That was typically what law enforcement did when they knew there was no longer a threat. Had I foolishly hypothesized that it was possible my father was a captive? It might have been a long shot, but it was our only hope of seeing him alive again.

Watching Harpreet fly into the bowling alley, I got a bitter taste in my mouth. "Damn him!" I said to my brother. "Didn't he just promise he would let us know what was going on?" Harpreet had chosen to play the part of FBI agent over friend. In that role, he was taught to keep everything close to the vest. Did he not understand our torment? Had he not taken pity on my mother, who was coming unhinged, waiting to know the fate of her husband? What if it had been his family who was suffering? I hated him at that moment.

I barely had time to vent my anger when Amardeep and I were summoned into the bowling alley. An Oak Creek police officer led us solemnly down the stairs and into a private room filled with law enforcement officers. As we walked in, the teenage boys who had been pleading for information about their mom all day walked out sobbing.

Amardeep and I took seats across the table from a team of FBI agents and local cops. Another dozen or so stood behind them, some in uniform, some wearing suits. Harpreet stood at the back of the room. One officer spoke for the group. "We regret to inform you that your father did not survive," she said. Why didn't I expect to hear that? Why didn't I know when the boys left in tears that those of us who were left at the scene would not have a good ending?

Bile surged from my stomach up into my throat. It didn't matter that this woman was just the messenger. The full force of my rage was upon her. Teeth clenched, hands sweating, heart racing, I glared at her. A million thoughts ran through my mind. *What took so long to tell us? How long did Dad suffer before actually passing away? What took the cops so long to enter the building? If they'd gotten inside sooner, could my father have been saved?*

Amardeep was crying, but I was too angry to shed tears. I didn't want to spend another second in that room with those people. *Don't give me your sad faces and official bullshit lines,*

I thought to myself. *You have no idea what you have put us through. You should have told my mom before she left.* But they'd waited too long and now I would have to tell her that Dad was gone. I stood to leave, asking Amardeep to meet me back at Mom's. I didn't want anyone to drive with me. I needed solitude.

Alone in my car, I raged. They were all cowards! The shooter was a coward for ambushing peace-loving people in their place of sanctuary. The cops were cowards for not going into the temple sooner and keeping us in the dark for so long. Harpreet was a coward for avoiding us when he knew that every minute was a minute more of suffering. Gurmail was a coward for hiding in the bathroom while my father was dying on the opposite side of the door. They were all fucking cowards! Every one of them!

I screamed all the way to my parents' house, so long and loud that my throat was raw. Was I going mad? I didn't know any other way to unleash the wrath and emotions attacking me. I was out of my mind with fear, fury, and an almost incomprehensible sadness. When I pulled into the driveway and saw my father's American flag flying in the front yard, I screamed some more.

I pulled myself together for the sake of my mother. Getting out of the car, I saw family members gathered outside the house, as if they were too afraid to go inside. Pausing to muster the courage for the task ahead, I asked myself, *How will I do this? What will I say?*

Mom was standing inside the front door. She searched my

face for answers. I tried to tell her, but the words wouldn't come. *Lord!* I thought. *I can't speak!* My mother fell to the floor, her body convulsing with sobs. I ran to her. First Amardeep and then the others followed. We all held each other and cried, as if our shared heartbreak might lighten the burden of our individual grief.

No one slept that night.

Arno

When I saw the first tweets, I was forty-five minutes outside of Milwaukee, working on a client's servers. *BREAKING NEWS: Reports of shots fired and officer down at Seik [sic] Temple in Oak Creek . . . Active shooter on the scene Shooting Report of Officer down & 3 to 4 victims. Active shooter on scene. Mutual aid from several PD's.*

I clicked on the hashtag #sikhtempleshooting, and all this stuff started streaming down the side of my laptop screen: *Getting reports that 4 people were shot at Sikh Temple. Police not giving out any information yet . . . Scanner reports indicate Oak Creek Police cannot find shooter at Sikh Temple—crew on scene says it is "chaos." . . . Multiple shooters reported.*

As soon as I heard the Sikh temple was under siege, my gut told me what no one was reporting yet. This was a strike by the radicalized American far-right movement. An attack to say, "You're threatening our race and we're going to eliminate you before you destroy us." It had all the markings of white supremacists—specifically, racist skinheads, the faction I helped to establish nearly twenty years before.

I didn't know anything about Sikhs except that they looked different than white American males. What I did know was that in my former world, "different" was all that was needed to provoke an attack. Didn't matter if you were black, brown, yellow, gay—anything but white, straight, and sympathetic to the cause, you were fair game.

Waiting for more information to come out, I did the only thing I could think of. Late that afternoon, I posted a video on YouTube, appealing for peace and understanding.

> This atrocity that happened today hits home for me not only because I live in Milwaukee and this is in my backyard but also because there was a time in my life that I practiced the hate and violence that was the raw material behind this shooting. I can remember my own sense of urgency as I engaged in the paranoid lie that my race was under attack and I had to do something about it, otherwise my people would be wiped out. It's a safe bet to say the shooter was attached to a very similar narrative that led him into a place of worship to murder people he's never met before.
>
> I'm driven to look for some kind of answer to this senseless violence. I understand the most effective measure I can take is to practice compassion and kindness, un-

conditionally, and to broadcast it to everyone I come into contact with. It is not a stretch to say an act of kindness could have diverted this shooter from where he ended up today. "Hate begets hate; violence begets violence," as Dr. Martin Luther King Jr. said. The same is true for peace and love.

I finished my consulting job and spent the evening switching between social media and TV news. It was late when I learned that the shooter was a white supremacist. Right from the jump I'd suspected as much, but having it confirmed made my stomach turn.

During my tenure of hate, I truly believed I was doing the crucial work of helping to save my imperiled race, as ridiculous as that sounded to me now. I was certain the shooter held the same reckless convictions, and six innocent people were dead because of it. Good people with families and friends and meaningful contributions to make to the world. Out of his own self-loathing and rage, the shooter had reached a point of disengagement from his own humanity and consequently the humanity of others around him. He didn't look at his victims as human anymore. They were the objects of his blind hatred. I had been that person. I didn't pull the trigger at the Sikh temple, but I had beaten people to near death. I had been terrified of the world around me. Everywhere I looked, I saw the work of the enemy. Anyone who wasn't white was out to wipe out my people. Anyone who didn't sympathize with the cause was a race traitor. I felt no remorse for the havoc I wrought—not until years later when I finally broke out of my cocoon of inhumanity.

I was fortunate to have done a 180-degree turn, thanks to a family that refused to give up on me, the birth of my daughter, and the kindness of people I professed to hate. Returning to that world, even if just through memory, made my skin crawl. I didn't need a name to know the shooter was someone so driven by hatred, so steeped in fear and ignorance, that the only way he could think to release his rage was by killing perceived enemies. People who, in his demented way of thinking, were a threat to him and his distorted worldview. What a complete fucking waste of beautiful human lives. *When will it stop?* I asked myself.

I slept fitfully that night. What if the killer was someone I knew from my previous life? What if the songs I wrote while I was with Centurion influenced him? *Crush your enemies with racial loyalty. It's a racial holy war! Centurion! Blood, soil, and honor!* White power music was seductive. It drew people in, provoked anger and violence, and sometimes even triggered murder, and our songs were iconic and easy to find on the internet. It hadn't been too long ago—long after I'd left the movement and years into my peace work—that a neo-Nazi from Germany contacted me to ask if I'd be interested in reviving the band. I didn't reply but I never forgot that the harm I'd set in motion was still hurting people.

I heard the name Wade Michael Page for the first time the next morning when I turned on the TV. The name wasn't familiar, and for that I was grateful. News reports said he had been on the watch lists of organizations that monitored hate groups because of his longtime ties to the white supremacist movement and his role as the leader of his own white power band. He attended Hammerfest, the white supremacist music festival inspired by concerts that I had helped organize back in the day. One photo showed him in a Confederate flag t-shirt, showing off a tattoo on his left arm. It was the number "14," representing the fourteen words that racist skinheads lived by—that I had once lived by: *We must secure the existence of our people and a future for white children.*

I left my white power skinhead self behind long ago, tossed him out, stomped on him, and swore that I'd spend the rest of my life atoning for his terrible acts. I knew that the shadow of that person and his crimes against humanity would follow me. Every time something like this happened, it reminded me that, as committed as I was to practicing loving kindness and working for a peaceful world, I would never be able to sweep away all of the fragments of my racist past. I would live with that until the day I died.

As I stared at Wade Page's photograph, I couldn't help but wonder if anyone had ever been kind enough to reassure him that he was better than that, as the brave black woman at McDonald's had once done for me.

It might have saved lives.

EIGHT

THE INVESTIGATION

Falsehood may be practiced a hundred times; it is still false.
Guru Nanak Dev Ji

Pardeep

A photo of my brother praying on his knees in the bowling alley parking lot became the face of the temple massacre. Newspapers featured it prominently on their front pages. Television stations led with it. Only two weeks earlier, a mass shooter had killed twelve people during a midnight screening of *The Dark Knight Rises*. I'd watched the coverage on TV. Now the image of our family's anguish was everywhere. At a time when we were at our most vulnerable, people were taking our picture. I wondered, *How did our tragedy become their entertainment?*

As a member of an already marginalized community, I felt even more victimized by the vague responses from law enforcement to everything I asked about my father's final moments. Sikhs believe that our destiny has been written, so I accepted my father's death as God's will. But, as his son, I needed to know what happened to him. I didn't understand the reticence of the local police chief and the FBI investigators working the case to answer the most basic things. What harm would come from telling us whether Dad was shot first or last, whether he died quickly or suffered longer? How would we ever get closure with so many open questions?

Out of pure frustration, and to satisfy my own gnawing need for answers, I set out to learn what I could on my own. I talked to people who escaped with their lives, as well as local cops who agreed to tell me things they'd heard around their precincts, provided I promised not to betray their confidence. Little by little, I was able to separate fact from fiction and piece many things together.

Sunday services at the Gurudwara typically attracted three hundred worshippers, but that day, because the shooter came early, only thirty or forty were there when the rampage began.

Mom and Dad drove separately that morning. Mom arrived at the temple first to help in the kitchen. Dad came in a few minutes later to begin setting up for the main service. After morning prayers, he went to the kitchen to fix his usual cup of tea. Mom and a dozen or so other women were already preparing the traditional Punjabi dishes of fried *samosas* and *poori* to be served at the afternoon *langar* meal. Dad was in good spirits, chitchatting with other congregants about raising money for Prakash Singh, a priest who had emigrated from India seven years earlier and had finally been able to bring his wife and two young children here. The family was about to move into their first apartment and needed help getting started.

As people arrived in dribs and drabs, Wade Michael Page left his apartment in Cudahy to drive the seven miles to Oak Creek. He got to the temple and parked his red pickup at the top of the parking lot. Dressed in a white t-shirt and dark pants and armed with a 9mm semiautomatic handgun, he walked to a spot where he could see everyone who came and went.

Sita Singh, a forty-one-year-old priest, pulled into the lot a moment later. Sita, who had moved from New York City only six months earlier, came to relieve his older brother Ranjit of his temple duties so that Ranjit could go to his job at a grocery store. At the same time Ranjit was leaving the Gurudwara, Sita was walking toward it. When they stopped to greet each other, Page opened fire.

Thirty yards away—the distance between bases on a baseball field—Amanat Singh and her eleven-year-old brother Abhay (whose name means "fearless") were playing outside the temple. Their parents were hosting that day's langar meal in honor of Amanat's ninth birthday and had run to the grocery store to fetch extra paper plates. The siblings were told to stay inside, but had decided to go out for air when the kitchen got too warm. They were sitting on a crate, singing and giggling, when they noticed the stocky, balding white man with glasses get out of his pickup.

For an instant, the children thought the man was lost and needed directions; but, without any warning, he pulled a gun from his holster and fired several shots at the brothers. Ranjit fell to the pavement, his chest and stomach riddled with bullets. Sita collapsed on top of him, struck several times in the back. Both had been mortally wounded.

Hearing shots outside, Dad ran from the kitchen toward the main entrance to see where the shots were coming from. At the same time, the terrified children ran into the kitchen to warn the others. "Someone killed the *babaji!*" they cried. *Someone killed the priest!* They had barely gotten the words out when Page stepped into the temple with his gun drawn.

I know that my father's first concern would have been the safety of everyone else, but I don't know where he was in the temple when Page started shooting. He may have been with the team of priests who'd been meeting in the foyer to plan the day's songs and scriptures. He could have gone back to the prayer hall, where early worshippers had been saying their morning prayers. Nevertheless, everyone scattered, some people toward the kitchen at one end of the temple, others toward the living quarters at the opposite end.

Prakash Singh ran to the room near the kitchen where his children were watching TV, waiting for Sunday school to begin. Bursting through the door, he tossed a set of keys to his daughter, Palmeet, and ordered her and her brother to lock themselves down in the basement. His distraught wife was close behind him. She and her children ran downstairs together. Others were already hiding there. In true character, Prakash ran back toward the prayer hall to try to help others. The decision would cost him his life.

From somewhere inside the temple, Dad made his first 911 call. In a loud but controlled voice, he said, "We are having a problem here at the Sikh Temple of Wisconsin. The guy is firing! We need 911 quick!" The sounds of gunfire and people shouting and screaming could be heard in the background.

All over the temple, people ran for their lives. They hid wherever they could find cover. Behind locked doors. In closets. Around corners. A bullet grazed one woman as she hid behind a large column in the main foyer. She ran into the kitchen, shouting, "I've been shot! I've been shot."

Mom locked the kitchen door, grabbed the two children and the injured woman, and led everyone into the impossibly tight quarters of the kitchen pantry. It was dark and sweltering inside, with barely room to turn around, but there was nowhere else to hide. Using the light from her phone, she quietly tended to the woman with the only thing she could find, a few paper napkins. As she dabbed the blood on the woman's arm, she heard shots and screams coming from the direction of the prayer hall. Everyone in the pantry started to pray. Many had loved ones outside. Mom prayed for Dad's safety. She knew he would take on the role of protector of the flock.

Page shot randomly from inside the foyer. One of his bullets penetrated the metal frame of the doors to the prayer hall. Mom believes the screams she heard were Paramjit Kaur, who had been praying in there at the *takhat*, the throne holding the Guru Granth Sahib, our holy scriptures, just before the shooting started. Paramjit was the mother of the heartbroken teenage boys I'd seen at the bowling alley. She hadn't been able to get out of the prayer hall fast enough and Page executed her as she knelt in a corner in prayer. She was forty-one.

After killing Paramjit, the shooter moved down the hallway toward the kitchen. A few seconds earlier, the women in the pantry smelled burning and two ran back to turn off ovens that were left on inadvertently in everyone's haste to hide. While they were rushing around the kitchen, they heard someone cry out a warning. "He is coming! He is coming!" Page appeared on the other side of the counter separating the kitchen from the fellowship hall. Taking a shooter's stance, he fired at the women, grazing both before they could get back into the pantry. Miraculously, he moved on to his next target. He must have surmised that the pantry door led outside. Had he pursued them, everyone in the pantry would likely have been murdered.

The sound of Page's wrath echoed throughout the temple, and panicked people called 911 for help. The first calls were garbled. Most of the callers spoke in faint whispers; many with accents that made them at times difficult to understand.

"Squad, I'm taking a report of an altercation, Sikh temple, 7512 S. Howell," the police dispatcher said. "I have a lot of noise. I'm unable to get much info, but there's a fight . . ."

More calls followed in quick succession.

There is shooting . . . There is shooting in this . . . He's shooting!

Someone is shooting us! Please hurry up!

We are just hiding now.

I don't know where my mother is.

My children are inside!

The initial radio dispatch was followed up with a report of possible gunshots. Seconds later, the dispatcher reported that "a bald male with glasses may have shot someone."

As police raced to the scene, Page made his way back from the kitchen to the main hallway. A few feet past the prayer hall he encountered eighty-four-year-old Suveg Singh Khattra, a devout man who came to the temple early in the morning and didn't leave until late at night, coming out of the library. He shot him in the head, killing him instantly.

He then went to the living quarters at the far end of the temple where Punjab Singh was hiding in his room. Punjab was a visiting priest from India. He was a gentle man who loved nature and could create a rose with multicolored petals. He had been tying his turban in preparation for the morning service when the first shots rang out. Barricading himself in his room, he was no match for Page, who was able to force the door open just enough to reach his gun inside and shoot the priest in the face. Punjab suffered catastrophic injuries to his brain and spinal cord.

Across the hall, Dad was locked in another guest room with three other priests, making 911 calls and watching out the window for the police. Prakash, who wanted to get to his children, unlocked the bedroom door and opened it a crack to look out. Page was on the other side. He shot Prakash in the eye. "*Maiṁ mara gi'ā hāṁ,*" Prakash said as he fell to the floor. *I am dead.*

The priest Gurmail was able to lock himself in the bathroom before Page could see. He could hear everything from inside. He heard Dad confront the shooter. "What is your problem?" he asked in English. Without answering, Page turned the gun on the third priest, Santokh Singh, shooting him twice, in the chest and the stomach. "What's wrong with you?" Santokh cried. "Why are you shooting me? Why can't we talk?"

Page pulled the trigger to shoot Santokh again, but the gun didn't fire. He was out of ammunition. When he reached down to reload, Santokh pushed through the slightly open door and ran for his life. He was halfway down the hallway when Page ducked out of the bedroom and fired after him. The shot missed and Santokh was able to get out of the temple and stagger to a nearby house. There, he collapsed on the front lawn, his white tunic soaked in blood.

While Page was stalking Santokh, my father made his final 911 call. Had he run out of the room and in the opposite direction of the shooter, he could have escaped through an exit that was no more than ten feet away. But my father would never have left when others were in danger. "Hurry, please!" he pleaded to the 911 operator. "He is shooting!" It was too late. The call cut out with the crack of gunfire.

OUTSIDE THE GURUDWARA, Lt. Brian Murphy, a tough New York Irishman and former Marine who'd served twenty years on the Oak Creek police force, was the first to respond. Murphy hadn't been scheduled to work, but he'd traded days off with another officer whose son was graduating from high school. It had been a low-key morning when he got the call about a fight at the temple, which quickly turned into shots fired, and a brief description of a possible shooter.

Murphy arrived at 10:28 A.M. He drove up the long blind driveway to the parking lot, where he discovered the bodies of the brothers. He called for an ambulance, then got out of his car to check their condition. It was clear they were dead.

Out of the corner of his eye, Murphy saw movement. A man wearing a white t-shirt and black fatigues, with a holster on his hip, was rushing out of the temple entrance. He fit the description from dispatch.

Drawing his service weapon, Murphy ran out into the open lot, shouting, "Police! Stop!" They made eye contact. Page seemed surprised to see him. They were standing a mere thirty yards apart. Both men took shots at the same time. Murphy's missed. Page's hit Murphy in the chin. The force of the bullet was so fierce that the officer's head snapped back violently. He felt like he'd been slammed with a sledgehammer.

The officer dove behind a parked car for cover. He was losing blood quickly and his adrenaline was pumping. He poked his head up to look for the shooter. Perhaps he'd hit him? By then, Page had circled around the car and was standing less than fifteen feet behind him. The guy obviously knew warfare, Murphy thought. Page fired again, shooting off half of Murphy's left thumb. The service revolver flew out of his hand. He was a sitting duck.

Page was all business. His facial expression was flat, pitiless. Murphy had seen more emotion on the faces of his colleagues at target practice. The man was obviously on a mission to kill. With Page bearing down on him, Murphy clawed his way under the car. Gravely injured, he was losing consciousness. Cocooned by a sense of calm and warmth, he caught himself drifting off. *Oh no!* he scolded himself. *I'm not going out like this. And I'm not going out in a parking lot.*

Murphy willed himself to stay conscious and alert. As he lay in a ball beneath the car, the shooter coolly reached down and shot him again. Mercilessly, he fired bullets into Murphy's arms and legs. Murphy wasn't going to give him anything. The pain of the bullets ripping through his body was crippling, but he refused to make a sound. He thought about the two men lying nearby and wondered how many others were dead inside the temple. If he didn't do something to stop Page, there would be even more carnage. His only hope was the rifle in his cruiser. If he could only get there.

When Page stopped to reload, Murphy made his move. He crawled out from under the car toward his cruiser. *Like that*, Page was standing over him. He pumped a bullet into the back of Murphy's head. *C'mon!* Murphy thought. *When is enough, enough?*

SAM LENDA WAS two minutes behind Murphy. With lights flashing and siren roaring, he ascended the temple driveway, not knowing what to expect. Driving over the rise, he thought he saw a man in white up ahead. His viewpoint was obstructed by distance and parked cars, but as he watched, he saw the man turn away from whatever he was doing and start walking toward him. He noted it wasn't a normal walk, but an aggressive march.

He radioed in to headquarters. "I got a guy in a white t-shirt walking out of the parking lot toward me."

"Where is Murphy?" the dispatcher asked.

"I don't see Murphy!" he responded.

Throwing the car in reverse, Lenda backed up to give himself enough distance to safely retrieve the locked squad rifle from his center console. Lenda was the best marksman around, with a decade of training for active shooters. Unlocking his rifle, he proceeded back toward the temple. Within seconds, Page appeared on the horizon again. Lenda saw Page either reload or check the magazine in his gun. He radioed in again. "I got a man with a gun in the parking lot!"

All hell broke loose. Within seconds, squads from surrounding towns began arriving. Sirens screeched. The police radio squawked desperately with requests for additional backup, ambulances, and questions about Murphy. No one had heard from him since that first transmission when he'd called for an ambulance. *Where's Murphy? Do you see Murphy? Is Murphy down?*

Lenda still didn't see any trace of Murphy. He rolled closer to the shooter. "Drop the gun!" he shouted. "Drop the gun!"

Page darted around the parking lot, aiming his gun. Lenda got out of his cruiser, taking cover behind his open driver's-side door. Once again, he ordered Page to drop his weapon.

From sixty yards away, Page took a shot. His bullet exploded through the windshield of the police car, lodging in the headrest of the seat where Lenda had been sitting seconds earlier. Lenda positioned his rifle and aimed at Page. He decided if he missed the shot, he would run him over. Page was not leaving that parking lot and he was not going back into the temple. Not on his watch.

Lenda grasped the wrist of his rifle stock and steadied his breathing so as not to throw off his shot. Aligning his sight with the target, he squeezed the trigger. Once, twice, six times.

My guys are here, Murphy thought, hearing the exchange of gunfire.

Lenda's second round wounded Page and he dropped to the ground. The officer saw him crawling. He shouted at Page not to move. The next sound was Page, shooting himself in the head.

I BELIEVE THAT my father died fighting Wade Page. My brother said an FBI agent told him there was a butter knife close to Dad's body, which they thought he used to fend off the shooter. I wouldn't have expected anything different. He spoke truth to power and didn't cower to evil. Dad was shot "multiple times," according to the autopsy report. Page was a right-handed shooter and most of Dad's injuries were on his left side—left abdomen; left arm; left chest; left upper back; left neck—which suggested a fierce struggle. While Page was killing him, had Dad picked up a knife to fight back? No one can say for sure, but I know his thought process would have been to do whatever it took to stop the attack. There were people to protect! His wife and his community were in trouble. He wasn't going down without a fight. If a butter knife was all he had at his disposal, he would have used it.

Lieutenant Murphy miraculously survived Page's attack. It ended his police career, and he'd had to endure months of grueling physical therapy, but he was lucky to be alive. Murphy is a legend in our Sikh community. After the shooting, he received thousands of cards and letters from Sikhs around the world, thanking him for his service. When he speaks publicly about the tragedy and people—rightfully so—applaud him for his valor, he often defers to my father as the real hero. He told me he, too, has heard the story about the knife found beside Dad and he believes Dad used it for battle. But he needed no more proof of my father's bravery, Murphy told me, than the fact he fought so valiantly to stop Page's rampage that his fingernails were ripped off. A man who was so devoted to his flock that he fought to the death trying to protect them was the epitome of a noble warrior. My father was the hero.

Sikh history is rich with examples of martyrs who sacrificed their lives for selfless causes and noble ends. Sikh scripture states, *"When all other methods fail, it is proper to hold the sword in hand.*" Dad martyred himself trying to spare others. That is his legacy.

Only the brave person dies a worthy death, the scripture says. *For he is accepted by the Lord after his death.*

NINE

BROTHERS

No one is my enemy and no one is a stranger;
God exists in all beings.
Guru Arjun Dev Ji

Arno   November 2012

Three months after the shooting, on Thanksgiving eve, 2012,
I was headed to the Gurudwara in Oak Creek at the invitation
of Pardeep. The occasion was "Heritage Day," a celebration
of cultures to honor those who were lost on August 5. Par had
asked me to be a guest speaker. The idea of entering the temple
for the first time, a place where such violence was wrought
such a short time ago, and as someone with the same history as
the man who brought evil there, was overwhelming.

A week earlier, Life After Hate had been hijacked by my
board—the same board of former white supremacists that
I appointed—and I was still smarting from it. My "firing" was
over some concocted bullshit, but it broke my heart. I had
kept the organization running on my own dime for the three
years it had been in existence. I often felt like it was a boat that

would sink if I stopped rowing, and I couldn't let that happen. By my own choice, I'd let my IT consulting business go to shit in order to be able to accommodate anti-violence programs and speaking invitations associated with the nonprofit. I saw it as my life's work, but it reached the point where my bank account was drained and I needed a salary, at least a small one, just enough to pay my bills, in order to keep up the momentum of the program. My board didn't seem to think my request was a priority, but they weren't struggling financially. I was.

There was a time when I would have gone down with the boat rather than speak up for myself. After I'd stopped abusing drugs and alcohol in 2004, I gained clarity and confidence, but I still beat the hell out of myself emotionally as a sort of masochistic penance for all the wrong I had done. When bad things happened to me, I reasoned it was because I didn't deserve good things. I deserved to suffer for the rest of my life, just as I had caused the suffering of so many others.

In an effort to try to forgive myself, I'd recently discovered meditation in the ancient Tibetan tradition of *Shine* (pronounced shee-nay), the Buddhist practice of calming the mind. Through my practice, I'd finally determined I was worth forgiving. Part of that forgiveness was realizing that I was a good person who did meaningful work and having the confidence to know I deserved to be paid for it.

After making many requests to the board for some kind of a compensation plan, the issue finally came to a head that November and, stressed by the ever-growing pile of unpaid bills on my desk, I blew my top. My board had never seen me lose my temper, and apparently it was not a pleasant sight. I regretted the tantrum the minute it was over and followed it up with a mea culpa email:

> My anger was directed entirely at myself for letting my expectations and desperation get the better of me, but it effected [*sic*] everyone and I'm deeply sorry for that. I tried to make it clear that I wasn't angry at anyone else but didn't do a very good job of that either. I am so grateful for your time and energy . . . I feel fortunate on a daily basis for all the help you have given me and LAH and for your friendship.
>
> I will be more mindful of expectations and desperation in the future. I know better with the former, and there is really no need for the latter, because I am grateful for life and especially to be able to share mine with all of you. I have lined up some IT work and speaking engagements so I can pay my bills, and I am confident that no matter how things shake down, it will be all good.
>
> I believe that the more people you have in your life who you can genuinely say "I Love You" to, the more successful you are.
>
> I feel incredibly fortunate to be able to say that I love each of you dearly.
>
> –Arno

Rather than accept my apology, the board informed me that I was to step down as executive director and take a leave from my organization until I got "professional help," at which point they would decide if I could return. According to them, it wasn't just one outburst that concerned them. One of them had secretly filmed me at other times when I'd lost my temper. They also slapped me with some trumped-up charge about "abusing volunteers." I was certainly intense and passionate about our mission, and I expected others to be, too—but abusing volunteers? That was a bunch of horseshit.

I told them all to take a great big flying fuck.

I was stunned and pissed off. Life After Hate was my concept, my online magazine, my organization, *my life*. I had built it with my blood, sweat, and tears for three fucking years, doing exponentially more work than the lot of the board combined, and here they were kicking me out of my own thing. And I put them in a position to do it by appointing them and setting myself up as an employee. All along, I'd discouraged the notion that Life After Hate was mine. It was a platform for everyone. Apparently that was an invitation for a hostile takeover.

On the same day I was so unceremoniously pushed out of my job, Pardeep called, asking me to join him at a talk he had scheduled at a local Milwaukee high school. After the shooting, Par had come up with a concept to introduce the Sikh community to the broader public through acts of service. He had a name, Serve 2 Unite, but it was still a nebulous idea waiting to be formed. He had put the idea of such an organization out to educators, and a local high school principal responded with an invitation to speak. I'd given plenty of talks during

THE GIFT OF OUR WOUNDS

my tenure as executive director of Life After Hate, and he thought our stories would complement each other. I accepted without hesitation. "But there's something I have to tell you," I said. "Those motherfuckers on my board just kicked me out of my own organization."

Pardeep listened patiently and responded with his usual aplomb. "Listen, Arno," he said. "You're right. They are motherfuckers. But if you'd been an asshole all the time, the way I am, this wouldn't have happened. They would have expected you to act that way and it wouldn't have been any big deal." Leave it to Pardeep to make me laugh when I was deep in the doldrums. "Secondly," he said, "this is great news! Now you can come and work with me on Serve 2 Unite!"

First, I had to get through the temple gig, I said. Then we could talk.

The theme for the Heritage Day was that all human culture is beautiful, and when we celebrate all together, we are one. It was very Sikh, and I thought it was brilliant. The Gurudwara was a virtual world map of cultures and teeming with Sikhs and others dressed in colorful native garb when I got there. Pardeep met me at the entrance and led me into the changing room, where I removed my shoes and picked a purple turban from the bin. The temple was pristine and peaceful. It was hard to absorb that such carnage had occurred there, except for the polarity of a bullet hole in the metal frame of the door leading into the prayer room. I lost my breath when I saw it. I had once been capable of such malevolence.

The prayer room was a sea of colors from the different

cultures represented. I looked out over the crowd, wondering how I, a former white supremacist, would be received. So many in the temple had been affected by the August attack. Some had been there when Page went on his rampage. Many had family members and friends who were injured. I couldn't imagine having gone through what they did, and then welcoming someone with the same past as the person who attacked their temple. If I expected blank stares or even looks of disapproval, I didn't see any. All I saw were expressions of encouragement and expectation and, dare I say, even love.

I listened with humility as Pardeep stood to introduce me. "My brother, Arno Michaelis," he said. I felt my throat tighten. Sometimes I wondered how I was so fortunate to be in the company of such a benevolent man. My hands shook as I began to speak, but I soon found the strength to deliver my message.

I've been very much honored to travel the country and the world talking about mistakes I've made and what I learned. . . . Initiating discussions with people of all ethnicities and walks of life in hopes that my mistakes can be learned from. One of the questions I am most often asked is, "How did I get out?" and "What led me to leave hate groups?" The answer is exhaustion. It's exhausting to practice hate and violence. And kindness. My father and mother let me know I was loved no matter how horrible I became. People I claimed to hate treated me with kindness when I didn't deserve it. Black. Jewish, Latino. Gay. The second most asked question I get is, "Will you ever go back?" My answer is, "Absolutely not." Because being a racist sucks. It sucks to deny the world around you and your connection to it.

My healing, I said, helped me to open myself up to the beauty of the world, the beauty of all cultures and all spiritual traditions. "To the point that I am incredibly humbled and honored to stand here today and call Pardeep and Amardeep my brothers, and to engage with them to bring forth the gift of their wounds."

TEN

JANESVILLE

When all other methods fail, it is proper to hold the sword in hand.
Guru Gobind Singh

Arno

It was our first trip together, a two-hour drive on a frigid
March afternoon to Wisconsin farm country. Our mission: to
talk about race relations in a town notorious for its association with the Ku Klux Klan. I picked up Par in my weathered
Toyota 4Runner, its hatchback lashed closed with climbing
rope, the odometer with as many miles as it is from here to
the moon. Par had a newer car, but he was kind enough to let
me drive when I told him I got carsick as a passenger. If he
noticed the big, red scar above the windshield from loading
my canoe on top or the multiple dents in the body from blazing through blizzards with death metal on blast, he didn't
mention it. He seemed, as he did every time we'd been together over the last four months, content to be in the moment,
wherever that happened to be.

I'd never met anyone as easygoing and grateful for being alive as Pardeep. While I had come a long way to feeling likewise, there always seemed to be a bit more weather in my skies. Back in my fighting days, I usually led with my face, and had since been diagnosed with post-concussion syndrome. The symptoms are chronic migraines, slurred speech, loss of balance, and, I'm sorry to say, moodiness. My bad moods, like passing storms, had become less frequent as I'd worked to cultivate inner peace, but sometimes the simplest annoyances— an early morning wake-up call, for instance—could still evoke downright hostility from me. Not Par. I'd never seen him angry. His unfailing good humor was at once maddening and awe-inspiring.

A few weeks after I spoke at the Gurudwara, Par had invited me to join him for a talk at Cudahy High School. It was our first time speaking together under the banner of Serve 2 Unite, and we'd made such an impact on the audience of a thousand teenagers that the local media came calling. A single news column about our budding but unlikely friendship precipitated invitations to more speaking gigs. This one came from the Rock County Diversity Council to speak in Janesville.

The road to Janesville was paved with memories I would have rather forgotten. I was anxious about the trip. The last time I'd been there was twenty-one years earlier, during my previous life, when television host Geraldo Rivera was filming a segment for his show about Wisconsin's white power movement. I was my hateful self then and I'd gone with some of my white power skinhead clan to kick up some dust, along with fellow haters from around the Midwest. "Hate in the Heartland" put Janesville on the map, not in a good way, and it had never fully recovered.

I was dubious about returning, but not only because it was yet another ugly chapter from my past that I had to face down. I was worried about Par. From what I knew, Rock County, where Janesville was located, had recently seen a resurgence of hate groups, and our speaking engagement had been publicized in the local paper. Back in the day, my crew would have made sure we were there to taunt the traitor and his little brown-skinned foreigner buddy.

If our first pit stop was a forecast of what was ahead, I feared not much had changed from the time I was there. We were somewhere between Milwaukee and Janesville when we stopped for gas. Par went to the restroom while I trolled for my third or fourth Diet Coke of the day. As I was looking around, I came across a bumper sticker for sale that read, "Illegal Alien Hunting License." I had to read it twice for it to register. When it did, I felt the heat of my anger travel from my neck to my forehead. I was steamed.

I hadn't heard Par come up behind me until he spoke. "You know it's not a Sikh who owns this gas station," he quipped, nodding toward the bumper sticker. He seemed as unruffled as I was incensed. *What grace this man has*, I thought. Not only did I respect him wildly, I cared about him and I felt protective of his dignity. "Don't worry," he said. "I'm kind of used to it." But how could I let the moment pass without doing something to illuminate how fucking ignorant it was to push that hateful bullshit?

The middle-aged white lady behind the register saw me coming with the bumper sticker in my hand. I placed it on the counter in front of her. "Is the idea of hunting people funny?" I asked politely. "You do realize you're advocating the killing of people, don't you?" Her face turned bright red. She stuttered and stammered, finally blurting out, "Oh . . . um . . . they just put those there. We're not in charge of what the stickers say." Bad answer, lady. "You decide whether you sell them or not," I said, looking her straight in the eye. "You should be ashamed of yourself." I turned to walk out, leaving her standing there with her mouth hanging open.

As much as I felt the need to defend Pardeep's honor, I would have had the same reaction if I'd been alone. See something; say something. That was my motto when it came to prejudice. It was as steeped in my soul as hatred had been when I was a racist thug. Dr. King got it right when he wrote, "Nothing in the world is more dangerous than sincere ignorance and conscientious stupidity." Part of my redemption was to point out sincere ignorance and conscientious stupidity wherever I saw it, the way that the nice, elderly black lady at McDonald's had once done for me.

Walking out of the store, I noticed Par had an extra spring in his step. "What?" I asked. He grinned and slapped my shoulder like I had just hit a home run. "Damn, Michaelis!" he said. "Let 'em know what's up!"

We climbed back into the truck and roared out of the

station, hip-hop music blasting. As we traveled south toward what was historically a hotbed of Wisconsin hate groups, my concern for Pardeep's well-being deepened. I wasn't sure he really understood what he was getting into when he decided to work with me, but he already had two strikes against him. He was brown *and* hanging with a race traitor.

Turning the music down a notch, I broached the subject with him. "Did I ever tell you about the last time I went to Janesville?" I asked. Of course, I hadn't. I hadn't known him long enough to spit out all of the details of my ugly past. I had given him the general picture, but the particulars were tough to rehash and I wanted to nurture our new friendship, not alienate him.

It was back in 1992, the same day that Geraldo came to town. I was headed toward the end of my racist skinhead days, I just didn't know it yet. My skinhead crew rolled down to Janesville to help "save the white race." Racial tensions had been smoldering in the town for months prior to that and flared up when the Klan placed ads in the local newspaper, soliciting new members. When a Klan leader announced publicly that he was holding a rally and cross burning on his property, Geraldo, who had a history of inciting white supremacists and brawling for ratings, was all over it.

Three years before Geraldo headed to Janesville, a neo-Nazi skinhead had broken his nose during a scuffle on his show. I thought I could do even better to make our point. The really fucked-up thing was that I'd convinced myself that going to Janesville for some street hooligan bullshit had something to do with being a good father. By acting out in racist, violent ways, I was somehow protecting the future of my white child.

I let out a nervous laugh, the one that sounded like machine-gun fire. Out of the corner of my eye, I saw that Pardeep had turned away from the window and was staring at me. Was he interested? Or was he wondering why he was even there? Why he had ever agreed to travel this road with me?

I needed to make sure that Pardeep understood the kind of people we were likely to encounter, so I cleared my throat and continued. I'd gone to Janesville with the intention of fighting with Geraldo, but I'd never gotten close enough to do any damage. That privilege had fallen to some farmer from Illinois, a Klansman who looked like he couldn't fight his way out of a paper bag. Turns out he couldn't. The Imperial Wizard's homeboy called Geraldo a spic and dirty Jew and threw the first punch. Geraldo went apeshit and decked him.

Pardeep let out a laugh. "C'mon, dude!" he cried. "How the fuck is someone going to get beat up by Geraldo?"

It was my turn to laugh. "The dude just threw some limp-ass punch, and Geraldo took him down and hit him a bunch of times—pretty soundly kicked his ass. So that made it suck even worse. If one of us got into it with Geraldo we would have whooped his ass!"

"Especially you!" Pardeep said.

"Oh yeah, especially me!" I said. "I was pretty confident I could have fucked up Geraldo."

Par knew enough about my past to know how revved up I used to get about fighting. He also knew I still felt a Pavlovian thrill at the idea of physical combat. The last time I put my hands on someone was 1995 on New Year's Eve, at the beginning of my transition from violent racist to erudite egalitarian, when a white guy used the word "nigger." I broke my hand on his orbital bone in the process of knocking him out and it felt good. Truth was, I missed fighting. There was no feeling quite like the adrenaline rush that comes with getting hit and hitting back. But now that I was an official emissary for peaceful coexistence, it probably wouldn't be cool if I hauled off and belted someone every time they said something stupid— even if they deserved it. Now when the urge to fight stirred within me, I observed it and let it pass. My Buddhist training helped.

As we merged onto 43 South, Par picked up the conversation again. "Why are you nervous about going to Janesville?" he asked. It was as though he could read my thoughts, which was creepy in a nice sort of way. He knew where I had been going with the conversation all along.

"You're right," I said. "I am nervous, but not for me. I'm worried about you." I told Par that it was possible we were headed into a beehive of hateful racists. For my whole life, I had walked a fine line between foolhardy and fearless. I was in danger when I was doing the deeds of the movement, and now I was in danger for having turned my back on them. There was only one kind of person that white supremacists hated more than browns, blacks, Jews, and gays, and that was people like me. A white guy who was once with them and was now working against them. Add to that equation a brown-skinned partner who most of those fools would mistake for Muslim and we were wanted men.

It wasn't as if Pardeep didn't know about danger. When he was a cop he'd walked the beat in some of Milwaukee's most forbidding neighborhoods. And he certainly understood that hate groups were capable of using extreme violence to get their point across. His family, after all, was a victim of it.

"I just had to let you know, and I know you know this already, but you are taking your life in your hands every time you go to do a gig with me," I said. "What we're doing is going to ruffle people's feathers. I don't want to sound ominous or paranoid. It's just how it is."

The tone in the car grew quiet. Par seemed to be mulling over what I'd said. "I get it," he said, finally. "I get that there are risks, but there are risks to everything we do in life. We've been given this—and I hate to say it this way—but it's almost a reluctant responsibility. If we don't do what we're doing, we're not doing what we're meant to do and that's a much bigger fear for me than losing my life. I don't know if it's something we were asked to do by a higher power, but ever since we met I feel like we have a responsibility to right some wrongs— either of our own choosing, or someone else's choosing. I'm not going to sit at home and think, 'This happened, but I didn't do anything about it 'cause I was scared.'"

Par's insight was Sikh wisdom. His religion taught that the only valid fear in life is the fear of God, and when one accepts that, all other fears retreat. I loved that philosophy. I told him that I wasn't particularly afraid to die, either. I had always lived on the edge without giving much thought to consequences. What I did agonize over was how my death would affect my family, especially Autumn.

I'd been thinking about my daughter the night before in anticipation of our trip to Janesville. I was never as scared as I should have been when I was giving talks that were critical of my former comrades, and, considering where we were going, I probably should have given more thought to security. Before I went to sleep, I had written Autumn a letter—in case something happened. I told her how much I loved her and how proud I was to call her my daughter. I asked her to celebrate my life and what I'd accomplished with my peace work rather than mourn my death. I'd hidden the letter in my room. "On the top left shelf by my TV, there's a papier-mâché teddy bear she made when she was a kid," I said to Pardeep. "The letter is rolled up under the teddy bear's arm. So if I get killed, I need you to make sure she gets it."

Pardeep nodded solemnly. "I will," he said. "I hope I never have to give her that letter, and we'll work to see that day doesn't happen. But one of the biggest lessons I've learned from August 5 is that when someone you love passes away, they've already given you what they needed to give you for you to move on and be productive."

Satwant Kaleka's gift had been teaching Pardeep the love and dedication it took to step into his shoes. Pardeep didn't know he had it in him until after his dad was gone. "I never thought I'd be able to do whatever was needed at the temple, or take care of the businesses, and Mom," he said. "There was just so much added responsibility. What I realized was that all of the tools and values I needed to get through what happened were already ingrained in me. Dad had already given me all those things before he died. You have given your daughter that foundation, too. The letter is there, and it will help her understand, but I think she already knows how you feel."

My eyes welled up, as they often did when I thought about my Autumn. She was grown, a wonderful, smart, caring young woman. Pardeep had a good point. Everything I'd written she already knew. I had raised her as best I could, loved her fiercely, and taught her how to survive by being confident, kind, and compassionate. Writing the letter had really been as much for my comfort as hers. "All the same," I said, "I think the letter can make a difference—it can help bring all those points home."

Pardeep agreed. He told me about his father's writings that he'd discovered after his death. They had provided him with a treasure trove of insight into his dad's thoughts and feelings. Satwant's reflections—about everything from the pain of leaving his homeland, to his struggles of integrating into American culture and the heartbreak he felt over cutting his sons' hair—were like a window into his soul.

"He wrote that when we got our hair cut, he cried after we went to bed because he had ultimately made a decision that went against our religion," Pardeep said. "He did that for us. For Amardeep and me. He would never have told us that, but he wrote it. His notes told me more about his feelings than he ever did. My dad wasn't that way. For him, for a lot of guys, we can't express ourselves. So, you're right, Arno. It's good to write it down."

Pardeep stared out the window at the passing fields of corn cut low, occasional yellow stalks poking out of the snow. Dusk was upon us and the vast, open landscape was tinted gray. It was beautiful, in a Wisconsin winter kind of way.

"I think I'm going to write a letter, too," he said after a few minutes. "I'm going to write to Jaspreet and the kids to let them know how I feel. So, if anything happens to me, you make sure they get those letters, too. Okay?"

"Word," I said.

We drove on in silence for a bit. I thought to myself how cool it was that a white guy who was born into the American dream and a brown guy who'd had to endure immense struggles to achieve it could have so much in common. *We are one* was a principle of the Sikh faith that Par had shared with me, and we'd chosen to emphasize it in our relationship and in our work for Serve 2 Unite. I truly believed in it. Having opened myself up to other cultures and befriended people with diverse backgrounds, I'd learned that we are all so much more alike than we are different.

So many people close themselves off from the world around them, as I once had, and never discover the joy that comes with having an open heart. It's normal to fear what we don't know, but not knowing isn't necessarily a cause for fear. In my own transformation, I'd found that everything I was afraid of in my early life—the people I'd hated because they looked different, the cultures and religions I'd discriminated against because they weren't mine—were the same people and cultures and religions I was drawn to once I was exposed to them. I now looked at skin as multicolored curtains that opened up to like hearts. Once I understood that, the window dressings were no longer scary to me. I embraced the *human race*, and that had set me free from the restrictions of hate.

The road sign said ten miles to Janesville. "Almost there!" I said, slapping my hand on the steering wheel. The dash lights flickered and Pardeep chuckled. He said his dad drove the same beat-up Toyota pickup truck forever. He bought it with tons of miles on it, way back when he was still working at a gas station. It was all he could afford at the time, but he'd kept it through all of his successes, from owning his first gas station to buying multiple gas stations, then rental properties, and a nice house in the suburbs. Even after he was in a position to drive whatever he wanted, he still chose the same tatty old truck.

That was the kind of guy Pardeep's father was. Until his death, he did all of his own maintenance on his properties. When a lightbulb needed changing in one of the canopies that sheltered the fuel pumps from weather, Satwant never asked one of his attendants to change it. He pulled the rusty Toyota up to the pumps, set a ten-foot folding ladder on the roof of the cab, then climbed the ladder to the top step—the one marked NOT A STEP. DON'T STAND ON THIS—and reached up with the fluorescent bulb without shedding a single bead of sweat on his turban.

It wasn't that his dad was cheap, Pardeep said. He'd give the shirt off his back to a stranger if they needed it, and he had. He was humble.

"That's fucking awesome!" I said.

"You know what my dad's favorite music was?" Pardeep asked, grinning.

"What?"

"Punjabi hip-hop. He had that broke-ass old Toyota, but he had a bumpin' audio system in it, with his music blasting, and everyone heard it, wherever he went. Sixty-year-old dude with a turban and beard *bumpin'* that shit!"

I could see it in my mind and I started to laugh. "No shit, man? Punjabi hip-hop?"

"Oh he could get into American hip-hop, too!" Pardeep said. "He used to rock out to Naughty by Nature when their song came on the radio. He didn't know what the lyrics meant, but he'd sing along."

Pardeep bounced up and down, throwing his hands in the air, singing, "O.P.P.!" with a thick Punjabi accent, the way his father had. It was too much to take. The thought of Satwant Singh Kaleka jammin' out to Naughty by Nature, waving his hands and shouting, "Uh-Pee-Peeee!" was hilarious to the point where I nearly had to pull over to the side of the road.

Par and I roared until tears streamed down our cheeks. Each time we'd catch our breath to try getting a glimpse of where we were going, one of us would bust out laughing again.

As I shook with laughter, my earlier fears about going back to Janesville seemed to retreat. In the back of my mind, I knew we could still potentially be walking into a dangerous situation, but Par and I were in it together.

We were still trying to compose ourselves when we pulled into the community college where the gig was being held. The campus looked pretty generic, with a lot of one-story buildings spread out over a wide-open space. Parking the car in a desolate lot, we went in search of the room where our talk was scheduled to take place. I had low expectations going in. I figured we might get a handful of white folks.

When we got to the right place, we found that the one-hundred-seat venue was filled to capacity. It was standing room only. Looking out over the audience, I saw one black man and an Asian woman. Everyone else was white. Why would that surprise me? The town was still 90 percent white. A uniformed security guard stood at the door, which brought back all of the concerns I had about being there. A rare bout of nerves set in. *Oh boy,* I thought. *This is going to be a party, an all-white crowd chomping at the bit to take off our heads.* Pardeep read my thoughts. "Security!" he said, smiling. "That's a good thing, Arno!" Yeah, I guess.

Pardeep

Arno's danger warning rang in my head as we waited to be introduced. You have to be hypervigilant, he'd said during our conversation in the car. He'd made the comparison between white supremacists and the Taliban and Al-Qaeda—people on the fringe who used terror and violence to gain attention and recruits. What better headline for a crew of racist skinheads than attacking a venue where a turncoat and the son of a murdered Sikh were speaking about peaceful coexistence? *Maybe I should be more worried than I am*, I thought. Except that I knew I was where I was supposed to be, doing what I was supposed to do. It was as if a spirit were pushing me. *A higher power has me*, I told myself. *A higher power has us*.

Arno

Waiting to begin our talk, I scanned the room, looking for any signs of potential trouble. No arms inked with swastikas or "14 Words." No shaved heads or black shitkicker boots.

The audience greeted us with warm applause. Smiling to conceal my suspicions, I told my story first. "On August 5," I said, "a man who I used to be walked into the Sikh Temple of Wisconsin and murdered six people because they had brown skin, because they had turbans on their heads. One of those people murdered was Pardeep's father."

I went on to emphasize that the reason I was no longer

that person was because of the kindness I'd received from people I'd once hated the most. "Black people, Jewish people, Latino people, gay people, who treated me as a human being when I refused to acknowledge their humanity," I said. "Their acts of kindness planted seeds that made it more and more difficult for me to keep practicing the kind of hate and violence necessary to hurt people."

Turning the program over to Par, I said, "Pardeep's dad would have been one of those benevolent people, if only I'd had the privilege of meeting him. So many times since I'd met Pardeep, I've found myself wishing I had."

Pardeep

I began with my parents' story of traveling from India to the United States with nothing more than a few dollars and assimilating into American culture through hard work and honorable intentions. They came here pursuing the American dream, and they had it until August 5. "Nevertheless," I said, "all is not lost. My father is as much an inspiration in death as he was in life. He would have told you that the storms in our lives are not the absence of God; rather, the response to those storms is the existence of God." God had been omnipresent in our lives since the tragedy. People of all faiths and all colors and all cultures—from around Wisconsin and the country and the world—had gone out of their way to embrace us when we were in the throes of grief. That was the presence of God.

I often wondered if Wade Michael Page had looked in my father's eyes before he pumped five shots into him at close range. If he had, he would have seen a man who exemplified the great ideals that our nation was built on: dedication. Hard work. Service. And, ultimately, sacrifice. I often wondered about how my mother must have felt as she hid in the pantry, not knowing what had become of my father. *I was told that lovers could feel each other's pain. Mom, did you feel the shots as they slammed into Dad's body? Did you feel the one that crushed his spine, leaving him helpless in the face of death?*

"My father was a deeply religious man whose dying words were a call to God to dispel darkness in the world with the light of love, compassion, and guidance. He died praying not for himself, but for this," I said, motioning toward the audience. "For you, the crowd that is here today in the spirit of love and understanding. And the next crowd. And the crowd after that. We have to be radically empathetic with each other, with the person next to us, with the person we just met today. Our message is to please commit to action for the betterment of humanity. My father and the others died praying for that."

Arno

Looking out over the audience, I saw quivering lips and tears of compassion as Pardeep spoke. I realized that the people who'd come out in the bitter cold to hear us were good and well intentioned. They were there, not for any nefarious reason, but because they wanted to understand. They wanted the same things Pardeep and I did. To make the world better through love and understanding each other.

We spoke for more than an hour. Afterward, a long line snaked around the room. No one seemed to want to leave. We hung around for a while longer, until everyone had been greeted. One woman in particular had really touched me. She said she'd grown up in Janesville and was always embarrassed by its reputation as a haven for racists. She had been planning to move away, but her daughter got pregnant so she'd decided to stay. In doing so, she promised herself that she would do something meaningful to make Janesville a better place. Staying true to herself, she had joined the diversity council, the group that invited us to speak. I was humbled by her story, and I berated myself for not giving the audience the benefit of the doubt simply because of the color of their skin. Judging them for being white was no better than when I used to judge people because they were black. I felt like an asshole. Another lesson learned.

ELEVEN

FORGIVENESS

The blessed will grow a crop of forgiveness while
the sufferers lose their roots.

Guru Ram Daas

Pardeep

Driving out of Janesville, toward home, I realized something.
I loved Arno, loved him like a brother. Yes, he could be direct
to the point of being brash. He had a tendency to be stubborn
and a little bit irritable, and you could never call him before
noon if you didn't want your head handed to you. But any lin-
gering doubts I'd had about his true self or his real heart had
completely evaporated.

Arno was quirky, no doubt about it. But he was also the
kindest, most genuine guy I knew. I'd watched him do things
quietly that spoke volumes about his character. The guy
walked down the street plugging expired meters for strangers!
The lattice of tattoos, the gravelly voice, the rough language
that rolled off his tongue like melting ice cream, none of it
could obscure his goodness. His commitment to redeeming

207

himself for the transgressions of his early life and his passion for social harmony were rock-solid real.

To me, Arno represented what was great about our country. He'd changed his ways and devoted his life to fighting the hatred he'd once embraced. That made him a hero in my eyes. In the short time I'd known him I'd learned so much about redemption and forgiveness. Arno showed me that people are basically good, but that sometimes one's pain and anguish translate to violence. People who are hurting sometimes hurt others.

One day Arno and I were talking and I told him I wanted to get a tattoo in remembrance of my father and the others who died at the temple. Arno was obviously an expert on the subject and he offered up his personal tattoo artist, who had inked the symbols of humanity and compassion over Arno's hate tattoos from his racist skinhead days. Then Arno had another idea. How about if we got matching tattoos?

We made an appointment together and decided on a tattoo with the date of the shooting under a splotch of red blood on our left palms. Scully, the tattoo artist, explained to us that palm skin sheds more than other parts of the body, so the tattoos would probably lose color over time. Go ahead and do it, we said.

Four years have passed since then and my ink is showing signs of wear. What the tattoo represents, however, will never fade: the impact that six beautiful souls have had on our world, even in death, and a friendship that was born of the tragedy that continues to thrive.

After my father's death, I wouldn't say the name Wade Michael Page. I wouldn't allow anyone to say it in my presence. That's how much I hated him. But spending time with Arno—understanding that this decent human being, someone who was changing the world, had once been motivated to hate by his own broken heart—opened my eyes to the possibility that Page, too, hated for lack of love. That made me sad. What made me even sadder was that no one had cared enough to show Page the love we all deserve. If someone had shown him love, my father and the others might still be alive.

One of our great gurus wrote, "Dispelled is anger as forgiveness is grasped." My brother, Arno, has taught me how to forgive Wade Page, and that has freed me to live the purposeful life my father would have expected of me.

Our Sikh scripture says, "Forgiveness is as necessary to life as the food we eat and the air we breathe.

"Where there is forgiveness, there is God."

TWELVE

SERVE 2 UNITE

Let wisdom be your food and compassion your guide.
Guru Nanak Dev Ji

Arno

Inspired by adversity, Serve 2 Unite began as a nebulous idea to educate the public about Sikhism. It quickly grew into a forum to address hate with an ongoing practice of creativity and compassion rooted in the Sikh principles of oneness, service to others, and the pursuit of relentless optimism. By 2013, with a lot of help from the brilliant nonprofit Arts @ Large, we introduced the concept of seeing "'yourself in the other" in Milwaukee schools and later in communities across the country. In collaborating with educators, policy makers, activists, and youth, Serve 2 Unite has inspired people of all backgrounds to value this common humanity and embrace the merits of living genuine, honest lives as peacemakers.

In our mission as brothers to bring about healing and wage peace, Pardeep and I have shared our stories and the

Serve 2 Unite philosophy with people throughout the United States and around the world. It was one of those endeavors that led to an invitation in the spring of 2017 to Groton, Massachusetts, a town not unlike Oak Creek, Wisconsin. Both are quintessential American towns where the citizens are generally good, hard working, and happy to lend each other a hand. But people in Groton were struggling with the difficulties that come with demographic shift, something we saw often in our travels. In recent years, the Hindu population in Groton had burgeoned from thirty families to three thousand, and some locals were voicing concerns about the building of a Mandir, a Hindu temple in a traditionally Christian town. Before the temple shooting, Oak Creek had suffered similar growing pains during an influx of Punjabi families a few years earlier when the Gurudwara became a beacon that led more Indians to Wisconsin. Understanding went a long way toward acceptance of the Sikh community in Oak Creek, and for many that came after the tragedy. We do not want this to be the case in any other town.

In response to the strife that was happening in Groton, the local interfaith group, in partnership with town government and the police chief, had organized a screening of *Waking in Oak Creek*, a beautifully crafted short documentary produced by the nonprofit Not In Our Town, about the shooting in Oak Creek and how the community came together in response by implementing policy and public reform. After the film, Par and I joined the police chief, Donald Palma, and the president of the Groton Interfaith Council,

Shua Khan Arshad, for a panel discussion. We had a great conversation with each other and the audience as we explored ways to think past fear to reveal a true understanding of the value and wonder of human diversity.

During the discussion we learned that Town Selectman Jack Petropoulis had introduced a measure to place stone monuments inscribed with ALL ARE WELCOME at the intersections leading into town as part of an initiative to welcome new immigrants and ease concerns of the townsfolk. The issue was coming up for a vote, and Jack worried it would fail. When he shared his frustration over the resistance he'd gotten to the idea, we urged him to press on with love, devotion, and faith. We also suggested adding service projects that all could take part in. Taking a page from our Serve 2 Unite student program, we suggested engaging the community in projects that gave members—old and new—equitable ownership and voice.

A few weeks after we returned home, Jack sent us this email:

Hi Arno and Pardeep,

I want to thank you for visiting our community last week, to tell you what it meant to me, and to tell you what I think it meant in a larger sense. First of all, thank you. I understand that you took time for us and I appreciate the commitment that it takes to do that. Secondly your message was heard loud and clear. Your encouragement to carry on buoyed my spirits and caused many of us to see things in ways that we have never experienced before. Lastly I want you to know that your talk inspired me to bring forward (the issue) to our town meeting with renewed commitment to the importance of the effort. Your comments of "even if it does not pass you will have moved the bar" were so true. More importantly your recounting of, and response to, the events of August 2012 served as both a warning and a roadmap for all of us. I went into our Town Meeting determined to carry the torch that I picked up that evening regardless of the outcome. I took the liberty of using your talk, your history and your encouragement in my message at Town Meeting. The vote passed by 27 in a room of 300. I know for a fact that there were people who came in ready to vote "no" thinking that they knew all they needed to know about the initiative, who changed their minds and voted in favor. . . . You made a difference in our town.

One of the many reasons Pardeep and I get along so well is that we both like to cause a bit of trouble. My taste for troublemaking almost killed me and others back in the day, but now Par has shown me how to use it in the best way possible: by defying hate and violence. Pardeep says that to him, forgiveness is vengeance. Kindness is the most devastating weapon against the suffering from which all violence stems. Love is the antidote to the fear and loneliness that seeds hate.

When Wade Page walked into the temple in Oak Creek, he sought to terrify the Sikh community, which in his eyes would have looked like a reflection of himself, into submission. He wanted them to be fearful and hateful. He wanted them to renounce their faith in *Chardi Kala*—relentless optimism, especially in the face of struggle.

He failed. Miserably.

Because of his pathetic attempt to sow strife and discord, the Sikh community of Wisconsin and of the world is that much more engaged with everyone else. More people know what Sikhs are all about: faith, love, and hard work.

Because of Page's desperate assault on everything that is good about being a human being, the town of Groton now has stones that say ALL ARE WELCOME at every intersection leading into town.

That's how we respond to violent extremism: By moving forward with good intentions and compassion for each other and ourselves. Whether the attacks come from white supremacists, far-right, far-left, or religious fundamentalists of whatever persuasion, we follow the universal truths of our common humanity to cultivate solutions defined by what we stand for—kindness, gratitude, forgiveness, compassion, courage, wisdom, love. We don't let hate dictate the terms of engagement.

This is what five years of *Chardi Kala* looks like.

Comments from Students

Arno and Pardeep, your amazing stories about your life experiences and the inspiration to found Serve 2 Unite have changed many lives including mine. The stories from Serve 2 Unite have changed my view entirely on the world and the people in it. The lessons I have learned in this program have taught me peace and compassion beyond anything I have ever known.

—Kiva, 7th Grade

Arno and Pardeep's stories, why they started Serve 2 Unite, were empowering and motivated me further than what I originally wanted. The love and respect Arno and Pardeep give you is enough to change anybody. This is why everyone should join Serve 2 Unite and make the world a better place.

—Logan, 8th Grade

The first day you walked into our classroom we were confused. Who are you? we wondered. Are they just going to give us another boring assignment that goes on our report card?

No, we were wrong.

That day two men came into our lives and told us inspirational stories of kindness and forgiving. We were inspired, and this inspiration was what drove us to create our projects.

I thank you for giving me and my friends this amazing opportunity.

See you next year!

—Aaron, 7th Grade

Through this experience I have learned a lot about myself and converting hate and negative energy into kindness and compassion for others. The end of the year project helped me boost my self-esteem and learn to speak in front of crowds with a better voice and attitude. The stories the adults and students have shared made me reflect on my actions and inspired me to reform myself in the future.

This project was a life-changing experience. The stories you told us about your past and to now is just amazing how someone could change so much. . . . I am really glad we got this opportunity at such a young age. Most kids don't get to do things like this and they don't get to speak. Thank you so much for doing this for us.

—Elana, 8th Grade

THIRTEEN

THE GIFT OF OUR WOUNDS

From Oneness came the many, and one day
shall merge back into the One.
Guru Arjun Dev Ji

Pardeep

As I look back at that fateful day in August 2012, I do so
free from disdain in my heart. For I bore witness to a great
human family that refused to be defined by the hate that
took seven lives and instead demonstrated the vast healing
power of love. Bearing witness is "to be evidence or proof
of." As the Sikh community grieved, we witnessed the truth
upon which our religion was founded. We call it *Ek Onkar*.
It means we are one, from a single creator, and we share
this divinity with all of creation. When our community
felt the most victimized, the most vulnerable and hurt, we
saw Christians, Muslims, Hindus, and Jews, people of all
ethnicities and backgrounds, gather together outside our
Gurudwara in the spirit of Oneness. Thousands of people,
in a rainbow of colors, speaking different languages, stood

together in kinship, engaging in communal prayer and helping each other to heal.

It was in this continuation of spirit and defiant love that we saw light in what had seemed like infinite darkness. Ours was a brotherhood of genuine honesty, compassion, understanding, gratitude, and joy. Together we were mindful of the truth that forgiveness is not forgetting, but rather forging a path to healing. It was not condoning the offense, but instead bridging individuals and communities—the ultimate vengeance against the cycles of suffering that will always challenge human existence. What I learned from that experience is that forgiveness is freedom.

The suffering caused by five hundred years of white supremacy has carved gaping wounds across our collective human psyche. We are bombarded with the misery of political and humanitarian crises around the world. It is important to remember that suffering happens not only because we are separated by constructs like race and nationality, but from ourselves. This split continues to breed blindness to the divinity that exists in every being on earth. Wholeness escapes us because we have overcommitted to the illusion of dichotomous ideologies dividing us, and undercommitted to the reality that in each person exists a good and evil spirit. Thus our identity is marked by the temporary roles we take on rather than the infinite truth of being part of the natural interdependence of the universal spirit.

To the world, it may seem that Arno and I met under the unlikeliest of circumstances. Our brotherhood may seem implausible, but to me it makes perfect sense: the spirit of intention was pushing us on a collision course. When I first met Arno, I immediately noticed that we both bore open wounds. Wounds that we could not heal on our own. It was clear that he could see mine, and I could see his. Peering into one another's souls, we saw each other's suffering and, uncomfortable as it was, found the courage to share our stories and our pain. It soon became clear that revealing was healing.

It is my greatest hope that by sharing who we are and what we have learned, we can inspire others to carry forward in *Chardi Kala*, the relentlessly optimistic spirit of compassion, forgiveness, gratitude and healing. That is the gift of our wounds.

ABOUT THE AUTHORS

PARDEEP SINGH KALEKA

Pardeep Singh Kaleka is a licensed therapist, specializing in utilizing a trauma-informed approach to treat survivors and perpetrators of assault, abuse, and acts of violence. A native of Punjab, India, Pardeep grew up in Milwaukee. As a former police officer and educator in the city of Milwaukee, Pardeep understands the difficulties our communities face, both locally and abroad. Both in and outside of his practice, Pardeep's passion remains one of healing and recovery. An example of this is Serve 2 Unite, an organization he founded in response to tragedy. This organization engages youth and communities at large in service learning, artistic response, and global engagement to build positive school environments and peaceful communal identity, addressing conflict from a trauma-informed lens. Over the past five years, the work of Serve 2 Unite has been locally and internationally recognized as the recipient of the Guru Nanak Award and the Parliament of World Religions for the work of building safe, inclusive communities. Partnership organizations include Arts@Large, Against Violent Extremism, the Forgiveness Project, Interfaith Council of Milwaukee, and Not In Our Town.

ARNO MICHAELIS

After spending over a decade as a successful information technology consultant and entrepreneur, Arno Michaelis is now a speaker, author of *My Life After Hate*, and very fortunate to be able to share his ongoing process of character development as an educator working with Serve 2 Unite. S2U engages students creatively with a global network of peacemakers and mentors in partnership with Against Violent Extremism, the Forgiveness Project, Arts @ Large, and Over My Shoulder Foundation. Michaelis has traveled to Abu Dhabi, Bosnia, Denmark, Ireland, Norway, Poland, Sweden, the United Kingdom, and all across the United States working in counterviolent extremism efforts. He has appeared on *The View*, CNN's *Anderson Cooper 360*, the BBC, and MSNBC and in *The New York Times*, the *Huffington Post*, and *The Washington Post*. His workshops and keynotes leverage the noble qualities of compassion, curiosity, and kindness to engage all human beings, building foundations for diversity appreciation and cultural agility. He also enjoys spending time with his daughter, art, music, and all forms of fearless creative expression, along with climbing things, being underwater, and the wonderful natural beauty of our planet Earth. Learn more at http://mylifeafterhate.com.

ROBIN GABY FISHER is a *New York Times* bestselling author of ten nonfiction books and a two-time finalist for the Pulitzer Prize in Feature Writing. She is also the recipient of a group Pulitzer Prize in Breaking News and the winner of the Nieman Foundation at Harvard's Fairness in Media Award. Her books have been published by Little, Brown; Atria; Touchstone; Penguin Books; and St. Martin's Press. She teaches journalism and narrative writing at Rutgers University in Newark, New Jersey, and lives in New Jersey and Woodstock, Vermont.

"*Preparing to Blend* is a kind and helpful guide for families who are merging two households into one. Ron Deal provides such valuable wisdom on this topic few are talking about, but many are in desperate need of. What a gift this book will be to all couples who want to navigate well and learn to thrive as a stepfamily."

—Lysa TerKeurst, #1 *New York Times* bestselling author; president, Proverbs 31 Ministries

"As you contemplate creating a blended family, reading and discussing *Preparing to Blend* is one of the best ways to prepare for success in creating the blended family that you envision."

—Gary Chapman, PhD, author, *The 5 Love Languages*

"There is absolutely no one better than Ron Deal to help blended families. No one. This resource is a critical tool in helping a couple prepare for their future together and the future of their blended family. Do the critical work now and your kids will thank you later."

—Dave and Ann Wilson, co-hosts, *FamilyLife Today*

"Ron L. Deal has provided parents and family members with a *hope-filled, practical, timely,* and *insightful* resource in *Preparing to Blend*."

—Dr. Tim Clinton, president, American Association of Christian Counselors; executive director, James Dobson Family Institute

"This beautifully written book is an extraordinary gift to stepfamilies and to those who want to help them. Ron Deal brings decades of experience, deep compassion, profound wisdom, and step-by-step practical guidance to forging a unity of heart for stepcouples and children journeying through the complexities of becoming a 'blended family.'"

—Dr. Patricia L. Papernow, author, *Surviving and Thriving in Stepfamily Relationships* and *The Stepfamily Handbook*

"I view Ron as the leading expert in the world of stepfamily issues. He brings his years of knowledge in the field to this most helpful book. I love it and will recommend it to anyone preparing to blend."

—Jim Burns, PhD, president, HomeWord; author, *Getting Ready for Marriage* and *Doing Life with Your Adult Children*

"Most premarital preparation doesn't foster the needed dialogue to prepare for blending families. But now, *Preparing to Blend* gives couples a roadmap they didn't know they wanted! Ron gifts us with a one-of-a-kind resource from a deep, practical well of decades of focused work counseling blended families and biblical expertise."

—David Robbins, president and CEO, FamilyLife®

"Ron Deal is a recognized expert on blended families; *Preparing to Blend* will equip you to face your future together and blend your family well. It's also a great guide for leaders wanting to offer effective pre-stepfamily counseling. I highly recommend it."

—Shaunti Feldhahn, social researcher; bestselling author, *For Women Only, For Parents Only,* and *Thriving in Love & Money*

"What are the practices and considerations couples should prioritize as they prepare for remarriage? Ron Deal is a foremost authority on blended families, and he has written an indispensable manual for engaged couples who want to successfully blend their two families."

—Jim Daly, president, Focus on the Family

"I thank God for Ron Deal! His advice is so practical, real to life, wise, and helpful. This will be my go-to book to give to couples who are about to blend their families."

— Gary Thomas, author, *Sacred Marriage* and *Sacred Parenting*

"Many books on blended families focus more on helping parents and minimize children's needs. *Preparing to Blend* boldly dives deeper into the struggles of family members. This is a powerful, effective, and easy-to-follow roadmap for every blended family. If you want a healthy and strong blended family, *Preparing to Blend* is a must-read."

—Meg Meeker, MD, bestselling author,
Strong Fathers, Strong Daughters

"Ron Deal's expert voice and years of experience provide a travel guide of wisdom through the issues of blending a family, such as what to expect, why it's different, how to handle unhappy kids, setting boundaries, the former spouse, jealousy, discipline, bonding, loyalty, and other issues that can cause conflict. *Preparing to Blend* is a must-read for blending couples, extended family, pastors, and therapists. I highly recommend this resource."

—Laura Petherbridge, speaker, author

"Ron Deal has studied and assisted stepfamilies for decades and knows more about them than anyone ministering to them today. *Preparing to Blend* needs to be required reading for any two people wanting to marry and blend their families."

—Steve Arterburn, bestselling author
and founder of New Life Live

"If you want to prepare yourself adequately to blend a family, read this book. Ron Deal has identified relational dynamics and everyday scenarios of stepcouples that prepare you for the road ahead and how to navigate it. Whether your kids are young, teenagers, or adults, this book is for you."

—Gayla Grace, staff writer for FamilyLife®; author,
Stepparenting with Grace

"*Preparing to Blend* is Ron Deal's crowning jewel! Packed with practical application for couples entering the stepfamily journey! You'll be delighted as a pastor, counselor, or one who is remarrying to heed the guidance in these pages. Knowing how to navigate the pain one has come from increases the success of remarriage legacy."

—Gil Stuart, MA, LCHMC, and Brenda Stuart, CTC, coauthors, *Restored and Remarried*

"Every couple who is preparing for married life in the proverbial blender needs all the help they can get. And Ron Deal is *the* expert on the topic. He writes with knowledge, compassion, and a wealth of practical insight. We'll be recommending this book for many years."

—Drs. Les & Leslie Parrott, #1 *New York Times* bestselling authors, *Saving Your Marriage Before It Starts*

PREPARING TO
BLEND

SMART
STEPFAMILY
SERIES

Books in the SMART STEPFAMILY SERIES

From Bethany House Publishers

101 Tips for the Smart Stepmom
(Laura Petherbridge)

Daily Encouragement for the Smart Stepfamily
(Ron L. Deal with Dianne Neal Matthews)

Dating and the Single Parent
(Ron L. Deal)

Preparing to Blend
(Ron L. Deal)

The Smart Stepdad
(Ron L. Deal)

The Smart Stepfamily
(Ron L. Deal)

The Smart Stepfamily DVD
(Ron L. Deal)

The Smart Stepfamily Guide to Financial Planning
(Ron L. Deal, Greg S. Pettys, and David O. Edwards)

The Smart Stepfamily Participant's Guide
(Ron L. Deal)

The Smart Stepfamily Marriage
(Ron L. Deal and David H. Olson)

The Smart Stepmom
(Ron L. Deal and Laura Petherbridge)

In Their Shoes
(Lauren Reitsema)

From Other Publishers

Building Love Together in Blended Families
(Ron L. Deal and Gary Chapman, Northfield Publishing)

Life in a Blender (booklet for kids)
(Ron L. Deal, FamilyLife Publishing)

The Smart Stepfamily Marriage Small-Group Study Guide
(Ron L. Deal, FamilyLife Publishing)

PREPARING TO BLEND

The Couple's Guide to
Becoming a **Smart** Stepfamily

RON L. DEAL

BETHANYHOUSE
a division of Baker Publishing Group
Minneapolis, Minnesota

© 2021 by Ron L. Deal

Published by Bethany House Publishers
11400 Hampshire Avenue South
Bloomington, Minnesota 55438
www.bethanyhouse.com

Bethany House Publishers is a division of
Baker Publishing Group, Grand Rapids, Michigan

Library of Congress Cataloging-in-Publication Data
Names: Deal, Ron L., author.
Title: Preparing to blend : the couple's guide to becoming a smart stepfamily / Ron L. Deal.
Description: Minneapolis, Minnesota : Bethany House, a division of Baker Publishing Group, [2021] | Includes bibliographical references.
Identifiers: LCCN 2021025321 | ISBN 9780764237935 (paper) | ISBN 9780764239694 (casebound) | ISBN 9781493433551 (ebook)
Subjects: LCSH: Stepfamilies. | Marriage counseling. | Families.
Classification: LCC HQ759.92 .D38 2021 | DDC 306.874/7—dc23
LC record available at https://lccn.loc.gov/2021025321

Cover design by Eric Walljasper

Author represented by MacGregor Literary

Baker Publishing Group publications use paper produced from sustainable forestry practices and post-consumer waste whenever possible.

21 22 23 24 25 26 27   7 6 5 4 3 2 1

To those who have loved and lost
and are willing to try again.
May coupleness be your haven
and familyness be your crowning joy.

Contents

Acknowledgments

This book is the culmination of a multi-book partnership with Bethany House Publishers (special thanks to Andy, Ellen, David, Steve, Holly, Deirdre, Eric, Julie, and Jim) and the guidance of my agent, Chip MacGregor. What fun it has been working with all of you to bring peace to couples and families.

Special thanks are also due to the leadership of FamilyLife®, our key donors for seeing the need for stepfamily education and support, and to my current FamilyLife Blended® team and bonus "adjuncts": Lynn and Larry, Gayla, Nicole, Kevin, Ann, Julie, Debbie, Sabrina, Tim, Kim, and Shannon.

And to my bride, Nan. Since 1986, the roller coaster we've ridden together has been full of ups and downs, sweet intimate vistas, and bitter sorrowful valleys. And through all of it, your love and partnership has given me a safe place to grow, mature, research, and share with others. I cannot thank you enough or thank God enough for you.

Introduction

This email is typical of the ones I frequently get through my website SmartStepfamilies.com.

> Hi Ron. A few years ago, I lost my wife of 34 years. We had two sons together and a wonderful family. Now there is a new love in my life. She lost her husband four years ago, has two children in their mid-twenties, and one grandchild. We're planning to get married but want to start this family off right. We're reading your books and listening to your podcast but think premarital counseling with someone who understands blended families well would be wise. Can you help us?

Yes, I can help them. And I can help *you*.

Many couples reading this are engaged and making wedding plans. (For the most part, I'm going to assume you're either engaged or are considering it. If you're not serious about engagement yet, you might read my book *Dating and the Single Parent*, then come back to this one.) This is an exciting time for you. But engagement is not just about planning a wedding; it's about planning for your marriage and blended family after the wedding. That's the focus of this book—to help you

Even though research confirms that premarital preparation strengthens relationships, most couples forming blended families don't seek it out.[1] Obviously, that's not you. *Good for you.*

continue the "family merger" you've already started and gain relational strength as you move toward the wedding. I've spent three decades working with families and developing resources specifically for blended families; it will be an honor to come alongside you as you prepare for the big day and what follows.

In case you're wondering, this book is appropriate for couples with young children and those with adult children, for those with a full nest and those with an empty nest. It's applicable if one or both of you are bringing biological children to the picture (and if you have a child together), and if death, divorce, or a dissolved relationship preceded your falling in love. Yes, stepfamilies come in many shapes and sizes—and I've tried to consider all while writing this book. Not every section will apply specifically to you, but most will.

In some ways this book is a continuation of the book I just mentioned, *Dating and the Single Parent*. If you read that book while dating, I'll pick up where it left off. If you're already engaged and didn't read it, that's okay. I'll integrate a few of the relevant points in this book. Now, having said that, if you are interested in learning more about any of the following topics, you may want to pick up a copy of that book since these are not covered in this one:

- Wise dating practices that consider children's emotional needs;
- Relational dynamics surrounding cohabitation before marriage;

- Questions about divorce and remarriage from a Christian perspective;
- How to know with confidence if forming a blended family is a good decision for you and the kids at this point in time.

This book assumes you are already headed toward the altar, but even then, preparing to form a blended family sometimes causes people to want to take a step back and explore the above topics. *Dating and the Single Parent* will help you do that.

Surround Yourself

In the early 1990s, when I first started working with stepfamilies, people would complain to me, "Ron, where are all the resources for blended families?" and they were right to do so. Practical resources for the general public were few and far between. But that's not true anymore. To date I have published more than a dozen resources and served as author and consulting editor of a series of books (SMART STEPFAMILY SERIES) for stepmoms, stepdads, and dating and married couples on a variety of subjects (e.g., money management and stepparenting), as well as multiple video curriculum and hundreds of online articles and videos. In addition, I'm teaching virtual classes, working with organizations and experts that cumulatively have produced many additional resources, dozens of national radio broadcasts, my popular podcast *FamilyLife Blended*, and worldwide on-demand livestream training. You can and should surround yourself with this trusted, research-informed, on-demand content, all accessible at SmartStepfamilies.com. Absorb as much of it as you can and decide now to be a student of stepfamily living. The more you know, the smarter you are, and the healthier your family gets.

General books on marriage can be helpful to you as well. For example, this book is a sister book to *Preparing for Marriage*, which is primarily for couples without children, getting married for the first time. That book lays an important Christian foundation for the purpose of marriage, describes various roles we play within marriage, and discusses healthy and unhealthy expectations for marriage. (I will not take the time to address those subjects here since that book does.) Another complementary resource is my book *The Smart Stepfamily Marriage*, coauthored with Dr. David Olson. Based on the largest survey of couples creating stepfamilies ever conducted, it includes an online relationship profile that provides personalized feedback about your relationship as you learn communication and conflict resolution skills, and gain insights about your relational styles, expectations, personalities, leisure preferences, sexual expectations, desired spiritual connection, and parenting strategies. It is a comprehensive examination of marriage in a blended family that can be read before or after the wedding and will complement what you find here.

Practical and Proven

In addition to emails like the one beginning this introduction asking if I can help prepare a couple for marriage in a blended family, I have also received thousands of emails, podcast reviews, and social media messages from couples who have been married for twenty years or more, thanking me for helping them navigate their family journey. The principles discussed in this book are practical and proven. However, if there's one truth about life, it's that none of us get to control it; no one can give you a recipe that will allow you to make every relationship just the way you want it. But having said that, I do know a few things that will help. I invite you to read this book with an open heart and mind. But don't just read it. *Do it.* That brings me to the central engine of this book, Growing Activities. Do them and you will be forever changed.

1

NOT JUST A COUPLE

Growing Activities, Bonding, and Becoming a Family

When it comes to blended families, *coupleness* does not necessarily equal *familyness*.

Right now you're a couple. The focus of your romantic love, and likely most of your dating, has been on falling in love and building a vision for your life together. But becoming a blended family involves so much more than just the two of you.

This book centers around several key Growing Activities that are designed to help you take steps toward family bonding—not just talk about familyness, but actually move toward it. So no, you can't read the chapter discussion and skip the activity. If you want to get the most from this book, you need to do the Growing Activities and include the children when indicated. I'll say more about the design of the Activities in a moment, but first I want you to consider something.

Join one of my virtual pre-blended family education groups for engaged couples at SmartStepfamilies.com.

Even though this book is DIY (do-it-yourself) pre-stepfamily training, I recommend you include one other person. As someone who has spent thousands of hours counseling and coaching couples, my advice is that you walk through the pages of this book with a relationship mentor, coach, or pastor. The best athletes, managers, salespersons, and even therapists have someone watch and coach them as they learn their craft. Sitting with someone who can ask probing questions and comment on your couple and family relationship dynamics will multiply the insights you gain and the ways you apply the wisdom of this book. I highly recommend that you take the time to find someone to walk with you. At SmartStepfamilies.com you can join my virtual groups for engaged couples and find a list of recognized Smart Stepfamily Therapy Providers™ (professionals who have been through my therapy training) who offer coaching and therapy to couples. In addition, many local places of worship offer premarital counseling. And organizations like Prepare-Enrich.com and SYMBIS.com can point you to certified coaches who make use of their online relationship assessments (which I highly recommend; you'll even find some of my Smart Stepfamilies material integrated into their resources).* Organizations like FamilyLife.com (I started the division called FamilyLife Blended®) and ForYourMarriage.org (Catholic Family Ministries) offer general marriage training, events, and small groups for couples, and FamilyLife.com/blended has a searchable map to help you find blended family ministries and

*Prepare-Enrich has a parenting assessment that I find especially helpful to blended family couples.

events around the country. You can walk through this book on your own, but I recommend you don't. Find a trusted guide who can walk beside you.

And in case you're wondering, making time for premarital preparation with a trusted guide is extremely valuable for couples in general. Numerous studies show that it really works. One study found that premarital preparation can reduce the risk of divorce by 30 percent.[1] Another meta-analysis of multiple studies found that overall, couples showed 79 percent improvement in all marital outcomes compared to couples who did not receive premarital education.[2] Taking the time to invest in your coupleness clearly matters.

Now, here's the catch: There are tons of pastors and marriage mentors or coaches, but not many have taken the time to become familiar with the unique dynamics of stepfamilies. Since you need to learn how to be a strong couple and a strong family, you need premarital preparation designed specifically for blended families. Go to the wrong coach, and you could end up getting misguided advice. My work trains and equips them for working with blended families, but many are still unfamiliar with it. So I've written this guide as a tool that can inform both you and them. Walking with them through each chapter, doing the Activities, and having the discussion will educate both of you and enhance your application of the material.

To the Pastor, Coach, or Mentor:

Use this book as your premarital counseling program and help close the gap in premarital education for blended family couples. A free downloadable guide is available along with suggestions for conducting blended family weddings. Go to FamilyLife.com /preparingtoblend.

Why Growing Activities?

If you want to make a new friend or deepen a romantic relationship, you must engage one another in a way that transforms the relationship. You can't just talk about having a better relationship; you have to do things *together* that make the relationship better and raise your emotional quotient.

The Growing Activities in this book are designed to move your step-relationships forward. Each chapter explains what the corresponding Growing Activity is meant to accomplish and why it is important to your family. Instructions for doing the activity are then outlined, and follow-up questions will help you process what you learned, identify insights gained from the Activity, and determine what steps your family might take next. Processing these questions with your mentor or pastor is wise as well.

Becoming family to one another—which is fundamentally what every blended family is hoping to accomplish—is an emotional process that requires active engagement by all parties. You can't just wish stepchildren, for example, into accepting, respecting, or loving a stepparent. They must develop mutual trust and affection through actual interaction. Growing Activities are intended to either move you in that direction or reveal what is standing in the way.

If you read *Dating and the Single Parent*, you may recognize a couple of the Activities. Even if you have done the Activities before, go through them again. Life and relationships are like a flowing river. You are further downstream than you were the first time you had the conversation, so go ahead and enter the stream again. You may find the outcome is different for a variety of reasons. Trust the process and jump in.

Include the children. It is critical that you include the children in Growing Activities when indicated. For years I've believed that children who feel included in decisions related to forming a blended family and can speak into the process find embracing the new family easier than children who aren't, and there's evidence of that. Researchers examining the importance of involving children in blended family educational courses concluded, "When it comes to strengthening couples in stepfamilies, the involvement of children is clearly implicated and should not be underestimated."[3] Here's why. The loss (actually, the *series* of losses) that children of every age experience leading up to a parent's marriage steals a sense of control and influence over their own lives. Anything you do to give them some voice in what's about to happen—and how it happens—restores some of that and may shift them from being a victim of their circumstances to a contributor to what is being built. And being a contributor makes it more likely they'll follow through with their part of the plan, because the message they receive from being included is that they are valued and important. Therefore, kids of all ages need some input into their future family; the Growing Activities help them do that in a tangible way.

By contrast, when children aren't involved in the planning, can't relate to the style of your wedding ceremony, or feel the ceremony dishonors their original family, they may experience your wedding as empty and meaningless.[4] To help you design a pre-wedding journey and family-based ceremony that is full of meaning and fosters family identity, chapter 4 goes into great detail about what is helpful to children of every age. By the way, if you are currently planning your wedding (e.g., the date and the details of the ceremony itself), you may want to skip to that chapter sooner rather than later so you can plan with wisdom. And share that chapter with your pastor, who likely also needs a little education about designing a blended family ceremony.

Giving children a voice in decisions that are affecting their lives and the family is important, but the most important reason you must include the children in Activities is that they need relational reassurance from their biological parent that they haven't been forgotten. Children are highly invested in maintaining relationship with their biological parent(s). When their mom or dad falls in love and gives their time and energy to another adult, it is natural for them to feel pushed aside, insignificant, and vulnerable. You need to move toward your children so you can move toward your new spouse. Therefore, it's wise from time to time when engaged in the family-centered Growing Activities for the future stepparent to step back and, for example, let the biological parent take the lead on the Activity or even have exclusive time with their kids to complete the Activity. You'll have to decide when to include the future stepparent and when not to, but occasionally compartmentalizing relationships in this way paradoxically helps children include the stepparent; when they are reassured of their parent's continued love and presence, children feel less relationally threatened by the stepparent (and perhaps new stepsiblings) and are more likely to open their hearts to them.

Some Growing Activities are couple-centered, others family-centered. In the end, the Activities aim to create for you three combinations of time together: biological parent-child time, couple time, and "family time" when the stepparent (and their children) are included. Even after the wedding, strive to keep this balance of time throughout your first few years. It feeds each person and helps prevent relationships from competing.

One more thought: In times of stress (whether caused by life events or the transition to a blended family), it is helpful for biological parents to increase parent-child alone time and decrease family time (while still maintaining couple time to continue nurturing the marriage in the midst of family stress).[5] This can feel to stepparents like they are being excluded, but long-term it has the opposite effect. When children feel safe

24

with their biological parent, they are more open to the step-parent, not less.

Building memories and a common language. Another advantage of the Growing Activities is that they build memories that the family can refer to after the wedding. For example, drawing your digital Blended Family Map (chapter 2) and helping to plan the wedding (chapter 4) create fun memories that stand on their own and represent the process of becoming a family. Positive memories serve a bonding function, and they give everyone a common language that they can utilize as they move through time. "Do you remember when we made that family map? I'll never forget realizing how hard it must be for Ashleigh to spend time with me when she can't be with her biological parent." Observations like this become points of mutual understanding that move individuals along the path of becoming family to one another.

Full steam ahead? By the way, if you experience significant resistance from children during the Growing Activities, you need to, at a minimum, spend more time and energy working through the barriers, and at a maximum, consider slowing your roll toward marriage. Children shouldn't get to dictate if and when you marry, but unwise is the couple who ignores the pushback or distress evident in a child(ren). Moving forward despite that is equivalent to shooting yourself in the foot. Instead, slow down. Talk through what you're seeing and what it tells you about the child. Consult with your mentor or coach (or small group), and together decide how you will move forward.

If, on the other hand, your Growing Activities experience affirms your wedding plans, full steam ahead.

Getting Started

I suggest that each of you read a chapter and discuss the concepts and the Growing Activity as outlined. Some couples will want two copies of this book in order to highlight what speaks to them most; others will share a copy. If you have a mentor or coach, you can discuss the chapter with them before and after doing the Activity (this makes a good structure for pre-stepfamily counseling). Feel free to modify the Activity for your family based on the ages of your kids, how well people are getting along, visitation schedules, and how much time you have. Make it your own. And if any Activity feels too risky, for whatever reason, feel free to skip it, but be sure to talk with each other and your coach about your concerns. What feels risky about it? What are you afraid will happen? These questions can be quite revealing.

After each Activity, share what you observed, what you think it means, and the implications for your journey forward. Each Activity is both an intervention—meaning it is designed to advance your family bonding process—and an assessment device—meaning it provides a feedback loop of information you didn't have before the Activity. Be sure to incorporate that information into how you move forward. For example, celebrate when you feel confirmation about the attitude of children or the family journey in general, and slow down to process information that suggests someone is struggling more than you realized.

Finally, let me make a comment about the order of the Growing Activities. There is a method to my madness. Activities—and the insights they bring—build on one another, so it's best if you go in order. The exceptions to that are "Planning Your Wedding" (chapter 4) and "Merging Money and Your Family" (chapter 9), which can be done at any point.

Co-Creating Your New Family

Unless you met as strangers on the TV program *Married at First Sight*, you have probably spent hundreds if not thousands

26

of hours investing in your coupleness. And if you had a few dating growing pains, keep in mind there were only two of you. You now endeavor to merge the lives of multiple children, sometimes from multiple homes, with perhaps a couple dozen extended family members for the rest of your lives. Let's just do the math, shall we? Biological families are often comprised of two parents and four grandparents. That means there are six primary parent figures directly responsible for childrearing and nurturing children through their lives—all of whom have a direct biological tie to a child who very much wants them in their world. Blended families often have between three and seven parents and stepparents, across three or more households, plus eight or more sets of grandparents, totaling nine to twenty-one parent figures. Now, keep in mind that many of these people don't like each other—which, of course, makes parenting far more complicated and difficult—and that on day one, children have strong preferences that some parent figures remain in their world while they would be fine with or without others. If you have invested hundreds or thousands of hours in building your coupleness, don't you think you need to be just as intentional *with children* to co-create your familyness? Let's get started.

TRY THIS

As you launch into this book, I encourage you to start a one-minute daily habit that will connect you and your spouse.

My one-year devotional *Daily Encouragement for the Smart Stepfamily* (with Dianne Neal Matthews) offers simple, practical thoughts to guide your journey to becoming family. Reading each day's thought literally takes less than a minute but can ignite important discussions as you strengthen your marriage and co-create your relationships and vision for parenting. And here's the bonus benefit: Reading that book on a regular basis, even as you work through *Preparing to Blend*, will establish a value-centered relationship habit that will stay with your relationship throughout the years. Now, *that's* a habit worth beginning.

2

SEEING IS EYE-OPENING

Drawing Your Blended Family Map

For close to thirty years in both individual therapy and large conferences, I've been using a tool familiar to family therapists called a genogram to help couples see the complexity of their blended family. Seeing is eye-opening. And when you do your family map, it is revealing, insightful, and hope-giving. Revealing because it removes the blinders romantic love has placed on your eyes so you can see the vast number of connections, dynamics, and factors affecting your family. Insightful because it helps you visualize the underlying relational dynamics that move your family through time and space. And hope-giving because the insights you gain empower your journey together as a family.

After completing their genogram and seeing how complex their multi-generational, multi-household family really is, I've had a few couples lose some optimism; instead of giving them hope for their future, they tell me I'm trying to crush their dreams.

But it's just the opposite! I'm trying to help you climb a mountain, together, with your eyes open. Romantic love, whether it's your first love or fifth, literally puts your brain in a kind of chemical daze. It reduces the activity of the frontal lobe (the part of your brain that actually thinks) and activates the parts of your brain that light up when someone is on cocaine. No, I'm not kidding. Let me put it this way. The Rocky Mountains look pretty small from a hundred miles away. It's easy to say, "Oh, that's nothing. We can climb that in no time." Romantic love makes you view building a new family that way. But move to the base of the Rockies and your eyes are opened. Climbing to the top might take a little more time—and the path may be steeper—than you thought. That's my job; to move you to the base of the mountain. For three decades, blended family couples have complained to me, "Why didn't anyone tell me this before we married?" Well, I'm telling you before you marry.

At this point, your heart may be racing a bit and you may feel like you're about to hear bad news. That's not the case. You're just going to hear truthful news—some of which will be encouraging, while some may challenge your assumptions about the climb. Either way, if I may borrow a phrase: The truth will set you free. Hope is found in an honest appraisal of your circumstances. Blind hope is no hope at all.

Your Digital Blended Family Map

My friends at Blending.Love have created a digital genogram that you can do online; they call it a Blended Family Map. Like a genogram commonly used by family therapists, a Blended Family Map can help you examine your family history, relationship patterns and roles, ethnic influences, and the unspoken rules for family behavior. In addition, you can use your digital map to anticipate how your family will look and interact after the wedding. Questions provided in this chapter (and throughout the book) will help reveal some of this, but much of this exploration you can do on your own just by being curious and asking each other questions. Plus, working with a pastor or counselor who is familiar with genograms can open your eyes even more as they ask probing questions.

Before they met, Juan and Hailey had each been married and divorced. Juan grew up in a first-generation immigrant Mexican family that very much valued traditional Hispanic family culture. His first marriage was to Maria, a woman with similar family values. They had three children together: Mia, Aria, and José. Juan and Maria would each tell you that they divorced simply because they grew apart, though Maria would add that she tried to save the marriage more than Juan did. Today, Maria, who is still single, lives just a few miles from Juan, and both sides of their extended family live nearby as well. Their children visit grandparents often and move regularly between their two homes; as former spouses who highly value a close extended family (a Hispanic cultural value known as familism), Juan and Maria have a fairly cooperative co-parenting relationship.

Hailey, a Caucasian woman from the Midwest, grew up in a single-parent home. Her father left her and her two brothers when she was young and continues to be an unpredictable presence in her life. Just before graduating from college, Hailey got pregnant with her daughter, Emma (now age fourteen). She married the father (Cameron) and had Mason (now age eleven). They divorced after Cameron had an affair; he later married a woman, Gabrielle, who had one child (Logan) from a previous relationship. Hailey and Cameron have a contentious co-parenting relationship, in part fueled by her resentment of his affair. Furthermore, both Hailey and Emma are bitter toward Gabrielle for "destroying their home."

The Juan-Hailey Blended Family Map (Figure 1) was created by Blending.Love. We've added relationship "temperatures" that I first discussed in my book *Building Love Together in Blended Families* with co-author Dr. Gary Chapman. Obviously, the details of your Blended Family Map will differ (and the icons used by the website may change with time), but you can still learn about your family from this example.

Family Structure and Ethnic Influences

There are many different stepfamily structures and configurations. Once they are married, Juan and Hailey's family structure will include five adults parenting six children spread over three different homes (Maria's, Juan and Hailey's, and Cameron and Gabrielle's). It also includes many grandparents in multiple households (not pictured here). You can see why I like to say that most blended families are tall and wide—that is, at least three generations tall and multiple households wide.

Juan and Hailey's Blended Family Map reveals the multitude of people and relationships that everyone must manage, not to mention the natural divisions they must overcome to bond and form a family identity. Seeing the reality of your family structure might also be eye-opening and sobering. When picturing the future, engaged couples often see their family as simple. Perhaps you imagine you, your children, and only your household. Former spouses (living or deceased), their new spouses, and the grandparents on their side of the family often don't get included in the imagined family portrait. But the first

Create your Blended Family Map at Blending.Love. Use discount code MAPDEAL30.

FIGURE 1

Hailey and Juan's Blended Family Map

blending.love
Map Your Blended Family

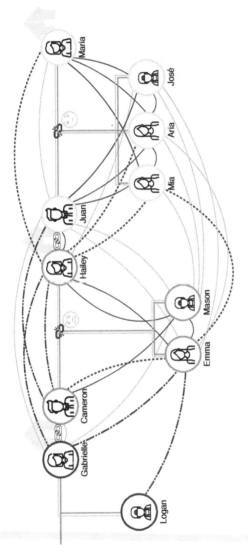

Relationship with Previous Partner

😊 Perfect Pals

😊 Cooperative Colleagues

😐 Angry Associates

😠 Fiery Foes

😣 Dissolved Duos

Household

Divorced

Married

Biological Bonds

Legal Bonds

Emotional Relationships

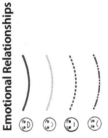

reality you must face is that everyone in your Blended Family Map is going to be part of your family. You might not think of them as being family, but your children or stepchildren do. Seeing the relational connections that exist makes that very apparent. Even former spouses are part of your family from an emotional, psychological, and practical standpoint. They impact your finances, your schedule, the climate of your home, parenting decisions, the well-being of children, the bonding process of new step-relationships, and on and on. Ultimately, everything and everyone is connected. It's important that you accept this so you can be proactive to respond to each dynamic and relationship connected to your home.

Relationship Temperatures

Each two people (called a dyad) have a relationship that could be described in general as "Cold" (awkward or conflicted), "Chilly" (fragile, weak, or in development), "Cool" (friendly or caring), or "Warm and Snug" (strong bond, committed). Of course, relationships evolve and change over time, so whatever label you use describes how you see it today; you might label it something else tomorrow.

Couples often see a few things differently. I encourage you to print two copies of your Blended Family Map so each of you can draw the temperature lines from your point of view. Then share your thoughts and listen to the other's perspective. You're not trying to decide who is correct; you're listening to their perspective (which may reveal their hopes, expectations, and beliefs about each relationship) so you can have a shared understanding of your family dynamics.

Another helpful reflection is examining how different people have differing experiences of the same family. For example, Juan has strong bonds with all three of his biological children and a mutually respectful relationship with his former spouse, Maria. So far, he is developing a friendly relationship with his future stepchildren, Emma and Mason. Hailey also has strong bonds with her two biological children and a friendly relationship with José (future stepson), but things are chilly with Mia and Aria. So while Juan may be feeling very optimistic about the family, Hailey may be apprehensive about her role as stepmom to the girls. Juan may love it when all five kids are together, and Hailey may vacillate between having fun and feeling anxious. It will be important for Juan and Hailey to empathize with each other and understand the other's experience (not take issue with it).

Look at the family structure from the kids' point of view. Because Juan and Maria's co-parenting relationship is cooperative, moving between homes may not be problematic for Mia, Aria, and José. But because animosity and resentment exist in Hailey and Cameron's co-parenting relationship, Emma and Mason will likely have logistical issues moving between homes (e.g., poor communication means things get left behind) and may experience, for example, anger (external behavior problems) or difficulties concentrating at school (internal anxiety issues). That means transition day may be exciting for one group of kids and depressing for another. So how will the parents respond?

And what about the relationship dyads of children—how do they differ? Aria has strong bonds with her mom and dad but is somewhat chilly toward Hailey, with whom she is just beginning a relationship. Emma, on the other hand, has a strong bond with her mother, a chilly relationship with her father, and a cold relationship with her stepmother, Gabrielle. Even though Aria and Emma are only one year apart in age, their emotional worlds are miles apart. How might this impact how each bonds with their new stepparent, or each other? This brings us to the topic of emotional triangles.

Relational Triangles and Patterns

Follow the triangle: What Peter tells you about Paul says more about your relationship with Peter than it does his relationship with Paul. It's easy to see that Peter's negative words about Paul reveal he doesn't like Paul, but what's just as important to notice is what his complaints to you about Paul reveal about your relationship with Peter. It might say, for example, that Peter feels safe with you. But it could also be that Peter is trying to form an alliance with you against Paul. Or maybe Peter is just trying to keep you for himself, moving you away from a close friendship with Paul.

And there's more. If Peter is successful in creating an alliance with you against Paul (albeit a surface, pseudo-alliance at best), your relationship will make it less likely that Peter is able to resolve his issues with Paul. Welcoming his gossip, as it were, fosters distance in the other two sides of the triangle. Your relationship with Peter (one side of the triangle) is greatly impacting the other two sides (his relationship with Paul, and your relationship with Paul).

There are numerous emotional triangles on Juan and Hailey's family map. For example, the fact that former spouses Juan and Maria have a respectful, cool relationship makes it more likely that each of their children can have a warm and snug relationship with them as parents. On the other hand, Hailey and Cameron's tense, conflicted, and cold co-parent relationship reinforces Hailey's super-close (we might say *overly* close) relationship with her daughter, Emma, and Emma's chilly relationship with her dad. What happens on one side of the triangle has an impact on the other sides, and vice versa. It doesn't dictate or determine the other sides, but it does influence it. For example, if Hailey and Cameron's relationship improved, it might release Emma to have a closer relationship with her dad—and perhaps even her stepmom, Gabrielle.

Trying to understand emotional triangles can be a bit overwhelming. I'm simply inviting you to look around and make observations—especially as it relates to relationships that seem stuck. For example, in general Juan has a cool relationship with his stepdaughter, Emma. It might help Juan (and Hailey) relax about that developing relationship if Juan can recognize how his conflictual relationship with Cameron and Emma's tense relationship with her dad impact her level of openness to Juan. Juan might understand more why Emma occasionally warms up to him but then backs off when longing for more from her dad. Empathizing with her dilemma can help him be more patient and not take her distance as disrespect. It can also help Hailey not pressure Emma into "going in 100 percent" with Juan. (I'll say more about this in chapter 3.)

Coupleness and Familyness

I invite you to create your own family map at Blending.Love. The questions at the end of this chapter will guide you into making many relationship observations.

Let me remind you that coupleness does not equal familyness.[1] Dating naturally focuses the eyes of most people primarily on their couple (or dyadic) relationship. But becoming a blended family involves so much more. You must now open your eyes to the familyness factors so your coupleness dreams can come true. Said another way, building a strong couple relationship is just part of what it takes to build a strong blended family. Each Growth Activity in this book is meant to strengthen your coupleness *and* move you toward familyness. Don't skip an Activity or leave children out of the ones designed for them; you can't grow familyness without their involvement.

1. Go to Blending.Love and create your Blended Family
   Map. This will be something you'll refer to throughout
   the reading of this book. (The Map is very afford-
   able; still, use this discount code to get 30 percent off:
   MAPDEAL30.)

2. Print two copies of your Blended Family Map. Draw
   a temperature line or label each dyadic relationship as
   Cold, Chilly, Cool, or Warm and Snug. Of course, relationship temperatures can change moment to moment.
   During conflict, for example, your marriage can be
   Chilly but will return to Warm and Snug after resolving
   the argument. We're not talking about that. Label each
   relationship as you see it in general. It's okay (and normal) if you label them differently as a couple.

   • Discuss your labels and perspective. Take turns shar-
     ing your Blended Family Maps. Consider the other's
     point of view and be curious. (For example, say, "Tell
     me more about that.")

   • Examine the emotional triangles. Pay attention to
     stuck relationships and the triangles of which they
     are a part. Discuss how changes in the other two sides
     might help the "stuck" side.

3. If you think it appropriate, use your Blended Family
   Map to begin a series of conversations with your children about your journey to become a family. You can
   even print a fresh copy of the Blended Family Map for
   each child and ask them to draw relationship temperatures as they see them.

   • Biological parents might choose to have this conversa-
     tion with their children without the future stepparent

present in order to encourage honesty and a candid dialogue. Share what you learn/observe later.

- Listen to your children's perspective on each relationship *before* sharing yours.

- This can be a very insightful dialogue with young and adult children alike.

- Resist the urge to push an acceptance agenda.[2] If your children express concerns, for example, don't try to argue with their logic or feelings in order to get them to accept your new partner or the new family. That may shut them down or make them feel like they are unimportant to you. Just listen and validate that they have questions or concerns.

4. Place Blended Family Maps in a common area of your home (such as on the refrigerator) so they prompt periodic conversations. Developing a common language between family members about the relationships in your home (and future home) is part of defining relationships and co-creating a new family identity.

POST-ACTIVITY QUESTIONS FOR REFLECTION

1. What did this activity open your eyes to? Regarding the process of becoming a family, what do you see more clearly now?

2. What did conversations with your children reveal? What did you learn about their perspective or feelings?

3. Describe your childhood family cultural and ethnic norms. For example, describe gender roles and expectations, social activities, and family celebrations (birthdays, holidays, and special events). Which of those

influences did you carry into any previous relationships (or marriage) and/or still practice today?

4. In light of your Blended Family Map, revisit the circumstances surrounding the end of any previous relationships (death, divorce, or a breakup). But don't just share what happened (the facts). Share the emotional impact it had on you (talk around your pain), any residue still on your heart today, and how the temperature of that relationship is impacting triangles that are forming in your blended family.

5. What did your experiences as a child teach you about the stability of marriage relationships? Share a story that illustrates this.

6. Describe your current co-parent circumstances. How cooperative is your co-parenting? What struggles does this create?

7. A wedding for one of the co-parents often ripples changes into the home of the other parent. (Everything is connected.) What changes do you anticipate in your child's other home when you marry?

8. Consider the temperature of each of your dyadic relationships. What could you do to change the temperature? How might that positively impact those connected to the triangles of which you are a part?

9. OPTIONAL: Share your Blended Family Map and observations with a mentor/pastor/therapist and ask them to help you explore relationship patterns even further.

TRY THIS

Take a stepfamily couple who has been married for a few years to dinner. Tell them what you've learned about your family from this Growth Activity and then ask them to talk about their family structure. Ask them what insights they have gained through the years about their family that they didn't see prior to the wedding and what they wish they had known.

3

HELPFUL EXPECTATIONS

It's helpful if your expectations are based on what is and what will be, not just on what you are dreaming about.

A single man who had never been married was dating a woman with four children by two different men, and two grandchildren. After his pastor helped him draw what would be their Blended Family Map if they married, the pastor said, "Your task in dating is to be sure you can marry this," and he pointed to everything on the paper.

Immediately, the man realized that the happy family he had begun to imagine was based solely on his relationship with his girlfriend; he hadn't fully considered what it meant to marry into a complex family system and be part of a parenting team that included adults in three households. It took staring at the Blended Family Map to realize that.

Maybe your Blended Family Map has begun to recalibrate your expectations as well. This is a good thing because it roots you in what is, not in unrealistic expectations.

43

If Only It Were So

Let's briefly explore some common unrealistic blended family expectations.[1] Recalibrating your expectations prepares you for what most families experience and puts the two of you on the same page so you can lead from a position of togetherness.

"**Family members will love each other right away.**" If only this were so! It does happen occasionally with some family members, but not with everyone. As it turns out, blended family relationships develop just like other friendships and close relationships: one step at a time, over time. Even when initial connections seem very positive, sometimes there is a "cooling off" once real life begins, then an "up and down, in and out" that continues over time. Sometimes the path to familyness starts with someone keeping another at arm's length. This, too, is normal, so don't be surprised or discouraged. Learn to be okay with one step forward, one step back, until time results in two steps forward, one step back.

One woman wrote to me saying that she and her fiancé were struggling to balance his time every other week with his two children, ages fourteen and twelve, with her feelings of being neglected. The father and his kids would take weekend trips together. He wanted to start including her, but the kids wanted to keep it just the three of them. The woman felt like an outsider and wondered if this would continue into the marriage.

I replied to her with a number of thoughts. "Yes, it probably will. Love takes time to develop, so his desire to include you doesn't mean they will want to include you in the same way. Find points of connection with the kids and slowly work your way in." I also told her something I knew she might not want to hear. I advocate for biological parents spending one-on-one time with their kids before and after a new marriage because it helps reassure children that they haven't completely lost their parent. But a couple hours a week or a weekend getaway every once in a while should be balanced with couple time and family activities that include everyone so the stepmom can build relationships and memories too.

And then I suggested that feeling neglected when he spent time with his kids was her job to manage. Yes, he needed to be sensitive to her and consider her feelings, but he couldn't make her okay. Only she could self-regulate. Expecting him to deter her every insecurity was unrealistic. "Is this revealing some vulnerability in you?" I asked. "Strive to manage your anxiety and not let it get the best of you, or you will grow to resent their connection. Their relationship is not the enemy; your fear is."

"This marriage/family will be better than the last." Don't try to convince your children that this family is better than the first or is somehow "God's plan" for them (which suggests their original family wasn't).[2] And don't think of this marriage as a test to prove, in light of a previous painful relationship, that you really are worth loving. It does make sense that if your first marriage ended in dissolution, you'd want this one to be a stronger, more fulfilling relationship, but don't live comparing everything to the past or you will be, ironically, still married to your past.

"We can merge traditions quickly." By definition, traditions aren't traditions until you've done them enough that people know what to expect and assume they will take place. So your family must wander a little in the wilderness until you figure out what you like and can repeat it enough that people become invested in the tradition. A birthday tradition takes years to develop. A holiday ritual only takes on meaning when it's expected and feels comfortable. And a fun vacation might be preceded by a few failed attempts. Relax your expectations around these experiences and trust that they will take on meaning over time.

"Our kids are invested in our marriage as much as we are." Even when kids love their stepparent and are in favor of their parent's marriage, they often feel a little divided about it as well. They love how their stepparent cares for their parent, but what they really want is for Mom and Dad to be together again. They value what the blended family brings to their life, but a part of them is sad that someone is missing from the family portrait. It cuts both ways. Bitter comes with sweet. Maybe the way to say it is that they just aren't as dedicated to your success as you are. They're not against your marriage necessarily, but they would be okay if you weren't together.

Now, here's what you need to keep in mind: These mixed feelings are the strongest in the early years of your marriage, and they usually subside over time. As the family bonds and they become more invested in what you are creating together, these feelings diminish. What you need to do is love your marriage and give them grace as they learn to love it too.

"My relationship with my children won't have to change." Morgan had two teenage children, and her husband, Aaron, had three daughters ages seven to twelve. Before they married, she saw some things that troubled her but decided they weren't a big deal. For one, he made himself available to his girls whenever they needed him. His attentiveness was admirable in one sense, but it had no boundaries. The reality of this hit on their wedding night when one of the girls called because she couldn't fall asleep without him kissing her good-night, and he suggested they go home and check on her. Did I mention this was their wedding night!

The couple discussed this and other similar actions from Aaron with their relationship coach. It became apparent that Aaron didn't think his relationship with his girls should have to change as a result of his marriage. "My kids didn't choose this," he said. "Just like their mom leaving, they didn't choose this. I did. They still need me."

46

No, actually, your relationship with your children must change. Sometimes fairly significantly. They should not lose you, and you will continue to make marital sacrifices of time, energy, money, and resources in order to care for them. But an abiding commitment to another adult will bring about some change. This does not, however, mean you stop loving your children—far from it. In fact, to embrace your new marriage they need to experience your consistent love, dedication, and presence in their lives. There will be tough decisions about where and with whom, for example, you spend your time, but this isn't a competition. You must choose both your spouse and your children—and invest deeply in each. Both win. Finding the balance in these two investments is not always easy, but working toward it as a marital team will make it more likely.[3]

"Things that trouble me will improve after the wedding." Without realizing it, engaged couples often assume that love will conquer all. You expect those little irritants that you've noticed in their personality to dissipate once real life together begins. The struggles you've had with a former spouse shouldn't affect your marriage much, right? And your fiancé's financial woes will get better once you are managing the money.

Before they married, Jeremiah noticed that Makala treated her two children more like friends than children. And the oldest, Aniyah, she treated more like a co-parent who was helping her raise the younger child. Jeremiah assumed that once he took his place in the home, his wife wouldn't need Aniyah to fill that role anymore. But the relationship was set—and, he would later learn, was part of a generational pattern between mothers and daughters even if a husband was present. Jeremiah found himself surprised that things didn't improve, he was frustrated, and he battled a dynamic that made him "the bad guy" who caused trouble in the family.

47

Don't assume like Jeremiah that minor or moderate dating irritants will instantly go away after the wedding. Yellow flashing lights send a signal to drivers to slow down and proceed with caution. Ignoring yellow lights or maintaining your speed through a caution zone is ill-advised for safe driving—and for safe preparation to become a blended family. Slow down, take a good hard look, and decide if what you see should alter how you proceed. Keep in mind that some yellow lights turn red.

By the way, because people sometimes assume that love will conquer all, engaged couples have been known to run red lights too. In my book *Dating and the Single Parent*, I review a number of yellow and red lights that dating couples should watch for before deciding to marry. For example, marrying someone who is a poor parent is one of them. Earlier I told you about Morgan, who saw that her fiancé, Aaron, had an overly connected relationship with his daughters (who couldn't go to sleep without him). She assumed it would change after they married. It didn't, and his inability to set boundaries with his girls ruined their wedding night. Jeremiah made the same mistake. Marrying someone means marrying not only their expanded, multi-household family structure; it means marrying their relationship patterns and dynamics, their personality quirks, their credit score, and their spiritual values. If you've been minimizing anything that troubles you, now is the time to name it and slow down before proceeding with caution.

"Blending is the goal of this stepfamily." Much of my writing and teaching career has been spent helping couples realize that you don't cook a stepfamily with a blender. I know some call them "blended families," and ultimately what you likely want is a family that has *merged well* together, but blenders have blades that cut people, their family history and connections, and hopes for the future into pieces. With intense force and Cutco®-like sharpness, blenders force ingredients to lose their identity and merge with other ingredients whether they want to or not. That doesn't create a family that is safe and comfortable for "ingredients." That creates a hostile environment that demands guardedness, caution, and self-protection.

As I detail in my book *The Smart Stepfamily*, the best cooking method to bring family ingredients together is a Crockpot.[4] Gently and persistently, slow cookers, as they are sometimes called, warm up ingredients and soften them so they can with integrity merge their flavor and being with other ingredients. Some ingredients warm up sooner than others; others need more time and warmth before they soften. But each, in its own time, gradually moves toward integration.

It's important that you create an environment of perpetual warmth and safety. Treating one another with respect, expecting people to be kind to others (even if you don't love them), and communicating another's value to you are all good examples of how to do this. But there are others. You could say that my SMART STEPFAMILY SERIES of books (found in the beginning of this book) are all about creating a Crockpot environment to help your family cook. You might complement this book with others that will also aid your cooking process, but understand that you can't rush the amount of time it takes. Like blenders, Instant Pots work fast, but they use pressure to do so. Crockpots work slowly, often taking hours. But that's how you get a good, authentic blend. A quick family integration is attractive, of course, but push too hard and you'll discover things slow down, conflict goes up, and so does stress. Instead, lower your expectations, grow your family slow and steady, and you'll find the taste gets better and better. The average blended family needs years for ingredients to share of themselves and combine (and not all ingredients combine to the same degree; some not at all). Warming, softening, and merging takes time. Embrace that truth with patience and persistence and you'll find more of what you're hoping for.

ACTIVITY INSTRUCTIONS

- This activity consists of guided conversations with each other and your children (and an optional family activity).
- Be honest to identify fears or concerns that arise. Don't avoid being candid. If you identify what might be a yellow or red light, say it out loud to yourself and a friend/mentor/coach.
- During conversations with your children, be sure to communicate your love and continued commitment to them.
- Step into grief. Talking about the future often brings up the loss of the past. Don't avoid this; step into it. Hug any hurt or pain that arises. Strive to let the pain of the past and the hopeful anticipation of the future coexist side by side.

Couple Conversation

1. Do you recognize your own thinking in any of these unrealistic expectations? Share which ones are hard to let go of and why.
   - New family members will love each other immediately.
   - This marriage/family will be better than the last.
   - We can merge traditions quickly.
   - Our kids are invested in our marriage as much as we are.
   - My relationship with my children won't have to change.
   - Things that trouble me will improve after the wedding.
   - Blending is the goal of this stepfamily.

2. Talk through how these expectations have been recalibrated by the chapter. What insights have you gained and how have your expectations been adjusted?

3. Say out loud or write down any concerns that have arisen for you while adjusting your expectations. For example, one person said, "Learning that it will take years to Crockpot our family harmony makes me concerned about my son who is seventeen and about to leave home. What if he doesn't have time to bond like the rest of us?"

4. Consider having some conversations with your children (ages five through adult) about their expectations. See the Parent-Child Conversation section below for a list of suggested questions. Chapter 8 will walk you through discussions about what will likely change after the wedding, but right now you can focus on their hopes and what they think you are expecting from them.

    Don't underestimate the power of these conversations. Not expecting your children to love everyone immediately is one thing; actually letting them talk to you about it is another growth moment for your family altogether. Not discussing these topics potentially puts psychological and emotional distance between you; talking openly about them and empathizing with your children's feelings closes that gap and gives you permission to connect again and again around these subjects over time.

    NOTE: In some cases, it may be best for the biological parent(s) to talk to their children individually or as a sibling group (i.e., without the stepparent); not including the future stepparent or stepsiblings may help children be more candid and open.

Optional Family Crockpot Exercise

Depending on the ages of your children, you might layer the below conversations on top of a fun dinner exercise (first shared in *The Smart Stepfamily*). This is optional. However, I think you might be pleasantly surprised how well children understand and make use over time of this metaphor about your family merging process.

1. Plan a fun Saturday. (This could be a combination of time with everyone together and/or subgroups, like a biological parent and children.) Start the day by gathering everyone in the kitchen. Have a Crockpot recipe ready. Let everyone add one ingredient to the pot. As they do, talk about how your family is like this dish.
   - Note that you are not stirring or blending the ingredients by hand but are relying on the Crockpot to bring everything together slowly over time.
   - Put on the lid and turn on the Crockpot. Wait a few seconds and ask why it hasn't cooked yet. Wait for responses.
   - Point out that for ingredients to merge, they have to warm up, soften, and then share of themselves—and that each ingredient has its own timing.
   - Then point out that the "ingredients" of your family will likely do that too, each in their own time.
   - Talk about how long it takes to cook food in a Crockpot. You might mention that just as it takes a few hours, your family may need a few years to fully merge.
   - Allow people to ask questions.

2. Go about your day as planned.
   - If you get a chance during the day, pause in the kitchen and ask people to observe how the cooking is going.
   - Make some observations (e.g., it's beginning to smell good, but it's not done yet; some ingredients haven't softened as much as others, etc.).

3. At the end of the cooking time, sit down together as a family and enjoy the meal. As you eat, ask what lessons people learned from the Crockpot experience. Pray together at the end of the meal, asking God to give your family patience as you "cook together."

4. Bonus: Incorporate some of the following questions into your day of fun and time together.

Parent-Child Conversation
Modify the following questions based on your child's age and development.

1. It took us a while to get back to normal life after the divorce/parental death. And remember how long it took for you to feel comfortable at your new school/church [identify something recent they can relate to]? How long do you think it will take for us to start feeling like a family after the wedding? Who will have the easiest adjustment? The hardest?
2. What's going to happen to how we do things around the house (like play our favorite game, eat meals, share the bathroom, etc.)?
3. If divorced: I think it's fair to say that you wish your mom/dad and I were back together again, right? Obviously, that's not happening, and I really want to marry

53

[name]. So, how are we going to do this if you want me
to be with mom/dad and I want to be with [name]?

4. If widowed: I know you wish mom/dad were still alive.
Me too. Given that, I can see from your point of view
how it's weird that I'm marrying [name]. I'm wondering how you can hold a permanent place in your heart
for your mom/dad while making room for the relationship with your stepparent?

5. What do you think my expectation is of you regarding
[name of fiancé]? I don't expect you to love them like
you love me or dad/mom, but do you sometimes think I
need you to love them like that?

6. What is your dad/mom's (other biological parent)
expectation of you regarding how you get along with
[name of fiancé]?

7. What do you think [name of fiancé]'s expectation is of
you regarding accepting/loving them?

Follow-Up Couple Conversation

1. Share as a couple what you heard from the children and
discuss the implications for your engagement and marriage. If working with a relationship coach or pastor,
share these observations with them as well to get their
perspective.

2. Finally, review this partial list of yellow and red
lights. Which, if any, are even the slightest concern for you? Now is the time to give voice to them
so you can begin working together toward their
resolution.

a. Yellow: Do either of you have an oppositional or
behaviorally troubled child? (Do you have a sense of

why this has happened? If nothing else, are you prepared to "marry" this dynamic?)

b. Yellow: Do either of you have difficulty trusting the
other? Have past hurts or betrayals left a residue of
distrust on someone's heart?

c. Yellow: Did either of you step quickly into this relationship after a big loss? Less than a year after a divorce or death is generally too quick and just delays
the grief journey till you are married.

d. Yellow: Is pornography a part of either of your lives?
To what degree?

e. Yellow: Are there character issues to deal with? Examples include obsessive-compulsive behavior, a
quick/repeating temper, blaming others for their life
situations, someone who won't respect your sexual
boundaries, excessive debt, excessive enmeshment
or disengagement with their family of origin, decep-
tion/lying, a diagnosed personality disorder.

f. Yellow: Do either of you have a difficult former
spouse or one who has a vastly different moral/
spiritual framework than you? (The values and parenting of the other home will dramatically affect
parenting and relationships within your home.)

g. Yellow: Do you get a sense that your fiancé would
like to change a relationship you have with one or
more of your children? What is their need? Do your
children feel threatened by this?

h. Red: Does either of you feel pressured to marry
quickly?

i. Red: Do you have extreme differences in parenting?

j. Red: Do either of you have a horrible former spouse who spreads contempt and bitterness throughout the family?

k. Red: Has cohabitation drifted into a decision to marry? To establish and maintain a strong commitment, men need the emotional space to freely choose marriage as opposed to waking up one day to discover they slid into marriage.[5]

POST-ACTIVITY QUESTIONS FOR REFLECTION

Many couples cautiously enter the conversations above and come out on the other side with a greater confidence that they are moving, with wisdom and intentionality, in the right direction.

If, on the other hand, the last two activities have raised a check in your spirit, listen to it. Many couples dismiss flashing yellow caution lights, or even red ones, because it means their dream may not be becoming reality as easily or quickly as they hoped. Don't be naïve. Give voice to your concerns and talk through them with a trusted advisor.

TRY THIS

Review the list of titles in the SMART STEPFAMILY SERIES (see the list near the front of this book). Which, if any, jump out at you as something you might want to explore after finishing this book? You might also start listening to my podcast, *FamilyLife Blended* (with Ron Deal), which provides practical guidance on many aspects of stepfamily living. Learn more at FamilyLife .com/blendedpodcast or wherever you get your podcasts.

4

PLANNING YOUR WEDDING

In an early outline of this book, I put this chapter toward the end. But after reading research on the role a well-planned wedding can play in the lives of children, I moved it toward the beginning. Let me explain.

In my book *Building Love Together in Blended Families*, co-authored with Dr. Gary Chapman, I explained that for blended families, a wedding ceremony culminates one process and begins another. Exchanging rings during the ceremony culminates a couple's journey into love and commitment; rings signify permanence. But the ceremony doesn't fully culminate the process of becoming a family. That process begins to a small degree before marriage, but it really expands and deepens for the entire family unit *after* the wedding.

Now, here's the opportunity. The process of planning and preparing for the wedding—and the ceremony itself—can play a part in facilitating family identity and bonding. It can accelerate becoming family to one another.

Have you ever heard about a blended family wedding that ended in disaster because the adult kids didn't show up or one of the children cried all the way through the ceremony? This happens because of the emotional gap that exists between the couple and their children leading up to and throughout the ceremony. The couple is happy and excited about the wedding, while their children are resentful, angry, or hurt by it. Weddings are intended to be moments of celebration that cast a vision for the future, but for some children, the event is empty, full of negative emotion, and a reminder of what has been lost. And for some, the ceremony—because of the way it is structured—actually delegitimizes the marriage. (I'll explain why later.)

But just as a poorly planned wedding can make things worse for your family, a wisely designed experience can improve it. Research confirms that when children are consulted about the decision to marry and the timing of it, when they are actively included in planning the wedding, and they are able to participate in a wedding that lifts high the couple's marital commitment and acknowledges both the children's family of origin and their role in the new stepfamily, they are much more likely to experience the ceremony itself as important and full of meaning.[1] A shared family experience that is positive and rich in meaning—not just for the couple, but for the children as well—contributes to the developing family identity. Though they might not have noticed it while it was happening, people can eventually look back at the wedding and say, "This is when we became a family."

To be clear, wedding planning and the wedding itself don't finalize the process of bonding (that process goes on for years), but they delineate a starting point for the family and can, if managed well, accelerate the process of becoming family.

You really want to get this right.

To that end, let me flesh out the essential elements of wedding planning to avoid and those to include.[2]

The Backstory Matters

What led to your decision to marry, the wedding itself, how events unfolded, and the biological parent's relationship to their children greatly impacts whether they view your wedding—and marriage—as legitimate. For example, a child's relationship with their stepparent initially goes *through* their relationship with their biological parent. As I said in chapter 1, in the beginning, children are most invested in preserving the relationship with their parent; as long as that remains strong, most kids are open to getting to know their stepparent. But a child who for whatever reason feels estranged from their biological parent or replaced by the stepparent in their parent's heart will likely struggle to embrace their parent's new love. A wedding under these circumstances tastes bitter to children. Ideally, a parent in this situation would re-invest in relationships with their children and reconcile before realistically expecting them to open up to the stepparent. (This is why it is so important that dating couples with children attend to the emotional needs of children while at the same time nurturing their new relationship.)

But there are other reasons a child might discount the significance of your ceremony. A parent who quickly remarries after being widowed or divorced, or who recouples multiple times (including serial dating and cohabitation), proving themselves untrustworthy, sacrifices the confidence of their child in their marital decisions. One young man said, "My mom would never let me date the kind of people she dated. I gave up trusting that any of her relationships could last." Or perhaps a child isn't drawn to the person you have chosen. A child who doesn't connect with or like the character of your spouse-to-be can't be excited about how such a relationship will impact you as their parent, them as your child, or the family as a whole.

And then there's the complication of grief. A parent's marriage always reminds children of the original loss. Watching Mom commit to love, honor, and cherish a man dramatically calls to mind the fact that Mom and Dad stopped loving, honoring, and cherishing each other. In the case of parental death, planning a wedding resurrects grief over the parent who died and the family unit that perished with them. You can't have one without the other.

Now, while you have some influence over the aforementioned elements of the backstory (e.g., you can attempt to draw closer to an estranged child), the story is what it is. And because of that, you should anticipate how your children might respond to the wedding and wonder what you might do differently at this point to come alongside any confusion or angst they may feel.

The Type of Wedding Matters

Interestingly, some children (especially those in their teens and adults) think a parental wedding should have some elements of a traditional wedding, but not too many. In other words, a big to-do with a white dress symbolizing virginity and "first love" can feel inauthentic and degrade the marriage of the child's biological parents (which the child still cherishes). But the opposite is also true. A civil ceremony doesn't feel traditional enough for some children. It can be criticized as too casual and not serious enough. As one child said, "Well, if you want everyone to take it seriously, it needs to be a little more than a barbeque."[3]

Worthy of note, cohabitation adds to the confusion. What is the role of a wedding when the parent has been living with the other person? *"Were we a family before, or is it just starting now? You're taking your vows now; were you not committed before? What's the difference?"* A casual wedding following cohabitation may not make a strong enough statement about the changing nature of the family. Weddings need to drive a stake in the ground and declare that something, that *everything*, has changed, or they run the risk of being insignificant and not altering the trajectory of the family.

Let the above research inform conversations with your children about the wedding. No, you are not letting your kids dictate what kind of wedding you will have, but in discussing it with them, you affirm their value to you and gain information that will inform your choices.

Involvement and the Elements of the Ceremony Matter

Unless a child is estranged from their parent, most want a fair amount of involvement in both pre-wedding planning and the ceremony itself. They want the messages of the ceremony to honor the past. And they want the wedding to not just be couple-centric, but family-centric. As one young adult indicated in hindsight about her mom's wedding, "I wish it would have helped create a family, not just a marriage."

A second or subsequent wedding for a parent brings three potentially competing emotional attachments into collision with one another: the couple's marriage, the child's loyalty to their family of origin, and the new blended family.[4] We typically think of weddings as being all about the couple (or for that matter, the bride), but a blended family wedding is also about the children, the family relationships that preexist the stepfamily, and the journey everyone has taken to get there. The trick is to acknowledge each of these relationships and not let one completely drown out the other two.

Get wedding officiant content and creative ideas for your wedding at familylife.com/preparingtoblend.

Consider the contrast. A wedding that ignores children, gives them no place in the ceremony, and focuses only on the couple could inadvertently send a strong message to a child that their family of origin is dead, their connection to the biological parent is insignificant, and the new marriage is all that counts. In light of the many losses the children have already experienced, a message like this will for some children strike a deathblow to their hearts regarding the marriage. However, a wedding that includes children in the decision-making, planning, and fulfillment of the ceremony helps children acknowledge the legitimacy of their parent's nuptials and receive the reality of their new family. Balance in celebrating the children's family of origin, inviting them to be part of the newly formed stepfamily, and holding up the new couple's commitment to each other can be a powerful turning point for your family.

Essentially, the three core messages to say to your children in your ceremony are: Our marital "us" matters; your past matters; and your expanding family matters. To overdo any one of those three messages to the neglect of the others could make the ceremony "empty" for a child, but the balance of all three makes it full of meaning and sends the most important message of all to a child: *You matter.*

The elements of a ceremony help send these balanced messages. Exchanging rings speaks to the importance of couple commitment establishing a covenant to last till death do them part. And planning a mother's wedding, for example, around the children's visitation schedule with their dad, and decorating the venue with pictures of the children with their father and extended family communicates an ongoing respect for their past and extended family relationships. And then to help each child see how they fit into the family being formed, the modern Blending of the Sands Ceremony (or a similar ritual) gives them a chance to symbolically pour themselves into what is being created. This doesn't, of course, complete that emotional process, but it does help to jump-start it, especially when children have helped plan that element of the wedding service. Planning helps them envision the moment when they will "give themselves" to the new family, logistical preparation helps them prepare their heart to do so, and participating in the ceremony symbolically marks the day and formally starts the bonding process—which is then walked out in real life following the ceremony.

Taken together, when various elements of the ceremony give all these messages (Our "us" matters; your past matters; your expanding family matters; you matter), children are more apt to legitimize the wedding, the marriage, and the new family in their hearts.

One couple, after reading an early version of this book manuscript, decided not to elope because her children would not witness them taking vows and certainly wouldn't play a part in the ceremony. Instead, Kristin and Jason planned a small but intimate wedding for family and let her children play the roles they wanted to play. Kristin's two boys walked her down the aisle and gave her away (answering the question of who gives this woman to this man with "My brother and I"), and her daughter carried the wedding rings and held her mom's bouquet. Jason added to his marital vows a promise to his new stepchildren to "love, support, and protect" them, and "nurture their growth in the Lord." By the way, in order not to mandate a reciprocal promise, the children were not asked to make any statements back to their new stepfather. However, they did feel comfortable, after the couple's vows and rings were exchanged, participating in creating a piece of family art that would later be placed in their home. Each adult and child painted their hand and pressed their handprint onto a blank canvas. The wedding officiant added meaning to the moment, noting that each of them—in a way they individually decide—now has the opportunity to put their own hand to this family and that each of them will stamp their unique fingerprints to the canvas of what this family is becoming. "And together," he said, "in your own timing and in your own way, you can create something beautiful." (Get more creative wedding ideas like this at familylife.com/preparingtoblend.)

ACTIVITY INSTRUCTIONS

This "activity" starts with a family meeting but might expand from there to a series of individual conversations with children as needed. The cumulative impact of the conversations is a process that includes children in decision-making (adding at least some sense of control to their lives) and lets them contribute to and participate in the wedding in ways that are meaningful to them.

Couple Conversation:

1. If you haven't already, start talking through your wedding and the elements you'd like to include.
2. Try to have a range of options that you are comfortable with—and what you are not open to. Carry this unity with you into your conversations with children.

Initial Family Meeting:

1. Decide who to include in the family meeting. Sometimes it's best to meet with children one-on-one from the start or meet with one group of children, then another. Don't forget younger children; they like to be included and may have more to offer to the conversation than you think.

2. Start by saying something like, "We are excited about getting married. But we also know you might have mixed feelings about it. It's okay if you are worried about how mom/dad might feel about this, or if you feel odd sometimes. We get that and we're not offended. In fact, we want to plan a wedding that celebrates the promise we are making to one another as husband and wife and acknowledges the many people you kids have in your life/family. We invite you to help us do that. So we've called you here to talk with you about the wedding ceremony. We won't get it all decided today, but we can at least hear one another's thoughts."

3. Ask: "Would you prefer a more traditional wedding or something different?"

4. Ask: "There are different elements of weddings these days. What do you think about [name a few you are considering , such as a Blending of the Sands ceremony]?"

5. Reception: "Here's what we're thinking about the reception . . . What do you think?"

6. Close by saying, "As plans for the wedding develop, we may come back to you and ask your opinion. And we'd be honored if you would help with some things. Would that be okay?"

POST-ACTIVITY QUESTIONS FOR REFLECTION

After the family meeting, process what you heard from the kids and move forward with wedding plans. Include them (invite their help and assign duties) when you can. Have additional family discussions or one-on-one conversations as needed.

1. In subsequent discussions, you might acknowledge the bittersweet nature of a wedding for the child.
   - If widowed: "Planning this wedding makes me think about planning my first wedding with your father/ mother. I miss him/her. And I know you do too."
   - If divorced: "I realize this wedding means your dad/ mom and I will never get back together again. I'm sure that makes a part of you sad."
2. Reflect on the weddings in your extended family. What message did they send and how were they received by you and others in your family? What message will others receive from your wedding?

TRY THIS

Watch some random blended family weddings on YouTube with your children. Ask them how they would feel about various elements of the weddings being in your wedding. You might also watch on YouTube my illustration of the Blending of the Sands Ceremony (search "Sand Ceremony, Blended and Blessed, Ron Deal") and what is really happening on the day of the wedding. Let family members share what they relate to in the video.

5

CO-CREATING FAMILYNESS

Deciding What to Call Each Other

Have you ever heard someone talk about a stepfamily member in a way that made you feel uncomfortable or worried about how the other person would feel if they heard it?

"This is my mom. And this is her husband."

"She's just my stepmom. My real mom is . . ."

"I don't like my stepsiblings—and I don't want them coming to my birthday party."

On the other hand, have you heard someone speak of others within their blended family in idealistic terms only to find out their family members don't speak of them in that way?

> Adult: "I love all the kids the same. There's no 'bonus kids' or 'stepkids' in this household. They're all just 'my kids.'"
>
> Child: "He's my stepdad."

What's Going On?

Language reveals so much. In these examples, the language used comments on the speaker's level of trust and connection—or desired level of connection—to the other individuals. It reveals their perception of the temperature of the relationship (see chapter 2). And it often reveals their needs as it relates to other people connected to the situation.

- A child (adult, teen, or young child) who when introducing their stepdad says, "This is my mom's husband," may be telling you that the temperature of that relationship is at least "cool" and "in development"— and perhaps that they are okay with that.
- From a triangle perspective (see chapter 2), a child's language for their stepparent is always a comment on their relationship with their biological parent of the same sex (e.g., stepdad and dad). The two are inseparable. A child's words about a stepparent might also be influenced by how their siblings feel about the stepparent.
- A parent who says, "There are no stepkids in this house," is telling you what they hope will be the case. They hope for warm and snug temperatures. They hope for healing, trusting, emotionally safe connections between stepfamily members. And in so doing, they reveal the deep-seated hope that preexisting biological relationships will have no bearing on the new step-relationships (something that is impossible).

It's important that you listen for these individual messages and what they reveal. But there's something else.

The difference in language between people also reveals the lack of shared clarity and definition in their relationship. When one person says, "There's no step-relationships in our home," and the other person says, "Oh, yes, there is," it is clear that there is no clarity in the family about who they are to one another or how they relate. "Everyone's the same in this family" may be a hopeful statement meant to bridge whatever gaps exist, but when it collides with language that acknowledges the gaps and declares them okay, conflict, cool temperatures, and entrenched hearts may result.

This gap must be reduced.

Co-Creating Familyness

Biological family relationships have the built-in luxury of non-verbal emotional and psychological connection. A newborn baby doesn't have to speak to their mom in order to be connected. Love just is. Parent-child attachment and identity just is. "You're my son and I'm your dad" doesn't have to be negotiated and decided; it's a given. A mutual, lifelong belonging, dedication, and willingness to care for each other—even if you don't like one another—just is.

Step-relationships don't have that advantage. From the outset they depend on communication. Unless people get to know one another and bring overt understanding to the nature of their relationship, trust will remain tentative and shallow. If they don't co-create shared agreement about the boundaries that will govern their relationship, the expectations they put on each other, the roles they will play in one another's lives, and the moral values that they will abide by, they may never have what we think of as a "family" relationship. Communicating about this takes time and intentional effort. While biological relationships are defined by what is (e.g., "You're my dad no matter what"), step-relationships are defined by what is communicated, negotiated, and co-created. You can't take anything for granted.

How we introduce someone to a third party says a lot about our definition of who they are to us. In addition, the term used to refer to them in everyday life says something about the relationship. For years, people have asked me what the best term is for a stepchild or stepparent to use in referring to the other or to another member of the extended family. Their question assumes there is a correct answer. There is not. It is far more important to their relationship and the developing family identity that people discuss and co-create this understanding. Determining a shared understanding of the terms they will use and why they use them can bring clarity to their ambiguous relationship. A conversation in which each party is heard, validated, and respected, and that results in a shared agreement of the terms of the relationship, moves the individuals toward familyness.

That is the purpose of this Growth Activity.

Terms and the Other Home

As you know from creating your Blended Family Map (chapter 2), some of the relational triangles of your stepfamily connect to people in another home (or to a deceased parent). The terms you negotiate for your home must be filtered through how it will impact relationships with those in the other home.

"Recently my stepdaughter called me 'Mom' for the first time and made a reference to it in her diary," shared Sandra. "Her mother read it last weekend and it created a lot of tension in both homes. My husband's ex-wife called crying and mad. She wants her daughter to call me by my first name only, but I'd prefer she call me 'Stepmom.' My stepdaughter is very much caught in the middle."[1]

I said earlier that a child's language for their stepparent is always a comment on their relationship with their biological parent of the same sex. If the child, for example, feels

70

secure in their relationship with their mother and believes she is comfortable with the child's relationship with the future stepmother, the child will feel more freedom to move emotionally toward the stepmom as soon as they are ready. (Sometimes this includes using terms of endearment for the stepmom.) But if the child is anxious about how their mom will react or perceives their mom to be jealous or in competition with the stepmom, they won't. (With very few exceptions, a child will preserve a biological parent relationship at the cost of the relationship with a stepparent.) Therefore, being aware of this dynamic for a child is critical to any conversation you may have with them. You cannot push them toward a label that makes you feel good but will jeopardize a relationship with a parent in the other home. Rather, they need your permission to respond as they see fit. But most important, they need you to take emotional care of you. Don't ask them to do that with a label.

ACTIVITY INSTRUCTIONS

1. Generally speaking, this is a Growth Activity that can include a future stepparent and stepsiblings. Co-creating something that is acceptable to everyone necessitates that. Having said that, it could be that you decide to include the stepparent but not their children or leave them all out of the initial conversation and have them join a later discussion. Proceed however you think best.

2. Depending on the ages and personalities of your kids, call a family meeting or go on a fun family outing. (You can easily have significant family discussions without the kids realizing it while fishing or hiking! And

71

side-by-side activity sometimes helps children open up because they don't have to look at you looking at them while they do it.)

3. Open the conversation with something lighthearted to avoid a serious tone.

   • For example, listen to or sing "The Name Game." Also called "The Banana Song," it was written and released by Shirley Ellis in 1964 and is a fun children's sing-along rhyming game that creates variations on a person's name. Have fun singing the names in your family.

   • Turn the corner: "That's a silly song. As we start our family, let's try to figure out what names or terms we're going to use to refer to one another."

4. Use other families you're aware of to make the point that there are many acceptable terms that people can use for stepfamily members. You should also talk around "temperatures" and the triangles kids are a part of so they will be more comfortable discussing these factors as well.

   "I've noticed that your friend Susan calls her stepdad by his first name. And your cousin Terrance calls his stepmom 'Mamma Tanisha.' My co-worker calls her stepmom 'Mom' when they are at home together, but in public she refers to her as 'Candace.' There's a lot of ways for us to do this. We're open to hearing what you would be most comfortable with.

   "But let me say this, we [indicate you're speaking for the couple] want you to know that we don't expect you to use any particular term when referring to us. You are free to use whatever label makes you comfortable as long as we agree to it as well.

"We know terms reflect how we feel about each other and that they may change over time. Whatever you feel today is how you feel—and it's okay.

"Plus, we know that you have a lot to worry about when choosing labels—things like whose feelings might get hurt or what another parent or sibling will think. Feel free to be honest with us about this stuff. Also, we know each of you [referring to different children] may have different preferences—that's okay. Just speak for yourself."

5. It's very important at this point for the children to hear the future stepparent say this:

"Please know I respect how important your relationship with your bio mom/dad is and I will never try to replace them. You only have one mom/dad in life; how you use that special term is totally up to you. If anything, I hope to be a bonus parent in your life—but that's my *role*—what you *call me* is up to us to figure out together."

6. NOTE: Children are always reading our nonverbals. If at this point yours communicate that you really aren't open to hearing their thoughts or that you really do wish they would call you Mom/Dad, then you will have defeated the point of the conversation. Check your agenda throughout the discussion.

7. Then ask these questions:[2]
   • [The biological parent might ask] "Once we are married, how would you like to be introduced to others by your stepparent? In general, should they say, 'This is my stepson/stepdaughter, or my husband's/wife's son, or something else?' What feels okay and what's weird about this?"

- "In private (e.g., in our home), what term would you like for them to use when talking to you or about you?"
- [The stepparent can now ask] "In public, how would you like to introduce me? When talking about me, what term feels most fitting?"
- "In private, what would you like to call me?"
- "What would you like to call your stepsiblings? Step-grandparents? Other family members?"
- "Now that we've decided this, when do you think these terms might be awkward (e.g., if your other parent is present)? What term would you like to fall back to at that point?"
- "We suspect that for all of us, these decisions will change at some point. Don't hesitate to let us know if you want to make a change. Can you imagine a time when we might start using different terms for one another?"
- "If your dad/mom were here (biological parent living in another home), what part of our decisions tonight would you be comfortable sharing with them? What part would be tough to share?"

8. Once the meeting is over, if you are co-parenting with your kids' other biological parent(s), you have a decision to make: Do you communicate to the parent(s) what you have decided?

   First, it's wise to check in with your child before doing so. How a child responded to the last question of item 7 above may help you decide how to proceed. Their response will also tell you something about what the child is having to do to manage this critical triangle of relationships.

In the best-case scenario, everyone agrees that telling the other home what your home has decided will add even more clarity to the uncertain nature of new stepfamily relationships and between-home relationships. In the worst-case scenario, a child demonstrates great emotional distress or panic over the idea—and it's clear that at this point, you shouldn't communicate what you've discussed. Most people fall somewhere in the middle.

The main objective is not to inform the other biological parent what specific terms will be used. The objective, rather, is to help the other parent understand the process your home went through to co-create language that is mutually agreeable, and for them to know that both the children and they were respected in the process. Learning, for example, that the children were not forced into using any terms brings a sense of peace to the outcome. And imagine a biological mother, for example, learning from her former husband that during the meeting, his fiancée (the stepmom-to-be) told the kids that she will always respect their mother, will protect their relationship with her, and fully expects them to reserve the term "Mom" just for their biological mother. That "no-threat" message has the potential to lower the biological mother's anxiety about the future stepmom because it communicates that the stepmom is not competing with the mother and that she knows the limits of her place in the children's lives.[3]

A sample phone call might sound something like this: "Hey, I just wanted to let you know that we had a conversation the other day while hiking about what terms we will use for one another after the wedding. To honor you, we made sure the kids knew we don't expect them to use the term *Mom/Dad*. In fact, we told them we were comfortable with many different labels depending on the context, and that we just needed to figure it out together. So we talked awhile, and David, Rebecca, and Teague all decided they are going to call my wife by her first name at home, but in public, David and Rebecca will introduce her as their stepmom; Teague, on the other hand, wants to call her his bonus mom.

"I'm telling you this because we know it affects you too. All the kids know I'm talking to you about this so you can speak with them about it if you want. Do you have any questions?"

Keep in mind while doing this Activity that what's more important than the terms negotiated is the co-creation of familyness that is happening in the process. Deciding how to introduce a stepparent to a teacher at school is one practical outcome; communicating openly about the ambiguity in your relationship and learning to trust one another even as you define how you will move forward as family is what you're really after.

Starting your family with intentional conversations around ambiguous and sometimes awkward topics likely means you can have more of them in the future. And with each conversation, you further define—and strengthen—familyness.

Additional Thoughts about Terms: A Rose by Any Other Name

Future stepparent, if a child uses a term of endearment for you sooner than you are prepared for, don't ask them to stop unless you have a significant concern (e.g., the biological parent in the other home will denigrate the child). The biological parent should be the one to ask the child not to. Otherwise, if a child wants to call a stepmother Mom, let them! (Even more, be thankful and enjoy it!) Out of an abundance of caution, some future stepparents have thought it best to reserve that term only for the mother, but a child who feels that drawn to you will likely feel rejected by your refusal. Besides, the whole point of co-creating definition in your relationship is empowering children, not controlling them. Most kids are good at measuring their loyalties and comfort zones. Trust them to do so.

As relationships grow and circumstances change, so will labels. A child who returns from weekend visitation with his father may refrain from calling his stepfather "Dad" for a few days. Leaving his dad heightens the child's sadness and, perhaps, guilt for referring to his stepdad with that special term. After a few days when the sadness wanes, the child may again call the stepfather "Dad" or something similar. Other children may use a term of endearment for a stepparent

Permission Denied!

Question: "My ex-husband makes our son feel guilty for calling my husband 'Dad.' How should I respond?"

Answer: I wish that your son were free to decide what label he uses for his stepdad. His father's feelings will surely impact his decision. If your son stops calling his stepdad "Dad," don't make him feel guilty or pressure him to start again. This creates a no-win emotional situation for your son. Further, your husband should strive not to take this personally. This isn't about him.

Some kids find a way around this, for example, by only using the term "Dad" when his biological father is not around. Tell him, "I know you are in a tight spot between your dad and your stepfather. Please know that whatever name you want to use is okay with us. The real joy here is you, not the labels."

77

(e.g., "Mamma Sara") unless the biological parent is physically present. Changing the label protects the biological parent's feelings.

A child's age can also be a factor in the name game. Very young children tend to use loving terms like "Daddy" and "Mommy" very quickly, but then may back away from them once they get older. The label change is often indicative of the child's greater sensitivity to loyalty issues or emotional changes in the relational triangle.

Please understand that the labels your children use are not crucial to your family's success. Co-creating relationship definition and bringing clarity to your ambiguity is what moves you toward becoming family. Labels are just labels. Love in the heart is what counts. A rose by any other name is still a rose.[4]

POST-ACTIVITY QUESTIONS FOR REFLECTION

After the family meeting, talk as a couple about what you heard from the kids. Have additional family discussions or one-on-one conversations as needed. In subsequent discussions you might explore how it has felt so far putting your decisions into practice by asking questions like these:

- "The other day I called you my stepson again. I know we decided that was okay, but now that I'm doing it, how does that feel?"
- "Are you having any second thoughts about what we decided last week? Is there a term or phrase that feels weird to say?"
- "Have you thought of something else we didn't talk about?"

1. Now that you know how to have a conversation defining labels, have the same conversation with your parents, extended family, and friends when you can. They are probably unsure whether to refer to you as a stepparent or bonus parent too, and themselves as stepgrandparent or "Pa Pa."

2. Should you call yourself a blended family or a stepfamily? Does it matter? Learn how this question parallels the focus of this chapter at www.smartstepfamilies.com/talking-blended.

3. Read more about how labels impact the loyalty conflicts children experience at www.smartstepfamilies.com/caught-in-the-middle.

6

PARENTING TOGETHER

All parenting teams disagree from time to time. Biological parents in first marriages disagree, and so do parent-stepparent couples and co-parents in blended families. Sometimes they fiercely disagree until they find a way to work through it. Whether the issue centers around an adult child who needs support, a teenager and their smartphone, or how you will divide responsibilities for the care of a newborn, disagreement is to be expected. But when parent and stepparent disagreement results in ongoing gridlock, conflict, and isolation, two predictable things happen: the marriage suffers and the family slows—sometimes stops—merging.

I wish I were overstating this, but nearly three decades of experience and research tells me I'm not. Occasionally a couple will ask if they can have two different parenting styles in one household. "We've each been raising our kids very differently and they're used to that. Can't we just continue parenting as we have?" "You can," I reply, "but your family will remain relationally separate—outsiders will remain outsiders—and there may be power games, kids caught in the middle, and resentment in your home."

If that's not what you want, you must take this chapter and your journey toward unity in parenting seriously. To be divided in parenting is to keep your family divided.

I've been making this point for decades, and still most couples ignore it; before marriage, they don't proactively work toward a common approach to parenting and don't plan for how the stepparent's role will differ from the biological parent's role. In our book *The Smart Stepfamily Marriage*, David Olson and I report on our study of couples creating stepfamilies. Taken in 2006, this is still the largest survey ever conducted of couples forming stepfamilies (with some follow-up analysis as well). Our book reports on what best predicts distressed and healthy stepcouple relationships and how you can strengthen your blended family marriage. (Consider it a great follow-up read after finishing this book.) As it relates to this chapter, we found that 41 percent of what contributes to a husband's satisfaction level in the marriage and close to half (46 percent) of the wife's satisfaction is strongly correlated to stepfamily adjustment and parenting issues. We also found that parenting matters cause increasing marital conflict over time unless the couple is working from a posture of unity.[1] And yet, the average couple doesn't spend focused time discussing these topics. Only about half of premarital stepcouples discuss issues related to child rearing as they prepare to form a stepfamily.[2]

This doesn't serve your future well. Some couples think talking about potentially divisive topics will slow their progress toward marriage. Some naïvely assume, as I discussed in chapter 3, that love will conquer all. Neither is true. David Olson and I found that compared to struggling stepcouples, happy couples were 1.5 times more likely before marriage to have discussed and agreed on how they will parent together after the wedding, nearly twice as likely to have agreed on how they will discipline their children, and twice as likely to have negotiated their religious expectations for the home.[3] Not having these conversations leaves your relationship vulnerable.

Now, let me close by saying this: If your parenting discussions result in some changes, don't make all the changes at once. If you do, your kids may experience expectation whiplash and behavioral confusion. Carefully talk through changes that will result in more unity and work into them slowly, one step at a time.

A Vision for Healthy Parenting in Blended Families

A complete guide for good parenting is beyond the scope of this book. I have written two specific books about this topic that I would recommend to you. *The Smart Stepmom* and *The Smart Stepdad* are written for stepparents and have chapters for biological parents to help you with the details of parenting and co-parenting in a blended family. In addition, my book *The Smart Stepfamily* and the revised and updated edition of my video series *The Smart Stepfamily DVD* (now available for streaming online) provide a comprehensive examination of every aspect of stepfamily living, including multiple layers of parenting and co-parenting, in order to equip you for the long journey. (I also contributed to another parenting resource that is worth watching, FamilyLife's *Art of Parenting* video series.) But I can lay out for you here, in brief, a vision of what is involved in smart stepfamily parenting. Like a syllabus for a college course, the below key aspects of parenting represent topics of study that will enrich your family journey. The Activity in this chapter will then invite you to step into a few of them as you begin to negotiate how you will parent together. If you get stuck, I suggest you consult one of the previously mentioned resources for a more thorough examination of parenting in a stepfamily.

Learn about good parenting.

Knowing principles of good parenting is a must. There is a multitude of books, resources, and courses available to help you learn the basics of raising children. Every parent needs a toolbox full of parenting skills, tools, and strategies to draw on as they walk with children over time. You also need to learn about yourself, what triggers reactivity in you, and how you can cope with it. Our love for our children and desire that they experience good things in life makes us vulnerable to their immature decisions and actions. Emotional dysregulation when a child rebels, for example, results in parents tossing their own parenting philosophy out the window, overreacting, resorting to shaming tactics to control a child, and a multitude of other coping strategies that hinder the parent-child relationship and train children to walk in shame and fear. Knowing how to emotionally regulate yourself—that is, having self-control—is one of your most important tools in parenting.

Learn about good parenting in blended families.

Most, if not all, resources on good parenting assume a parenting system comprised of two biological parents. Be careful in how you apply them. Blended families, when you include all the parenting authorities from each home, have multiple people and multiple intersecting dynamics that these resources do not address or take into consideration. Before you can apply their parenting advice, you must lace in an understanding of stepfamily realities.

You will learn about some of these underlying dynamics in the section that follows, but let me give you one example. Many good biological parents find becoming a stepparent confusing and exasperating. The relational equity that they held with their own children isn't a given in their developing relationship

84

with stepchildren, so their ability to guide, influence, and punish is frustrated. Add to that the dynamic forces of living in the shadow of a deceased parent or having a biological parent in the other home undercut their position in the family, and stepparents can feel powerless very quickly. An ambiguous role in a child's life does not allow parents to implement the good parenting advice found in many books (remember, most parenting advice is meant for parents in a two-parent biological family). What is needed is an understanding of stepparent-child bonding, how stepparents evolve their relationship with stepchildren over time, loyalty conflicts in children, stepfamily development, and the role of the biological parent (spouse) in creating an environment of respect for stepparents (discussed in part below).

Study good co-parenting across households.

Have you ever wondered what it would be like to be the ambassador from the United States to one of our arch enemies? The hostile, sometimes war-infused nature of the countries' interaction would make negotiation and mutual respect difficult, if not near impossible. Well, if you are a co-parent and have an angry, embittered relationship with your child's other home, you are in just that position.

Co-parenting has the goal of working with the adults of your child's other home in order to raise the child well. If the climate of your co-parent relationship is generally cooperative, you will find that goal much easier to accomplish. If it is fiery, unworkable, or unreliable, you will not. Commit yourself to learning as much as you can about effective co-parenting and to gaining skills that will aid your between-home cooperation. Here are a few guidelines from my book *The Smart Stepfamily: 7 Steps to a Healthy Family.*[4]

1. Work hard to respect the other parent and his or her household. Agree that each parent has a right to privacy, and do not intrude in his or her life. Do not demean the other's living circumstances, activities, dates, or decisions, and give up the need to control your ex's parenting style.

2. Schedule a regular (weekly to monthly) "business" meeting to discuss co-parenting matters. You can address schedules, academic reports, behavioral training, and spiritual development. If you cannot talk with your ex face-to-face due to conflict, use instant messaging, email, or text. Do what you can to make your meetings productive for the children.

3. Never ask your children to be spies or tattletales on the other home. This places them in a loyalty bind that brings great emotional distress. Celebrate the positive relationships they have with those in their other home.

4. When children have confusing or angry feelings toward your ex, don't capitalize on their hurt and berate the other parent. Listen and help them explore their feelings without trying to sway their opinions with your own. If you can't make positive statements about the other parent, strive for neutral ones.

5. Children should have everything they need in each home. Don't make them bring basic necessities back and forth. Special items, like a specific shirt or a smartphone, can move back and forth as needed.

6. Try to release your hostility toward the other parent so that the children can't take advantage of your hard feelings. Manipulation is much easier when former spouses harbor resentment toward each other.

7. Do not disappoint your children with broken promises or by being unreliable. Do what you say, keep your visitation schedule as agreed, and stay active in their lives.

8. Make your custody structure work for your children even if you don't like the details of the arrangement. Update the other when changes need to be made to the visitation schedule. Also, inform the other parent of any change in job, living arrangements, etc., that may require an adjustment by the children.

9. Help children adjust when going to the other home:
   - If the children will go on vacation while in the other home, find out what's on the agenda. You can help your kids pack special items and needed clothing.
   - Provide the other home with information regarding your child's changes. A switch in preferences (regarding music, clothes, hairstyles, foods, etc.) or physical, cognitive, or emotional developments can be significant. Let the other home know what is different before the child arrives.
   - When receiving children, give them time to unpack, relax, and settle in. Try not to overwhelm them at first with plans, rules, or even special treatment. Let them work their way in at their own pace.

10. If you and your ex cannot resolve a problem, agree to problem-solving through mediation rather than litigation.

Teamwork

Let's turn our attention to how you will parent in your home. All good parenting involves teamwork. In blended families, the biological parent and stepparent must work hard to find their harmony, to support one another, and to play to one another's strengths. As you prepare to blend, here are five keys to becoming a good team.

Key 1: Biological Parents Must Be the Parent

Before championing the stepparent's role, the biological parent must first function consistently in the role of primary parent. Hopefully you are doing this now, because you have to continue doing so after the wedding, especially around matters of nurturance, affection, and punishment. Until the stepparent has had time to develop a bond with the kids and earn respect as an authority, you need to clearly be the authority. Look at it from your kids' perspective: You are the safest, most well-defined parent figure in their life. Be that parent.

Here's the problem for those of you who haven't been *that parent*. Making the change to become the primary nurturer and manager of their behavior may be met with resentment from your kids and a blaming of the stepparent even though it isn't their doing. Let's say, for example, that during the single-parent years, you lowered your behavioral expectations, and your children got used to not obeying. Raising your expectations now will likely result in some conflict in your new family. Nevertheless, you need to do what you must to become *that parent* because you have the leadership authority to raise the standard (the stepparent does not). Find the courage to lead.[5]

Key 2: Biological Parents Must Pass Authority to Stepparents

One challenge to stepparenting is developing a relationship with a stepchild that affords the stepparent the needed authority to follow through with rules and impose consequences for disobedience.[6] Until such a relationship is built and trust between stepparent and child established, how does a stepparent

88

function as a parental authority? They must live on borrowed power from the biological parent.[7]

Parents pass authority to the stepparent when they make it clear to their children that the stepparent is an extension of their authority. Saying something like, "I know he is not your dad, but when I am not here, he will be enforcing the household rules he and I have agreed on. I expect you to be courteous and respect him as you would any authority figure," communicates your expectations clearly. Be sure to then back up the stepparent just like you would a baby-sitter or your child's teacher at school.

Key 3: Biological Parents Should Build Trust in Stepparents

One of the greatest barriers to entrusting your children to your spouse is a fundamental lack of trust in the stepparent's intentions. In a two-parent biological home, couples don't seem to question the motives of their spouse. They may not agree with the specific parenting decisions of their spouse, but they don't question their spouse's love or commitment to the child. Parents generally assume the best about the other biological parent's motives. Stepparents are not always granted that same benefit of the doubt.

Zachary loved his wife, Brianna, very much, but he just wasn't sure why she was critical of his two daughters. Brianna complained that Zachary was too easy on them and she feared they would grow up to be "spoiled, boy-chasing girls." Zachary believed that Brianna's real problem was jealousy; he interpreted her criticism of the girls as her attempt to step between Zachary and his daughters. Therefore, he ignored her input and discounted her efforts at discipline.

In order to give your spouse the benefit of the doubt, you must force yourself to trust their motives. Sometimes stepparents *are* jealous, but that doesn't mean they are mean-spirited toward your children. If you don't strive for trust, you'll continually defend your children, even when ill-advised. Your children will learn that obeying the stepparent is optional (since you'll stick up for your children), and your spouse will truly grow to resent your children. Open yourself to the stepparent's input and trust her heart. Talk, listen, and negotiate.

Zachary and Brianna's story illustrates another point. It is very common the world over, says stepfamily expert Patricia Papernow, for stepparents like Brianna to want more limits and boundaries with their stepchildren and for biological parents like Zachary to lean toward understanding and mercy for their children.[8] This is as natural as grandparents wanting to—and feeling the right to—spoil their grandchildren. Each parent must find their way toward the middle. It doesn't help things when parents label the other as *permissive* or *strict*; that just creates defensiveness in the other and closes your mind to their perspective. Consider the other's point of view and resist the temptation to polarize toward the opposite end of the love/limits spectrum.

Key 4: Stepparents Should Move into Relationship and Discipline Gradually

Since authority is based on relationship and trust with the child, stepparents should move gradually into relationship first, then discipline. Good parenting, you may have read, involves a balance of love and warmth on one hand and firm boundaries and correction on the other (what is generally referred to as "authoritative" parenting). To start your family off well, it is crucial that the biological parent reflect both ends of this continuum and the stepparent focus almost exclusively on warmth and relationship building. (Some stepparents will need to remain on this end of the continuum indefinitely.) To be more specific, it is very important that limits and boundary setting come from the biological parent.

Researcher James Bray says one of the most important step-parenting skills is *monitoring the children's activities.*[9] The focus of monitoring is strengthening the relationship with the child. It involves knowing their daily routines, where the children are, who they are with, and what extracurricular activities they are involved in, but does not necessarily include being involved in the child's emotional life. It is parenting that is sensitive to the pace of the child, not pushing too hard for closeness, but continually being an active presence in the child's life in order to allow for relationship to grow. Monitoring stepparents check homework and daily chores and befriend stepchildren yet refrain from emotional closeness that is unwelcome to the child. Bottom line: Good stepparents listen to the child's level of openness, and they keep trying to nurture a relationship with their stepchildren, even if they are rejected again and again. They are persistent and gracious. And in the end, much of the time, a connection is created that is beneficial to the child, the stepparent, and the marriage.

Once a stronger bond is built between stepparent and stepchild, a natural authority to teach, train, and discipline begins to grow. There are two kinds of authority: positional authority and relational authority. Positional authority is what your boss at work has over you, and it's what a teacher has in the classroom. Their position in that context gives them authority. Relational authority is much more influential—and difficult to obtain—because it is based on trust. Caring about your boss's evaluation because you're hoping for a raise is one thing; caring about her opinion because as friends you have come to respect her is another.

Stepparents come into the stepfamily with positional authority. That is, because they are an adult, they are afforded some authority as is any adult, teacher, or neighbor. When children come to care about the stepparent as a person and

91

value their relationship with them, then a stepparent has gained relational authority. Initially, positional authority is dependent upon the biological parent's backing; relational authority stands on its own. Obviously, relational authority is an attractive goal for stepparents, but it must be earned the old-fashioned way—you have to earn it by nurturing a relationship with the child. A stepparent who walks into a family claiming the rights of relational authority without having earned them frequently finds resistance from children (or at least one child) and resentment from their spouse for being heavy-handed.

A child's trust, respect, and honor grow out of a relational history with a stepparent that comes with time and positive experiences. Successful stepparents are dedicated to relationship building over the long haul and don't try to force their way into the child's heart. They also understand the limitations of positional authority in the first few years of the stepfamily and rely heavily on the biological parent to manage the children until their own relational influence grows.[10]

Helen called to complain about her husband's parenting of her son. "Larry's not abusive, but he will always say no to whatever Brandon asks, and when he walks in the room, Larry tells him to do chores or some task. He doesn't make conversation with Brandon, relax, or open up to him. I feel like I am always running defense for my son, and it is the biggest cause of fights in our marriage." Larry was critical and nonaccepting of his stepson, and it was pushing both his stepson and wife further away. Larry needed to learn ways of connecting with his stepson. Lightening up, being humble and willing to engage Brandon in his interests, sharing his own talents and skills with Brandon, complimenting him, and showing appreciation for how he contributes to the home are just a few ideas he could implement.[11]

Key 5: Align Your Parenting Strategies

I started the chapter by saying you cannot have two vastly different parenting strategies in your home. Aligning your parenting is a significant aspect of your family merger. By the way, if your children are adults, this principle still applies. No, you aren't directly responsible for their behavior, but you are still influencing and mentoring them, and the boundaries and expectations around emotional closeness and your involvement in their lives are still being played out every day. All these aspects of parenting need to be brought in alignment with adult children too.

I've decided there are many good ways to parent children. Good parenting tactics are one element of parenting, but what matters just as much (or more) is that you decide together how you will parent. Unity is vital. As was said earlier, reading good books on parenting and discussing the principles will help move you toward a common parenting posture. You can also watch other parents and learn from them, invite an older couple with a solid track record to mentor you, or attend formal classes on the subject. Over time I suggest you do all of the above, but you might as well start now.

The following Activity is designed to start you on the journey of finding unity. Don't rush through it. Let each part surface what needs to be discussed. Your goal is to co-create a plan for how you will move forward *together* as parents. This is not your definitive plan for all time! It's just a starting point. Beginning to walk out your plan will inevitably bring about revisions. Let life teach you what you need to change. Just get started. Can you begin to implement some of your strategies now, even before the wedding? Yes, absolutely. Test it out, knowing that what you discover will inform and help revise how you move forward after the wedding (when life gets very real for everyone).

ACTIVITY INSTRUCTIONS

Use the following questions to learn more about your current parenting practices and each other's ideal parenting philosophy while co-creating a plan of how you will parent together. You will not be able to work through these questions in one sitting; rather, pace yourself with a series of conversations. Some questions will open big topics that may last awhile. If you are talking with a mentor or pastor on a regular schedule, discuss as many as you can between meetings, then, if needed, continue your parenting dialogue even after moving on to subsequent chapters.

1. If you are a biological parent, what's one aspect of your parenting that you're working on and why?

2. Say out loud or write in just a few sentences your basic philosophy of parenting as it relates to each of these subtopics (consider the developmental ages of your children):

   a. Teaching spiritual values and beliefs

   b. Expressing love to a child

   c. Motivating children toward responsibility

   d. Punishment for misbehavior

   e. Being friends with your children versus being an authority figure

3. How did your parent(s) handle these aspects when you were growing up? How is your style similar or different from theirs and why?

   Discussing how you were parented as a child is important. We know that most people get their practical parent training from how they were parented. Couples who were parented similarly find it easier to come

94

together around their parenting philosophy and practices. In our research, 82 percent of all couples acknowledge they were parented differently by their parents as a
child, but those who were parented similarly were 11.5
times more likely to have higher quality couple relationships.[12] So explore your history openly. Being parented
differently as children likely means you will need to be
very intentional to bring your stepfamily practices in
line. Also, as you explore these questions, go back to
your Blended Family Map (chapter 2) and indicate how
each parent (stepparent, grandparent, and any authority figure in your childhood) parented you and your
siblings. Tell each other two sets of stories: Ones that
symbolize the everyday parenting you received (and how
you felt about it) and stories about the extreme moments you experienced. This last group of stories might
be difficult to tell, but include them, as they often leave
a residue of either joy or pain on our hearts.

4. Review the following descriptions of parenting styles.[13]
   Which best describes your childhood parents/authori-
   ties? Which best describes your parenting style over
   the past few years? If you have a co-parent, which best
   describes their parenting style? Again, it might be helpful to record these labels on your Blended Family Map
   for easy future reference. You can also note how children respond(ed) to that form of parenting; this may
   help you notice patterns between homes and across
   generations.

   a. Democratic Parenting. Sometimes referred to as
      authoritative, these parents establish clear rules
      and expectations and discuss them with the child.
      Although they acknowledge the child's perspective,

they use both reason and power to enforce their standards. They balance being emotionally connected with their child (having solid, loving relationships) and being flexible (providing structure, clear expectations, and limits). When behavioral lines are crossed, children are firmly admonished, but love remains. This combination of emotional warmth and boundaries brings out the best in children. (A quick note: as discussed above, initially in a blended family the biological parent should be the one setting boundaries and enforcing consequences when boundaries are violated.)

b. Authoritarian Parenting. These parents have more rigid rules and expectations and strictly enforce them. They expect and demand obedience from their children. The authoritarian style is characterized by very structured parenting while closeness and loyalty to the family are highly demanded. (A quick note: In general, authoritarian parenting by stepparents in the first few years is toxic to stepparent-stepchild relationships and should be avoided.)

c. Permissive Parenting. These parents let the child's preferences take priority over their ideals, and rarely force the child to conform to reasonable behavioral standards. Expectations and rules are chaotic at times and easily manipulated because these parents prefer to keep the peace with their children. A warm, affectionate friendship with the children is the parent's most important priority.

d. Rejecting Parenting. These parents do not pay much attention to their child's emotional needs but have high expectations regarding how the child should behave. These families have little emotional connection; children are not sure they are loved due to the parents' disengaged style. An environment with high expectations and little emotional support creates children who feel they aren't good enough; failure comes with great insecurity and shows itself in low self-esteem, immaturity, and a variety of psychological problems.

   e. Uninvolved Parenting. Also called neglectful parenting, these parents often ignore children, letting the child's preferences prevail as long as they do not interfere with the parents' activities. Like the rejecting parent, uninvolved parents are emotionally disengaged, but they don't have rigid rules or expectations. Rather, they are overly flexible in their structure, leaving the child alone without consistent boundaries.

5. Which of these forms of correction have you/would you utilize? How frequently? Give an example. If there is a co-parent, which do they frequently utilize? NOTE: Just because a strategy is listed does not mean it is a recommended form of correction.

   a. Explaining or talking to a child about their misbehavior and how it affects others

   b. Spanking, slapping, or swatting (corporal punishment)

   c. Discussing right and wrong/appealing to the heart

   d. Yelling

   e. Criticizing the child

   f. Ignoring misbehavior

   g. Reviewing rules and codes of conduct

   h. Demeaning or shaming the child

    i. Lecture

    j. Making the child feel guilty

    k. Coaching (e.g., helping a child apologize to a sibling or decide how to cope with a friend in need)

    l. Counting to give them time to correct behavior

  m. Time-out

    n. Giving extra chores

    o. Taking away objects (e.g., toys) or privileges (e.g., going to bed without a meal or taking the car keys)

    p. Withholding love or yourself from the child

    q. Natural consequences (e.g., if a child forgets their lunch they go without)

    r. Logical consequences (e.g., if you spill your milk, you clean it up)

    s. Rewarding improved behavior

    t. Other: What additional strategies do you/might you utilize?

6. Discuss why it's important to "catch kids doing something right," that is, pay attention to good or respectful behavior and applaud it. How often should this strategy be utilized, in your opinion?[14]

7. On a scale of 1–10, how good are you at:

    a. Managing your anger toward a child, especially when feeling disrespected or ignored?

    b. Following through on what you said you would do?

    c. Looking for improved behavior?

    d. Helping children know what is expected?

    e. Listening to your child when they feel a rule is unfair or something needs to change?

f. Separating a child's behavior from your identity? For example, not feeling personally embarrassed by poor or unwise behavior?

g. Not being manipulated by guilt trips or a child's sadness?

h. Encouraging a child, building them up?

8. On a scale of 1–10, how well would your children say you remain self-controlled and calm when they misbehave? What do you need to improve to emotionally regulate yourself better in these moments?

9. In general, would you rather tell a child what to do or help them make a decision for themselves? Explain why.

10. What are your boundaries around money and the use of family assets? How and when do you share money with children?

11. What responsibilities do you expect children to have as they grow (e.g., chores)? How should they contribute to the home and the family?

12. What are your ideal behavioral boundaries and expectations for smartphones, the internet, social media, and screen entertainment?

13. Hot topics: What current behavioral matters are you concerned about? What can you anticipate in the months/years ahead?

14. Discuss these common mistakes of biological parents and stepparents. Which have you made already? Which might you be vulnerable to make in the future?

a. Common Biological Parent Mistakes

• During the single-parent years, becoming soft with expectations and/or not following through with discipline.

- Refusing to do the hard things of parenting (e.g., taking the lead in punishment or telling a child no). This creates a gap in the home that stepparents try to fill before they have enough relational equity, which usually increases family conflict and sabotages the stepparent.
- Not trusting the stepparent's heart for the children.
- Not making space in parenting decisions to include the new stepparent (leaving them out).
- Becoming easily defensive or dismissive when the stepparent makes suggestions or questions a parenting decision or pattern.
- Allowing past pain and hurt with a former spouse to sabotage your co-parenting cooperation.
- Going behind the stepparent and undermining their involvement.

b. Common Stepparent Mistakes

- Acting like you're trying to replace their biological mom/dad (whether living in another home or deceased).
- Expecting children to embrace you without hesitation.
- Not making fun a priority.
- Expecting children to immediately accept the stepparent's authority at the same level as a biological parent. Not growing into your role.
- Taking a child's hesitation to accept you as rejection (it's often just confusion about where to put you in their heart).

100

- Making unilateral decisions without the biological parent's agreement.
- Expecting to make right the "wrongs" that exist in the biological parent or the routines/patterns of the household (e.g., changing foods or birthday traditions to suit your preferences).
- Being harsh, temperamental, or cold with stepchildren.
- Not allowing the children to spend time occasionally with their parent (your spouse) without you. In the beginning, children need reassurance they still have access to their parent and some things will remain the same.
- Speaking poorly of the child's other household in front of them.

15. If your children move between homes, what co-parent dynamics/patterns are you currently facing?

   a. Which movie title best describes your current co-parenting relationship (e.g., *Die Hard, Jaws, Singin' in the Rain*, or something else)?

   b. What are the parenting rules or values of the other home that stand in contrast to yours, and how do you cope with them?

   c. To what degree do your children get caught in the middle of conflict between homes?

   d. What leftover hurts interfere with cooperative co-parenting?

   e. Future stepparent: What observations or questions do you have about your fiancé's co-parenting situation?

POST-ACTIVITY QUESTIONS FOR REFLECTION

1. Based on your discussion so far, say or write a few sentences about what you've learned about how you will parent together. What is your plan? What needs to change and who needs to own the change?

2. Begin to implement some of what you've discussed (even before the wedding). Children should be told *by the biological parent* about significant changes before they begin.

TRY THIS

- Listen to episodes of my FamilyLife Blended podcast addressing stepparenting, co-parenting, between-home transitions, and navigating the holidays, and discuss the key principles you hear. Use these podcasts over time as a catalyst to conversations that move you toward oneness in parenting.

- For more strategic ideas for bonding emotionally with stepchildren, read my book *Building Love Together in Blended Families: The 5 Love Languages and Becoming Stepfamily Smart,* co-authored with Dr. Gary Chapman (Northfield Publishing, 2020), and take the Love Languages Profiles, modified for blended families, in the book.

7

CREATING A SHARED
GRIEF JOURNEY

Your wedding is about your family's future. So why do we need to step back into the losses of the past? In most chapters to this point, we've been thinking forward as we examined relational expectations, planning the wedding, introductions and bringing definition to family relationships, and parenting together. But it's time to reflect again on your Blended Family Map (created in chapter 2) and take note of who has a place in your family story but is not living in your home. Blended Family Maps create a present-day snapshot of an intergenerational family narrative, but you cannot fully understand the present without tying it to the past. Said another way, you and your children must occasionally step back into the past so you can understand it and, in some cases, grieve it, because it is always a part of your present and future.

People on your Blended Family Map who are absent from your home today (e.g., a parent) represent a plot line of your family story that is carried into the present. Their map icon symbolizes positive memories and emotions like love, comfort, belonging, stability, trust, and peace, as well as hard realities like conflict, hurt, betrayal, cancer, anger, uncertainty, pain, tragedy, financial distress, and broken dreams. That one little icon represents every joy and longing, comfort and pain—and everything that led up to their departure and what has happened since. Likewise, the addition of new people to the Blended Family Map again points back to the original loss (i.e., what happened that made their presence possible) and brings new losses and transitions to the family in the present (e.g., changes in family roles and routines, parenting, living conditions, social network, etc.). I find that many stepfamily adults want to run from this reality. For example, they want to pretend that a deceased parent will not impact the role of a stepparent in the home or that a fiancé's former spouse's values and lifestyle will not affect parenting decisions in the new blended family home. Not true. You cannot avoid these realities, nor should you. To attempt to blend your families without acknowledging loss or the presence of the past is to remain blind and disconnected from one another. You cannot truly love one another and ignore this elephant in the room.

My goal in this chapter is to foster both individual and family grieving. You will not complete it—you never finish grieving significant losses—but you can grieve forward, *together*. Even more, family grieving not only helps individuals reposition the past and carry it with them in healthy ways, but it fosters emotional bonding between new stepfamily members.

Each person has their distinctive individual grief journey. Most of us seem to be aware of that. But far less recognized is a family's grief journey. For example, a biological parent and their children have a collective journey following a death or divorce. It may come in the form of conversations around what has changed, what it means, and how they are going to cope. It may come in the form of hugs and shared tears. It may come in the form of mutual indignation and frustration with God and each other. And it may require shifts in chores or responsibilities around the house, economic adjustments, new ways of caring for each other, and different living conditions.

Some families do this well. Others have never grieved together at all, only separately. They grieve in isolation from one another. Whichever the case, I want to help you and your children grieve with more intentionality—and now add others to the collective grief dialogue, namely stepparents, so children experience them as caring, compassionate friends with whom they are emotionally safe.

Just consider the alternative. When a stepparent lacks sympathy for a child's sadness, it may harden the child's heart toward the stepparent. Without saying a word, a stepparent's coldness communicates messages like, "Your dad is dead; I'm your new dad now," or "Aren't you over this yet? Your loss isn't a big deal," all of which thicken a child's loyalty to the person or reality they are grieving (e.g., a deceased parent or the idea of their parents still together) and increase their rejection of the stepparent. Stepping on a child's grief is for some stepparents a mortal sin from which they never recover, but the opposite is also true. A stepparent who compassionately enters a child's grief, gives permission to it, and by their willingness to grieve with the child, sends the message, "You should grieve your father; I respect that and will help you," or, "I understand you grieving that your parents aren't together anymore; I can give you space to wrestle with that." Besides helping the child, this has the added benefit of fostering bonding between stepparents and children and furthering the "cooking" process of the entire family unit. When new people and old ones become safe harbors for one another, respect develops and familyness deepens.

Earthquakes and Aftershocks

I know a lot about grief and family grieving. Unfortunately, I've been there and am doing that. In February of 2009, my wife, Nan, and I went to see the movie *Taken*. The movie is about a father whose daughter is abducted—that is, taken—for sex trafficking. After the movie, we returned home to find our middle son, Connor, complaining of a headache. Little did we know that at that very hour, Connor was being taken. A MRSA staph infection had contaminated his body and was systematically destroying his lungs. Over the next ten days we rode the roller coaster of hope and fear until finally descending into the valley of the shadow of death. Connor was gone from this life. Taken.

There is no recovery from this. There is only surviving and trusting God for enough grace to get through (which he has graciously provided). For Nan, me, and our other two sons, life is forever changed.*

At first after a monumental loss like this, life stops. Completely. You are in a fog, a daze of disbelief and overwhelming sorrow. You can't imagine going on. For what? How? Why? I didn't seem to care about anything. Everything was trivial at that point and our grief was all-consuming. Questions filled my mind. *What do I do with this hole in my heart? How do I love my wife and other boys? How do we grieve together? We have different emotions, intensities, needs to talk or be silent, questions, and perspectives on what happened and God's place in the situation.*

And then life forces you to start living again, but you don't know how. I had to go back to work. Our boys had to return to school. We still had responsibilities that wouldn't go away;

---

*Hear Ron and Nan recount their story of loss, grief, and their journey to find grace on this podcast: www.familylife.com/podcast/series/connors-song.

birthdays, holidays, and anniversaries we couldn't celebrate; and spiritual rituals that seemed powerless and lifeless.

As life moves ahead, the questions persist. *Where was God? Where is he now? What good is prayer? How do I love my family when I don't care about anything? How do I parent when I'm so distracted? How do I cope with the varied reactions from others—some of whom are angels of mercy and others just plain stupid and without compassion. And how do I be around people who are shallow and hollow in their perspective about life—people with "normal" complaints that I, too, once had, but now I find petty and ridiculous?* Questions, questions, questions. Pain, pain, pain. It's inescapable and completely overwhelming.

Loss of this magnitude is not a onetime event. It starts with the original earthquake and is then followed by a series of ongoing aftershocks that add to the destruction. Aftershocks that may continue for years and years—or a lifetime.

I think you, too, have had a similar journey. Yes, the specifics of your grief journey are different, but maybe you and your kids can relate to the process. First came the death, divorce, or breakup, and then come the aftershocks:

- A lost sense of self, identity, and struggles with your self-worth.
- Fun family rituals, like a pizza and movies on Friday nights, become hollow, empty reminders of what was but isn't anymore.
- A loss of social belonging: Friends or family members who won't engage you as they did before or church members who treat you differently.
- Feeling helpless to help your children wrestle with their grief and the realities of what is happening.

- Worrying that your kids will doubt God, when you yourself doubt him.
- Financial struggles.
- Changes in parenting, values between homes, and not knowing how to respond.

This list likely goes on and on. Without much effort you can probably list five to ten aftershocks that you're dealing with right now. Yes, in many ways, the impact of the original earthquake has subsided in intensity and you've gotten back to life, but the residue of dust still coats your heart and relationships.

Just a few minutes before writing this, my wife and I had a phone call with our oldest son, Braden. He is twenty-six and has COVID-19. We've known this for a few days, but now his throat is hurting badly and he's wondering what he can do about it. He's tried over-the-counter medicines with little relief. He called the Teledoc (because the clinic won't let him enter), but they couldn't prescribe anything stronger. Should he go to the ER? Another doctor said he should avoid that unless his breathing is labored. Too many questions and not enough answers. Bottom line: This is triggering a lot of fear in my wife and me. We've been down this road before, and we can't help but be fearful of what could happen. Others might brush this off and say, "Oh, he's young and healthy. Odds are he'll be fine." But you can't say that to us. Life has already taught us—with severe permanence—that what we think will never happen to us, can happen to us.

And it's taught *you* that unfortunate lesson as well.

The best of intentions don't always produce the outcome you desire. Tragic stories are not just about others; hurt is something that happens to you. You can't unlearn this. But you—and we—can strive to put your trust in God, manage your fear (so it doesn't manage you), and share your anxiety with others around you so together you can share the load.

Here's the point: Tragic and terrible loss requires intentional grieving. The trajectory of your life is forever changed (dare I point out that you wouldn't be getting married if something tragic hadn't happened), and you must be proactive with each other and your children to cope with it or you will fall prey to grief's heavy weight. Grief is an emotion that will not be denied. For a moment you can pretend it doesn't exist or isn't relevant, but you cannot erase its presence.

After twelve years, Nan and I can tell you that our grief is far less intense and debilitating than it was the first several years. We can smile again. Laugh again. And release ourselves to enjoy life. But our sadness is not gone. There are moments when it rushes back on us like a massive ocean hurricane wave. And triggers, like another son's illness, bring it all back and fill us with fear. (By the way, our oldest son recovered from COVID and we are grateful to God for it.)

Do not ignore grief. It is unkind to those who grieve. View it, instead, as a companion in your family's journey. An unwanted companion, most certainly, but one you must pay attention to.

Family Grieving Starts with You

I'm wondering what the last section has resurrected in you. Has it reminded you of your grief (past or present)? Do you feel it in your body (head, neck, or back pain, stomach tightness)? Did you find yourself restless as you read that section? Take notice, right now, of what is rising up in you. It is telling you something about your grief, and your response is telling you something about your typical coping method. Do you talk about it? Are you swallowing your feelings? Are you feeling sad, angry, helpless, bitter, confused? Listen to yourself.

If you have never been through great suffering but are marrying someone who has (and their kids), you may not be feeling much of anything. Or maybe you are aware that you can't really relate to their pain. That is important to be conscious of because it can inadvertently translate into a lack of compassion for their sadness and minimizing their pain. Not only will that result in your being unable to grieve with those who grieve, but it will put an emotional gap between you and them that could be offensive or make you unsafe, someone to avoid and hide from rather than someone with whom they can trust their inner emotions. It's important that you can come alongside their grief.

I'll say more about that in the section that follows, but for now, let me emphasize that good family grieving starts with the adults in the home. Whether you are the biological parent or stepparent, you have a role to play. During the Growth Activity, you will discuss the following strategies.

Grieve out loud. Make sure you talk openly about your sadness. This communicates that it's okay to grieve, be angry, not know how to feel, and have concerns. Sometimes parents want to convey strength and inadvertently communicate that sorrow is off limits. Children and teens need to know how to think about loss. When you go first, you show them how to grieve and give them permission to do the same. Don't confuse talking about your sadness with making your children your emotional caretakers. While not putting the burden of your well-being on their shoulders, talking openly about your grief essentially says, "We're in this together," and invites children to lean on you with their sadness.

Connect faith and life. When you communicate your grief through the lens of faith and moral values, you help children see how faith and life connect at an important level. This matures children as you grieve together. First, it teaches that vulnerability

110

and "not knowing" is a part of life and does not equal weakness. And second, it shows children how to think through a situation from a faith-informed, value-centered perspective. Grief is innately self-centered. Infusing it with a spiritual perspective informs pain with that which helps us transcend it.

Listen, affirm, and validate . . . don't try to fix. To do this means being able to endure the child's pain because you cannot fix their pain; you can only hug it. A small child who falls and skins their knee will most assuredly cry out in pain. You can put a little medicine and a bandage on the abrasion, but mostly what they need is a hug. A little TLC somehow helps the hurt. It doesn't fix the skinned knee, but somehow the child feels better. This is the way you help children of every age with the scrapes on their hearts. Time and again you pull them into your lap, letting them cry over what hurts. Wrap listening with compassion and, when you can, physical touch. Somehow it helps.

Practice emotional coaching. One compassionate way to respond in those moments is with emotional coaching. In his excellent book *Raising an Emotionally Intelligent Child*, Dr. John Gottman says that parents should teach children to recognize how their emotions are impacting them and how to self-regulate their behavior despite their emotions. He outlines several steps to emotion coaching.[1] Begin by being aware of your own emotions and what you are feeling in the moment. Managing yourself appropriately models what you are teaching the child to do.

Next, seek out the key emotions in what the child is saying, and label them. Small children in particular often don't have a vocabulary for their emotions. They know how to act mad, but they don't recognize the sadness beneath. You will have to point that out to them so they can connect their experience with the emotion ("I can tell you are really angry and perhaps a little

111

sad right now. Do you know what you are sad about?"). This is important because it gets to the heart of the matter. Focusing only on the above-the-surface issue won't help them deal with below-the-surface grief.

After labeling the emotion, remember to resist the temptation to fix it. "Don't feel bad. Everything will be okay." "Your dad doesn't mean to hurt you." These attempts to fix sorrow won't work. Even worse, they minimize the child's pain and shut them down. The message is, "Stop feeling and talking about this." We want just the opposite: for them to talk more about this—and share it with you. You must find a way to endure a child's sadness or you will never really hear it—and you won't be able to help them walk through it.

By the way, why do we say such things? Because we are uncomfortable with their pain and want to relieve them of it. I'm sure you want to stop seeing them suffer. Perhaps you feel guilty or somehow responsible. Whatever the reason, wanting to make a child's sadness go away is, of course, understandable, but trying to make it go away only distances you from their heart. What goes away is you, not the pain. Don't try to fix it.

Finally, while labeling the emotion is a good first step, try to, in effect, open the wound to hear more. Consider this example of a child who returns home after a weekend at his mom's house. Ten-year-old Brennan walks in the door snippy and curt. Not his usual self, he speaks to his stepmom, Carmen, with a disrespectful tone. In the past, Carmen has interpreted such behavior as rejection. She would snap back at Brennan and the two would bicker until she sent him to his room "until his father gets home." This time, she calmed down and focused in on his experience.

Brennan: [in a harsh, disrespectful tone] "Do I still have to do my chores tonight? I already did some at my mom's

112

house. It's not fair!" [Stepparents make easy targets for the frustrations children feel; try to remember that much of what is directed at you is not about you.]

Carmen: [in a calm tone; she momentarily sidesteps the disrespect and begins to label the emotions she hears] "Hold on a second. I can tell you are really irritated about having to do chores twice. Am I getting that right?"

Brennan: [his response baits Carmen to take the issue personally] "Yes. Your son only has to do chores in one house, and I have to do them at my mom's house and here. It's not fair."

Carmen: [she skirts the lure and stays centered on Brennan's emotion, wondering what's behind it] "You're feeling put upon because you have to do chores twice. I can see how you might feel that way. [That last part disarms Brennan a little; he's not used to her empathizing and not taking the bait.] I'm also wondering if you are angry you had to leave your mom's house and come home. It's hard to do that, isn't it?"

Brennan: [now refocused on what is painful] "I guess so."

Carmen: [digs a little deeper] "It hurts when you enjoy being with your mom and then have to leave. I can see why you might come home a little grumpy and sad."

Brennan: [calming down] "It's not fair that I have to leave; I only get three days there and Mom cries when I leave. I hate that."

Carmen: [now realizes how deep his sadness is; replies softly and gently with compassion] "I'm sorry. That really stinks for you. I know your mom loves you very much and you love her. It's very hard coming back to our house. [There's no attempt to fix his emotions, just acknowledgment. She pauses . . .] Could I give you a

113

hug—or do you need a little more time first?" [TLC at its best. She gives him a verbal hug just by saying she wants to physically hug him. She also gives him permission not to hug her if he can't do so comfortably right now.]

Brennan: [showing how torn he is] "I'm not quite ready yet."

Carmen: "Okay. I'll hug you later when it feels okay for you."

[At this point, Carmen has earned the right to address the initial disrespect that started the exchange. Her emotional coaching has refocused Brennan and proved herself safe for him. Connection before correction increases her authority. She continues calmly . . .]

"You know, a little while ago you spoke harshly to me. I know you came home feeling cruddy, but I don't deserve to be spoken to that way. I don't appreciate it and don't want you to do it again. Next time, if you come home feeling yucky, I'd rather you walk in and tell me that so I know to give you some space until you feel better. That way we won't argue. Could you do that?" [Waits for response.] "I forgive you, but I'd still appreciate an apology." [Waits for a response.]

[smiling big] "I'm still going to give you that hug later. You can go now."[2]

It might be that this exchange will help Brennan to better manage his emotions and disrespect and the two of them just might have started down a different path together. Notice how they got there: Carmen managed her fear of rejection, shifted away from her own emotions to Brennan's, helped label his emotions for him, validated that he had reason to feel that way, and pursued connection with his emotions before correcting his misbehavior. By coaching Brennan through the moment, she prevented grief from putting distance in their relationship and instead turned the moment into an opportunity for shared grieving. Now catch this: What made all of this possible was Carmen's self-control.

At some point, if Brennan can't stop being disrespectful when he's sad, Carmen and her husband may need to impose a consequence for his behavior. Either way, the emotional coaching should continue.

Stepparents, don't erase and replace. Send a message that you are not competing with the object of the child's grief, but respect and honor it. In the previous case study, Carmen affirmed how hard it was for Brennan to leave his mother. This not only validated his sadness, but communicated that Carmen was not trying to replace his mother. It's very important that children understand this about you so they don't toughen their resolve to make sure you don't.

Step into a child's grief at strategic moments. Because we carry grief with us through time, look for opportunities for family grieving. When a song triggers a memory in yourself or a child, reflect on it. Tell a story related to the song and what it reminds you of. Or when a picture, meal, movie, or circumstance calls attention to what has been lost, acknowledge it. Special days (e.g., birthdays, religious rituals, anniversaries) and holidays predictably trigger sadness because of who isn't present or a tradition that can no longer be kept. Anticipate this and plan how you might comment on the elephant in the room.

Before their father died, Eric's stepchildren spent every Labor Day weekend four-wheeling with their father. They'd fish, camp, and go on long walks together. Even before he married their mother, as Labor Day approached, Eric asked the kids to show him pictures and smartphone videos of their time together. Not all the kids wanted to share their memories, but most would. He

115

laughed at their stories. He shared his sadness that they could not make more together. And when Labor Day actually came, he didn't try to replicate the scenario. Instead, after talking it through with their mother, he made it possible for her and them to go to their paternal grandparent's house for the weekend . . . without him. Giving them time to be with that side of the family—and not inserting himself into the weekend—was a huge blessing for everyone.

Other thoughts to keep in mind:

- If your child doesn't seem to be grieving, keep monitoring. Children grieve in spurts. Just because you don't see it doesn't mean the pain won't resurface later. Plus, they could be hiding their feelings to relieve you of the burden of worrying about them. Children who don't cry worry me the most. Remain open to the possibility that future life circumstances may release emotions that have been hibernating, and continue sharing your feelings so the child will know it's safe to talk when the day finally comes.

- Some young children will express their feelings best through art or play, which allows them to tell us about their pain without having to use words. Finding a qualified art or play therapist can be very helpful.[3]

ACTIVITY INSTRUCTIONS

1. Before talking with children, discuss the following as a couple: If you have been through a significant loss, describe your initial earthquake and then list a few past and current aftershocks that you experience and/or see in your children.

116

2. Revisit your Blended Family Map and make a list of each family member and the losses you believe he or she has experienced. You might print off a new copy of the Blended Family Map and write the losses beside each person's name. Imagine what it has been like to be that person at each point along the way: before the breakup/divorce or death of a parent, after the divorce/death, during the single-parent years, and after your engagement was announced. Finally, anticipate what each may experience after the wedding. Share this list with your fiancé. (Seeing this accumulated list of losses may help you recognize how much each person has been through.)

3. Now, make a list of grief triggers that resurrect these losses for each person. Triggers can be anything—sights, words, smells, songs, places—that tap into sadness and resurrect feelings of grief, anger, resentment, pain, depression, or other strong emotions. Triggers can change over time, so try to capture the most recent that you've noticed in yourself and others.

4. As a couple, discuss the grieving strategies listed above in the "Family Grieving Starts with You" section. Which are you doing well at this point and which need some attention?

5. Ignite conversations with your children about loss, some one-on-one and some as a group. It's best not to call a family meeting in order to foster family grieving, but to take advantage of the symbols and situations of life that naturally tap into grief. A casual bike ride with your kids can be an opportunity to remember how their deceased mother taught them to ride. A movie or dinner out can be symbolic of a previous time the family spent together. Use these moments to ignite

conversations and nudge hard emotions to the surface. When children do express themselves, stay curious (e.g., "tell me more about what makes you sad about that").

6. If you haven't done so already, have a family conversation that sets the boundaries for how you will talk about feelings of sadness going forward. Your goal is to let each person share when and how it is best for them to be involved in grief conversations (e.g., one-on-one, before special days, during, or after). Because they are uncomfortable with grief, someone may say, "never," so make sure you also communicate that this will be something you bring up from time to time even if they don't want to go there. Hearing what is helpful to each person helps you respect their needs to the degree you can.

7. If a parent died, make a trip to the cemetery with whoever wants to go. Ask kids if they are okay with the future stepparent going—and if not, respect their wishes.

8. Start conversations with statements/questions that get below the surface.

   a. "My guess is you will feel two very different things at the wedding. Happy for me and sad that your dad/mom and I are not together anymore. Can you see yourself feeling that way?"

   b. If you were widowed: "I got to thinking about something the other day. As excited as I am to marry Jane/John, it makes me miss your mother/father. I miss the way she/he would . . . Has my engagement made you miss them too?"

   c. If you are divorced: "I know our divorce has put you through a lot, and I grieve what cannot be for you. I was thinking, if I were you, I'd be a little sad that . . . (e.g., you're going to have to get used to a stepmom/

CREATING A SHARED GRIEF JOURNEY

dad/stepsiblings in the house). Or maybe you're feeling hurt or angry that I'm getting married because . . . (e.g., this means your mother/father and I can't get back together). Or maybe you are worried how this will impact your mom/dad. Is any of that on your mind?"

d. "What's difficult for you to get used to as you think about the wedding, my marriage, and our new family?"[4]

POST-ACTIVITY QUESTIONS FOR REFLECTION

1. Revisit the list of losses you made for each family member in item 2 above. After talking with the kids, what else can you add to their list?

2. Discuss the implications for parenting and stepparenting your children based on their accumulated losses. What might you do differently and what will you keep the same?

3. Knowing that guilt and sadness for what children (of every age) have experienced can result in permissive parenting, how can you guard against this?

TRY THIS

- Review the expanded section on loss, grief, and menacing emotions in *The Smart Stepfamily: 7 Steps to a Healthy Family*, chapter 9. It reviews common losses for both adults and children after death, divorce, or the dissolution of cohabiting households.

119

8

ANTICIPATING WHAT
WILL CHANGE

Standing in a large, empty tank and having six inches of water added will not cause alarm to the average person. You get wet, but you don't feel anxious. But it would make you anxious if you were already up to your eyeballs in water. What feel like small changes to adults can feel overwhelming to children who are already nearly drowning in a sea of unwanted changes. You can't always lessen the amount of water coming in around them, but you can hold their hand and tell them they aren't treading water alone. The ultimate purpose of this Growth Activity is to acknowledge with children that more change is coming and to communicate, "You're not alone in this. We are with you. Let's find our way through." By the way, there are times when adults need to try to lessen—or stop—additional water being added to a child's tank. Signs of distress in your children may be a signal that their tank is filling too fast or making it hard for them to breathe. For example, you may not think you're rushing to the altar, but your kids might. And changing homes, schools, churches, social circles, and making it more difficult to get to their other parent may not seem like much to you, but it can be overwhelming to them. If they are "drowning," your family is going to struggle. Monitor each child's tank; if your child is struggling to cope with the water pouring in, do something to slow it down. For example, the biological parent might spend a little more one-on-one time with their child(ren) and ease off time when everyone is together. Your presence will reassure the child that they are not alone in their tank.

A secondary purpose of this Growth Activity is to draw kids into the logistics of forming a stepfamily and help your family learn to problem solve together. Inevitably, there will be practical and relational changes that will occur when you blend two families. This activity will help you put them into perspective and discover how you will manage them together. You may want to talk through some of these items individually with children, teens, or adults, but talking through them as a group shows everyone the value of family meetings—a helpful strategy you may continue periodically or regularly. Giving children a voice in decisions helps them to feel valued, teaches responsibility and critical thinking skills, and helps your family take on a team spirit. In some cases, group decisions will provide long-lasting, workable solutions to matters; in other cases, the decision will be just the beginning of a live-and-learn process. Feel free to revisit and adjust decisions over time as the family learns what really works best.

Learn more about Family Meetings at SmartStepfamilies.com /family-meetings.

Discussing changes—and clarifying what they mean and don't mean—also helps you keep logistical changes from inadvertently negatively impacting relationships. Sometimes children, when insecure because of the many changes going on around them, equate logistical shifts to mean there has been a relational change. An adult child may wonder if changes to your will reflect a shift in your commitment to your grandchildren. Or a younger child may think, "Mom doesn't pick me up from school anymore and we don't get that car time to talk like we used to, so I guess I'm not as important to her." Despite being inaccurate, this conclusion will have significant negative psychological impact on a child. This Activity provides a chance, for example, to explain why it will be more convenient from now on for someone else to pick the child up and to reassure the child that they are just as loved as ever. By the way, in a case like this, try to replace some of the lost one-on-one time however you can. As I explained in the introduction of this book, during times of stress and transition, kids need more exclusive time with their biological parent, not less.

The following is not a comprehensive list of changes that may occur when a blended family is formed, but it will focus your thoughts and help you see them from a child's point of view. Please add other areas to your discussions as you think of them. When it comes time to discuss them as a family unit, start with what you think is most pressing, and feel free to spread them out over multiple conversations.

A Seismic Shift

In chapter 7 I described loss as a series of earthquakes and aftershocks. Because single-parent families often reorient themselves around the parent-child relationship, your marriage is yet another earthquake to your children. Committing yourself to your spouse "till death do us part" at your wedding is a seismic shift to the emotional climate of your home. Of course, this does not mean you stop loving or caring for your children, but there is a new significant relationship in your life that will be reflected in your dedication to each other and how you spend your time and energy. Do not hear me say that you must choose one over the other; you are choosing both your spouse and your children. But the marriage will change how some things get done and how time is spent. Acknowledging this while at the same time reassuring children of your continued love and dedication to them will be part of the Activity.

Let's drill down on this a little further. This also activates the emotional triangle that impacts child(ren), parent, and stepparent, and it can feel like another six inches of water to a child who is already struggling to keep their head above the waters of loss. It's critical that you gain empathy for each person in the triangle.

Let's begin with the children. After the wedding, when a child witnesses their parent relationally turning toward the stepparent, it often feels as if the parent is turning away from them. (I've repeated this a few times throughout the book because it's important that you receive this truth.) This change might activate nervousness ("Did I just get replaced?"), competition ("I'd better position myself between my parent and stepparent"), and anxious pursuit of the parent ("Complaints, anger, sadness, depression, or whiney behavior might draw my parent back to me"). Why would this happen? Because the child is manipulative or controlling? No, because six inches of water just got added to the tank. They want, and need, to feel reassured of their parent's love and presence during this change.

It's important to note here that some engaged couples begin to feel this tension before a wedding (especially if they're living together), but others may not feel it in a significant way until after the wedding when they merge family households. Until then, many dating couples are able to naturally compartmentalize their developing couple relationship from the children. Until everyone moves in together, children don't have to face on a regular basis moments when their parent turns toward the stepparent and away from them. But once you live under the same roof, this change becomes obvious, and their "insider" status with their parent becomes challenged by the "outsider" stepparent.

This is also when stepparents—the second party in the triangle to consider—feel the temperature of their relationship with the children growing cooler. They seemed to warm up to you before the wedding but now are cooling off. This emotional whiplash is confusing unless you recognize what has changed for the children and the emotional work it requires of them to keep their heads above water.

The biological parent—the third part of the triangle—is generally trying desperately to remain close to both their child(ren) and their new spouse. And given "cooler temperatures," the biological parent often feels caught in the middle. To turn toward one party is to turn away from the other. Not really, of course; you still love the other. But you are aware that the other is unsure of your love, which makes you feel stuck and at times guilty for every choice you make with your time or energy.[1]

It's important that you recognize that this insider-outsider push-pull dynamic is unavoidable; it is inherent to the nature of how blended families are "born." Some of you enter the Crockpot as insiders (biological family), and some don't. One way to mitigate this dynamic (I don't think you can prevent it) is to begin talking about it even before it happens—and then calmly continue to talk about it once it kicks in. This chapter's Growing Activity is designed to get that conversation started and helps each of you turn toward one another. Putting words on the experience of children helps them feel cared for and creates awareness of what they are feeling. Having empathy and respect for what others in the emotional triangle are experiencing during each conversation will help you validate and connect to one another because those qualities make it easier to adapt to the unwanted relational changes that are occurring. A stepparent, for example, might compassionately say to a child, "I imagine it's hard for you when your mom sits by me instead of you when we're watching a movie. How does that feel to you?" Or a parent might say to both the stepparent and their children at the same time, "I know this is hard, but I love all of you. When I spend time with the other, I'm not saying I've stopped loving you. It's just the other's turn. I hope you can hold on to that."

Here's one last tip to help you manage this triangular push-pull: carve up the triangle on occasion. Yes, your entire family needs to spend time together developing connections and building memories, but it is crucial that couples spend time alone. *And,* as I shared earlier, it's vital that a parent spends one-on-one time with their children. Whole family time is what adults often want after the wedding; make sure you are just as, if not more, intentional about the individual relationships. Don't over-orchestrate familyness, or it may become harder to find.

Daily Routines and Time Together

As your wedding approaches, you may have already changed some daily routines. Although many couples begin to integrate their lives well before the wedding occurs, officially merging your households and every aspect of your lives will likely change your schedules and daily routines significantly.

Walking through your day with kids to explore how having new people in the house will change breakfast, chores, getting to and from school or work, etc., will help everyone begin to think through the logistics and get used to the idea that such changes are coming. Routines, as well as cherished rituals and traditions, help to tell us who we are and give definition to relationships. Your new life may require that routines change, but try not to lose the meaning or connection the old routine offered. Having breakfast together each morning and talking about the day ahead, for example, is more than just a routine. For a single-parent family, it gives everyone focused time together before the day begins and schedules take everyone in opposite directions. It also gives a parent a regular opportunity to affirm each child. Having that routine changed by the presence of a stepparent and stepsiblings not only dilutes their planning time for the day, but it steals the regular dose of nurture the biological parent gets to share with their child(ren). When routines like this need to change, strive to find another way to share meaningful connection, or children may feel that six inches of water has just been added to the tank.

Rituals, Traditions, Holidays, and Special Days

As with routines, holiday traditions, annual activities, religious rituals, and how you celebrate birthdays make statements about family identity and belonging. So in general, try to change as few as possible in order to retain the value behind the ritual or tradition, but when a change is needed, talk it through.

Negotiating that change is not easy. For example, when it comes to combining traditions, be flexible and keep something old, make something new, and borrow from each other till you find something that works. He and his kids open Christmas gifts on Christmas Eve. She and her kids open them Christmas morning. You might try to pull something from each tradition forward while you figure out what will work long-term. To start, you might open gifts both Christmas Eve and the next morning, but run it by the kids first so they can speak into the changes.

Remember—and this is important—there's no one right answer. What works the first year may need to change the next, and what works for you may be entirely different for another blended family. Be considerate, talk through the options, and maintain a live-and-learn attitude.

Primary Residence and Physical Space in the Home

"I used to have my own room. Now I have to share. And she's a pain and there's not that much closet space!" Just like married couples have to learn to share a bathroom, family members have to learn to share the Wi-Fi, TVs, screens, toys, furniture, and yes, the bathrooms. They also have more people to compete with to sit in Mom's lap, and someone else is sitting in their designated chair at dinner. Every one of these changes has the potential to be annoying and to affect how someone sees themselves and their place in the family.

Some couples merge into one person's household; others move out of both and buy a new home. There are many necessary considerations and good options. Changing living situations can be welcomed or unwelcomed by children. Help them anticipate the change and what it will mean for them.

Faith Perspectives

Increasingly, blended family couples come from differing religious backgrounds. They may be more similar than different (e.g., two different Christian denominations) or more different than similar (e.g., totally different faiths with deep cultural rituals attached to them). In either case, there is need for a family discussion about what will change. By the way, in this area I

128

encourage you as a couple to determine the direction you will lead your family in before talking to them. They need to see your conviction and unity.

School

Changing schools is a significant adjustment for kids, especially older children and teens. It means making new friends and losing old ones, finding their place, forming new routines, and adapting to new educational expectations. This should not be a short conversation. Spend ample time helping children prepare for the change.

Social Life

The older children are, the more invested they are in their social connections. Unless there is good reason for change, this is one aspect of a child's life that I would encourage you not to touch, especially for teens and young adults. Having stability in their friendships can help mitigate the other changes going on in their home.

Visitation Schedule and Logistics

Here's another area of their life that should not change unless it simply cannot be avoided. Significant changes in access to the other parent will make accepting and enjoying the new family more difficult. Children of every age need consistent contact with their biological parents. Do what you can to preserve that. If you move farther away from the other parent, then you should carry the burden of making sure contact continues.

Other topics include, for example, how things will change when part-time children visit the home or who will be responsible for certain chores based on who is physically present. Adult stepfamilies may need to discuss how time with the grandparents will be divided and who will host Thanksgiving. Adult children who are married have in-laws to consider, so this can get complicated quickly. Try to plan early, make sacrifices, and be flexible.

Vacation

As with traditions, family members sometimes have definite ideas of what vacations should entail. You'll need to discuss differing preferences and negotiate where you will go, how the time is spent, and what it will cost. By the way, some families find that retaining some meaningful getaways for the biological parent and children while creating new traditions for the entire stepfamily affirms established relationships and builds the new ones. It may take you a few years to figure all this out, but agreement in this area may contribute memories that positively impact family harmony.

Money and Spending Habits

How financial decisions are made, attitudes about spending, and how money is shared with children are elements that might change after your wedding. Helping children anticipate these changes eliminates surprises and gives you an opportunity to teach them about wise money practices.

I highly recommend that you get your money plan together prior to the wedding. Learning to "finance togetherness" is the topic of an entire book I co-authored with Greg Pettys and David Edwards, called *The Smart Stepfamily Guide to Financial Planning*. You'll get a small taste of that material in chapter 9, which might be helpful to absorb before you share any significant financial changes when children are involved (e.g., changing the names of beneficiaries on insurance policies).

Roles in the Home

While a single mother, Lavonda worked extra hours and relied on her mother to pick up the kids from school and watch them until she got off work. Her oldest daughter, Jasmine, looked after her siblings and helped make lunches for them before school. Between Lavonda, Grandma, and his big sister, Daniel, the youngest, had three "mothers" to care for him. He relished being the baby of the family and often took advantage of it. But after Lavonda married, she no longer needed to work as much, Grandma didn't see the kids as often, Jasmine lost part of her contribution to the family, and Daniel, who now wasn't the youngest child, found himself competing with a younger stepsibling for attention.

Changes in roles can be substantial for family members. In some situations, the person receives benefit. Jasmine, for example, was released of having to make lunches in the morning because her mom could now do it, but Jasmine found herself feeling less significant to the family. In other cases, the person experiences a disadvantage. Grandma, Lavonda's mother, will likely experience a loss in not being able to spend time with her grandchildren as she had in the past. But then, maybe that is a welcome relief.

Help both adults and children anticipate how their roles within the home may shift or change. If a child has fulfilled a critical role for a long time, be sure to celebrate their contributions and thank them for their service and sacrifice. If they will not be needed as they were in the past, reframe the change like a graduation or milestone birthday; that is, from this point forward, they have an opportunity to discover new roads.

Parenting Expectations

Chapter 6 gave you the opportunity to explore your parenting strategies and how you will parent together following the wedding. Now is the time to begin making small changes in that direction and informing the children of what will change. But this should not be a one-way street. Ask them questions about what they would like to see change as it relates to your parenting style and consider their input. No, they don't get to dictate how you parent or what the rules will be, but healthy parents have an ongoing feedback loop in their parenting that helps them refine their attitudes and behaviors.

ACTIVITY INSTRUCTIONS

Review each of these items first as a couple. You may have definite opinions about some of them that you need to agree on before you inform the children. But whenever possible, as much as is developmentally appropriate, let children have input. This makes it more likely they will own responsibility for implementing the solution. When you must make the call on a decision, it is helpful if you let kids speak into some aspect of the changing situation (e.g., bedtime on school nights is nonnegotiable, but on weekends is negotiable). Share power when you can.

Be as practical as you can in these conversations and explore all relevant topics. The examples below are just a few possible questions. Start by saying something like, "You know, we got to thinking about all the things that will change once we get married and move in together. Some of them are going to be welcomed changes, and others will be beyond your control. Let's try to think of as many as we can and talk about them."

1. "What's one thing you are really looking forward to? Who wants to go first?"
2. "What's one thing you aren't looking forward to? I'll go first on this one."
3. A Seismic Shift: Explain to your children that you are bringing a significant relationship into the family and you know it will bring some changes. Then reassure children that this does not mean you will stop being their parent or loving them in a unique and special way. Then, if developmentally appropriate, ask them what changes they've already noticed in how you spend your time with your fiancé and if they have felt in competition with that relationship.
   a. Parent and stepparent: Be sure to respond to children with empathy (e.g., "I can see how tough that would be for you").
   b. Parent: Resist the temptation to change the child's attitude or feelings in order to move them emotionally toward your fiancé (e.g., "You don't have to worry that I spend time with him/her"). Just listen and affirm for now. Carving out one-on-one time with your child is what will actually reassure them.
4. Routines: "Let's walk through a typical day. How do you think things will change with more people in the house? Breakfast? Getting to school/work? Evenings? Bedtime? Weekends?"
   a. "What will you miss about how things used to be?" [Sometimes this question reveals a hidden emotional anchor that you can try to replace some other way.]
   b. Remind people that a change in your time with them is not to say that they are less valuable to you.

5. Rituals, Traditions, Holidays, and Special Days: Use an upcoming special day as a case study to discuss traditions, their meaning, and how you will manage things going forward. Don't try to negotiate every tradition, just discuss a few examples and note that you'll have to figure out the specifics of each as they come up.

   a. "Lori has a birthday coming up soon. What do you guys usually do to celebrate birthdays?"

   b. "Lori, what is meaningful to you about that? What would you never want to lose?"

   c. Holidays: "Both sides of our family have a special tradition on Christmas morning. We can't do them both like we have in the past. How should we handle that in the future?"

   d. Remind everyone that your family won't get everything right the first time. "We may have to learn from our mistakes, but we will try to consider everyone's feelings."

6. Primary Residence and Physical Space in the Home:

   a. "Let's talk about how things might feel different around the house. The boys are going to share a room. What do you guys think that will be like?"

   b. Share a situation that you anticipate will change, and invite others to talk about it. For example, "On Friday nights for a long time, David (son) and I have enjoyed sitting on the couch, watching movies, and eating pizza. There will be a lot more people in the house now. David, I know I'm going to miss that alone time with you a little, but I'll enjoy having others with us too. What do you think it will be like?"

134

c. "With stepsiblings in the house together, it might be wise for us to have a dress code. What should that be? Under what conditions can you enter someone's bedroom? If you have a problem, who do you talk to?" (Read more about personal boundaries in step-families and awkward physical touch in my book *The Smart Stepdad*.)

d. Discuss changes in bedrooms, bathroom use, kitchen use, TV/computer/media time, etc.

e. More people in the family means less time with a parent. Anticipate what this might mean for them and reassure them of the things that will continue (e.g., a special nighttime ritual with a child). Acknowledge openly what needs to be grieved (e.g., going to lunch regularly with a child).

7. Faith Perspectives: Point out your similarities and differences and discuss how you will manage them going forward. If changes need to be made (e.g., finding a church your whole family will attend), start a dialogue about what people value in a church and why.

8. School and Social Life: Because these can be so unique for children, you may want to talk with them individually but have collective discussions about how school changes will impact the family calendar.

9. Visitation Schedule and Logistics:

a. Regarding visitation, biological parents should explain any frequency or schedule changes to their children—and explain how you plan to honor the other parent's time with the child.

b. Discuss what might change in terms of logistics. For example, "We will live closer to your dad's house, so it will take less time to get there—that's a good thing!"

   c. Talk through days when some children will be present and some gone and how it will impact room situations, responsibilities around the house, etc.

10. Vacation: Start talking about your next vacation and what people want to do. Listen to their past experiences and what they liked. Start dreaming of what you might do together.

11. Money and Spending Habits:

   a. Tell children who they go to for lunch money or to make college payments.

   b. Explore what you anticipate changing as it relates to the overall household income. Give practical examples of what might change. (Example: "We're going to have a lot more kids in the house once we get married, so all of us are going to have to limit our outside activities to one per semester. I know that stinks. We are giving up some things as well. What questions do you have about this?")

   c. Let children know of any negotiated changes in how you will manage or distribute money (e.g., allowance).

12. Roles in the Home:

   a. Start by making a quick list of how each family member contributes to the home. Then anticipate with the group how those roles will stay the same or change.

   b. Remember to honor people for significant roles they have played in the past that will no longer be needed, and celebrate their new freedoms. Be sure to also acknowledge the loss they may feel at not being able to contribute in a familiar way.

13. Parenting Expectations:

    a. What general expectations/rules will be the same, and which will change?

    b. What chores will children be responsible for?

    c. Explain what the kids should expect if they misbehave and who they will hear from.

    d. If developmentally appropriate, give kids a chance to speak into what is expected of them. This sends a message that you are open to (but not required to) listening to them. Ask what rules or expectations they would like to see change in the future (e.g., teenagers may want more freedom to make decisions about their time). Note: Kids are observant. Likely they have already experienced the differences between you as parents and have opinions about what they like and don't like in a future stepparent. Ask them to share their thoughts.

POST-ACTIVITY QUESTIONS FOR REFLECTION

How many new changes will your children need to adapt to? Pause and reflect on all that will be required of them. Remember that change, especially unwanted change, brings loss and a sense of powerlessness (for kids and adults alike) so prioritize the changes and move slowly. To increase stability, strive to reduce unnecessary changes for children and be compassionate when they react strongly to what is, for them, another six inches of water.

TRY THIS

Talk with a friend about their blended family transition. What changes did they not anticipate well? Depending on their age, invite your children to talk with a friend and ask the same question. Your family might even interview another family all together so kids and adults alike hear what everyone has to say.

9

MERGING MONEY AND YOUR FAMILY

I was being interviewed on CNBC about *The Smart Stepfamily Guide to Financial Planning*, when the program anchor questioned something important: "Why do most blended family couples avoid talking about money?"

She was right. One study found that fewer than 25 percent of premarital couples forming blended families discussed financial matters,[1] and yet research by Dr. David Olson and myself found that happy, thriving stepcouples have an 80 percent agreement rate on spending and saving.[2] That's twice the rate of unhappy couples! Not talking about money is a bad idea, but for more than just financial reasons. Ultimately, as I'll explain in this chapter, stepfamily financial planning is about financing relational and emotional togetherness in your marriage, in your family, and on behalf of your collective financial futures.

Did you know that long after a divorce, a former spouse is entitled to a portion of your retirement and stock options?

Did you know that, unless you've made legal arrangements, if you die and your former spouse marries again—and then your former spouse dies—some of your assets can end up going to their new spouse and their children, not *your* children? What if you decide not to update insurance beneficiaries or your will and something happens, leaving someone without financial provision—and family members bickering over assets and what you intended in the event of your death?

This doesn't have to be part of your future. To avoid these difficulties, devote some time to the Growth Activity in this chapter. For a few couples, this chapter will be enough to help you create a unifying plan, but most will benefit from reading *The Smart Stepfamily Guide to Financial Planning*, which presents a comprehensive process for merging your money and your family. After doing the research for that book, I now tell premarital coaches, counselors, and pastors that I believe we have a moral obligation to push couples into this discussion because if we don't, they can get blindsided quickly. I don't want you to get blindsided. The benefits of a healthy discussion are great, and the problems avoided are many. If you find yourself a little hesitant to jump in, trust that now is the time to start the conversation. You don't have to settle all the questions, but you do need to get started.

By the way, my reply to the CNBC anchor's question about why couples often avoid talking about finances was twofold: First, because even though partners flippantly say to each other, "I'll take care of yours and you'll take care of mine," they don't really know what that means or how they'll do it. The attitude may be romantic, but their good intentions often get overrun by stepfamily realities, including legal restrictions, complex multiple-home parenting, relationship challenges, and extended family members. I shared that you need more than just good intentions; you need a plan. And second, most couples think they don't have enough money to worry about. That's not true. Everybody has something, even if it's debt. Everything matters. At this point you may have a significant retirement nest egg saved or not many assets at all, but starting to plan now will help you get your new family started off on the right foot. Remember, this conversation helps you merge more than just money. It merges your values and dreams and, most important, helps you decide how money will serve your family. I'll add a third reason pre-blended family couples avoid talking about money: They have already studied one of the many popular money management systems and feel equipped. These courses offer much, but rarely, if ever, do they talk through the unique financial issues impacting blended family couples, nor do they address relational trust issues and parenting dilemmas that can complicate or sabotage most common financial programs. Merging money and merging family relationships are always tied together in blended families. Get ahead of the game; start planning now.

On Merging Money and Family

A stepfamily is a complex spaghetti of loyalties, cultures, traditions, DNA, expectations, parenting styles, losses, fears, and people—both those in the home and outside the home. As this book has discussed, merging means attending to all these pieces.

What does this have to do with financial planning and money management? Everything. If older stepsiblings got a car when they turned sixteen, once you marry are you obligated to do the same for younger children just to keep it fair? What do you do if the other home lets your child be on a traveling sports team and then expects you to help pay for it with time and money? How many bank accounts should stepcouples have? Do you put your new spouse's name on the house, or buy a different house? And what do you do, for example, if for financial and child development reasons you decide not to buy a child a smartphone, but the other home does it anyway? Are these solely money matters? Not at all. When you look underneath, it's obvious that many financial conflicts in stepfamilies are much bigger issues of belonging, loyalty, trust, power, control, acceptance, perceptions of favoritism, and fears of relational uncertainty.[3]

"My husband often spends money on his kids without discussing it with me first. He brought three children to the marriage, and they are older than my two. I just want to be included and considered. Leaving me out makes me feel unimportant, and I'm suspicious of what else he and his kids may be hiding." This woman's primary complaint is not about money; it's about trust and feeling unimportant in the marriage and, therefore, unsafe. An issue about decision-making and spending has revealed these feelings, but ultimately, this isn't about money. Said another way, financial conflicts are often just a symptom of much deeper blended family dynamics and relationships.

Below the surface. Michelle wasn't trying to shut Jamar out. Eventually, he learned more about Michelle's past and understood more about her apprehensions. Her first husband had abandoned her for another woman and left Michelle with little except debt from a stack of maxed-out credit cards. It took her many years to get out from under the constant worry about how she would pay the bills. Now, she admitted, she was guarded and cautious with her finances and children.

I've met many couples in blended families who have similar concerns. When below-the-surface issues come up, it's important for both partners in a relationship to exercise great patience with each other's fears before dealing with financial decisions. As Jamar and Michelle came to understand each other's pasts, they found compassion and grace for each other. They lowered their demands related to money and became much more patient with the merging process. Accommodating each other while they continued to work through their fears was an act of love that, ultimately, helped make true oneness more possible.[4]

Dealing with hidden issues. In any situation where there is a below-the-surface issue, seek to resolve that first, even if that means delaying a money management decision. The most important conversations you will have as a couple are around matters of commitment, companionship, and cherishing each other. In blended families, conversations may also need to address parenting and stepparenting priorities, coping with ex-spouses, and other stressful dynamics. Finding agreement about these matters while setting boundaries to protect and guard your family affirms your love for each other and raises confidence in the long-term dedication of each partner. When those below-the-surface insecurities are relieved, return to above-the-surface financial decisions and find an agreeable solution.

The necessary element of trust. With every step of this journey, each partner must act in a trustworthy manner. One woman wrote to me feeling trapped. Her husband forced her to sign a prenuptial agreement before they married without much discussion of the items included. He controlled their finances after they married and gave her little decision-making power. Then, in a move that cost him the little trust she still had in him, he set up a trust to provide for his kids but wouldn't let her speak into the details. Ironically, his financial trust came at the great cost of relational trust with his wife. Building trust between you is worth every conversation, every awkward moment, and every sacrifice. Without relational trust, your financial decisions will fail.

Stop and reflect. What are the below-the-surface issues in your relationship right now? Which of those are yours to manage and/or change? Begin to recognize below-the-surface emotional and

143

relational issues that must be addressed so that you can later consider the above-the-surface, practical matters of merging your financial lives.

Practical Steps to Financing Your Togetherness

How do you orchestrate a healthy family and financial merger? Here are a few practical steps discussed at length in the book *The Smart Stepfamily Guide to Financial Planning*.

Step one: take stock. Taking stock of yourself and your family relationships is an important first step to developing a financial vision for your blended family. Since stepfamilies are born out of loss (the death of a parent or the dissolution of the parents' relationship), understanding the past and your present emotional health is important in understanding how your blended family is functioning—and how well you'll be able to negotiate financial matters.

You also need to take stock of your financial situation. The Activity below will help, but for now, think in generalities: What are your major assets and remaining debts? Who are the people you are financially responsible for (e.g., children) or to (e.g., aging parents)? What happens to all of this if one of you dies?

Step two: create a Togetherness Agreement. A Togetherness Agreement (TA) helps you plan to succeed. A TA is a detailed financial vison of your life together. Essentially, it involves putting everything on the financial table—your assets, debts, dreams, and obligations—and deciding how you can meet your needs and facilitate the permanency of your marriage. This takes work, but the net result is a stronger relationship as you design your positive and secure future together.

Some will choose to have their TA drafted by a lawyer so that it is binding (a legal contract). Others will be satisfied to talk through the matter on their own (with or without an attorney) and design a path forward. Both create a shared vision for life together.

The specific stipulations included in a Togetherness Agreement vary by couple but will give consideration to your specific blended family. Your TA might include general agreements about handling finances, such as whether you will keep some bank accounts separate and have a joint account, and how you will manage retirement portfolios, debt, insurance, and businesses. It might also include agreements regarding the financial support, rights, roles, responsibilities, and overall well-being of spouses, children, stepchildren, grandchildren, stepgrandchildren, parents, stepparents, grandparents, stepgrandparents, and other significant relationships.

The TA is not just about money; it's a plan for how money will help care for your family over time. And therein lies an important attitude distinction that influences whether money matters help or hurt blended families: A prenuptial agreement is done *to* your spouse when you want to protect yourself in the event of a divorce. A Togetherness Agreement is done *for* your spouse. Better yet, when it is created *with* your spouse, both persons make promises on behalf of the other and lay a positive foundation for their life together.[5]

Negative reactions. If the idea of a Togetherness Agreement brings up a strong negative reaction in your partner or in you, consider how you might respond.

Consult with your pastor, mentor, or financial planner. Having a third party guide your discussion can be very helpful. In addition, recognize that strong reactions may be indicative of deep fears in your partner or in you. Recognize the fear and articulate it. Put aside conversations about the details of your money matters, and as a couple talk about your past experiences and what's driving strong emotional reactions now. Then you can return to making financial plans.

Below are some specific elements of the TA that you may want to discuss.

Bank accounts. Discuss how many bank accounts you'll have and who has access to the money therein. Should you have just one account that both of you have complete access to, two pots based on your differing incomes and liabilities, or three accounts (or more) with a combination of his, hers, and our money? Some people think this decision is symbolic of each person's level of trust in the other. "If she won't put all her money into our account," one man told me, "then she isn't really committed to me." Can you hear his below-the-surface insecurities? Until these are addressed, he likely won't be open to anything other than a one-account system. But know this: There are many good ways to manage your money. The number of accounts matters less than the fact that you discussed it, decided on a system that you can both support, and you feel trusted by each other. Unity does not mean one account. In this case, it means unity of heart. It's also very helpful if you have the bigger picture agreed to as well. Knowing how assets are being used to provide for both yourself, your spouse, and your children in the event someone dies, for example, means you trust the heart of your spouse beyond how many bank accounts you have.

Money boundaries with kids. Significant changes in money boundaries can, for kids, add water to their tank (see the be-

If you find it difficult to manage conflicts about money or any other subject, consider consulting *The Smart Stepfamily Marriage* by Ron Deal and David Olson, a book that helps couples develop practical skills to strengthen their marriage.

ginning of chapter 8). As a single mom, Taylor was quick to hand money to her children whenever they asked. They had been through a lot when their father left, and there wasn't much she could do about it; this felt like something she could control for them. Heading into marriage with a man who would rather give his children a set amount and see them manage it for themselves, this is a potential problem. Together they need to define how much money is appropriate to give kids, as well as how often and under what circumstances they will give it. If this changes anything for Taylor's children, she needs to be the one to communicate it.

If boundary issues like this arise during your conversation, pull back and slow down. A situation like this has many elements to it (parenting, money, family history, emotional security, etc.). Explore them together, but ultimately in a case like this, the biological parent needs to be the one making the changes with their children. This clearly communicates that the parent is in favor of and responsible for the change.

Money boundaries with a previous spouse. Let's consider another example that includes a former spouse. Victor is a successful businessman who regularly negotiates big financial deals. But ever since his divorce, he's catered to his ex-wife. In an effort to avoid conflict, he's agreed to give her more custody time and money than required by their divorce decree.

Then he married Felicia, a highly successful consultant who's not afraid of controversy. Victor and Felicia agreed that she would manage their finances. As soon as she looked at the books, she told Victor's ex that they were no longer going to give her extra money every month. Felicia was simply trying to help her new family be better stewards of their money, and she believed setting limits would help Victor's children learn to do the same. The decision sent waves crashing through the co-parenting relationship, Victor and Felicia's marriage, and

147

Felicia's relationship with her new stepchildren, who heard their mother's side of the story first.

The primary problem here was not whether Victor and Felicia should reduce paying for things, but that Felicia acted without first discussing the situation with Victor. Decide *together* how you will implement changes. Felicia should have seen that there would be strong feelings about finances on both sides and many layers to consider, and that there would likely be numerous conversations before they could agree on what to do. Whatever it took, finding unity would be well worth the effort because it would support their new, fragile marriage, their parenting and stepparenting, and the foundation of their home.[6]

Should your current spouse get into the negotiation mix? This is a common question for blended families who experience mid- to high-conflict co-parenting situations. (Low-conflict co-parents are generally able to talk through parenting and money issues.) Ideally, biological parents work together for their children, but sometimes they can't and the question arises whether a stepparent should step in and negotiate on behalf of their household.

Every situation is different, and that's why there's not one right answer to this question. Some couples intuitively know that involving the stepparent will make things worse. However, if the stepparent is willing to be involved and has the temperament of a mediator, give it a try. For example, if a stepdad and biological dad can have a productive discussion about between-home parenting and money matters, then the biological mom doesn't have to take part in the conversations if she doesn't want to. But she should most certainly talk with her husband before and after he speaks to her former husband.

Some stepfamilies find that this is a temporary arrangement that helps everyone through a challenging season, and others find it is a good long-term solution. In any case, it is important

148

for the stepparent couple to talk a great deal in advance of the negotiation so the stepparent can represent their household well when talking with the other home. Once the conversation with the other home begins, the stepparent should not make any commitments before talking again with their spouse in private unless they are confident the biological parent will be okay with the decision.

Between-Home Communication Strategies That Help

When it comes to negotiations with a former partner, sometimes the outcome of a money or boundary conversation depends largely on how you start it. Having a business mentality in your exchanges can be helpful.[7]

Open with an invitation, not a demand. Instead of saying, "I need more money today to cover this," say, "Ella's travel team is adding games, and they're farther away. It's getting expensive. Could we meet to discuss her plans?" You've had time to consider the situation and arrive at the conclusion that more financial support is required; give the other person the chance to do the same. If you just declare what needs to happen, you can create a control issue. Give the co-parent a chance to think about it and process the information. At that point, a collaborative decision to contribute money is more likely.

Open with a question. "Dillon wants a tutor. How do you feel about that?" Starting the conversation like this respects the other parent's opinions and gives them a chance to process the situation. Again, you've had a chance to do that, so make sure they get to as well.

Show gratitude. Whenever possible, begin the conversation with gratefulness for what your co-parent has already done before discussing additional expenses. "I appreciate you paying for the band fee and instrument rental. I've paid for the uniform and competition travel costs as agreed. But now the school is asking we pay for the hotel at the competition." Asking for more without acknowledging what both parties have already done feels cold and is likely to make your co-parent feel taken for granted. Keeping your heart appreciative makes openness from them more likely.

"You go first. What do you think is fair?" Especially if there is friction between you, this approach changes the dynamic from one of you trying to be in control of the solution ("Here's what should happen") to one where the co-parent can take the lead and be responsible for finding what's fair. Of course, there's no guarantee their opinion will match yours, but it might at least shift the climate of the dialogue away from power and control to collaboration.

Know your triggers. It's vital you know what your personal hot buttons are, why you react the way you do with a co-parent, and how you can regulate your emotions in the midst of tension. Divorces and nonmarital breakups tempt people into viewing the other person as the bad guy and themselves as the victim. This false narrative can leave you blind to any contributions you may bring to ongoing conflict; it's easy to blame the other person and focus on their faults and totally miss your own. Managing money with former spouses starts when you look closely in the mirror, know what sets you off, and then manage yourself well.[8]

Getting Started

The Growth Activity questions below will get you started building a simple, verbal Togetherness Agreement. There isn't space in this book to explore all the topics you might need to discuss or the various financial tools and strategies available; you can explore *The Smart Stepfamily Guide to Financial Planning* or consult with a CFP (Certified Financial Planner) or estate attorney for a thorough discussion of merging properties, managing a business, insurance and retirement plans, legal issues, boundaries with adult children, and more. But for now, let the Activity get you started. Identify any emotionally charged issues for your family, affirm your commitment to the permanency of your marriage, and begin exploring how you will provide for each other and your children.

ACTIVITY INSTRUCTIONS

As a couple, first discuss some general subjects to explore your attitudes about money. Then you'll address some logistics.

1. State aloud your overall goal as it relates to utilizing money as a tool to care for your spouse, children, and stepchildren. What would you like to see happen as you walk out your marriage together? What would you like to see happen financially when one of you dies? Would you like to pursue creating a formal Togetherness Agreement?

2. Once married, how do you envision merging your assets and debt? Are there things you'd like to keep separate? What implications does this have for daily money management, paying bills, and caring for the household and children?

3. Under what circumstances can one of you spend money on, or give money to, children without the other knowing about it?

4. Some stepparents feel confused by the ambiguity of being responsible to care for stepchildren but not always being included in financial decisions that affect them (or

151

their biological children). It's also confusing if they are expected to financially support stepchildren but then are left out of parenting decisions that affect everyone. How might this be a factor in your marriage?

5. What spending habits of the other make you a little nervous? What habits do you appreciate?

6. How important to you is tithing to your place of worship and doing good works in the community?

7. What below-the-surface issues has this chapter surfaced for you? Make a list of emotionally charged financial matters.

Now discuss some practicalities of money management.

1. Write down everything you own and owe (assets and debts). Assets include bank accounts, retirement accounts, investments, real estate, personal property, vehicles, insurance, pensions, etc. Debts include home mortgage, vehicle loans, credit card balances, personal or consumer loans, unpaid income tax, and any other bills or debts that are not paid off monthly. Review your insurance and investment documents together.

2. Create a general plan for day-to-day and monthly expenses. Walk through a typical month as a good case study.

   a. Daily money management logistics: How do we anticipate managing day-to-day expenses, deposits, and accounting?

   b. How many bank accounts will we have?

   • Who has control and access to the funds? Who can use a debit card (or write checks), make deposits, or transfer money into or out of each account?

Who will be responsible for paying bills from and managing a joint account?

- Who gets each account in the event of a death?
- How transparent are the financial transactions? Even if your spouse is not named on an account, should you provide some way for them to see what's going on with it, through paper statements or online access?

c. Health, auto, and home insurance.

d. Parenting: Discuss, for example, how you have handled giving children money in the past and what you will do once your families merge.

e. What is your philosophy about saving for emergencies?

3. Begin estate planning. What are your general thoughts about these subjects?

a. Wills? What happens if one of you dies?

b. Investments and retirement savings?

c. Insurance beneficiaries?

d. Paying for your cars, college, and computers (devices)?

e. Social security?

f. Family business?

g. Do you expect to receive an inheritance at some point?

4. Once you agree to a general plan, how much of it do you think you should communicate to your children or

---

To learn more, *The Smart Stepfamily Guide to Financial Planning* discusses updating beneficiary designations, managing debt, investments, real estate, and businesses or closely held corporations, saving for college, end-of-life disability and health-care wishes, and more.

extended family? When would you like to communicate this?

a. Keep in mind that adult children often appreciate being told of any significant estate changes before the wedding—and need to hear it from their biological parent (with the new spouse present as well).

b. Older children and teens should be told about logistical changes that impact their daily lives and expectations.

TRY THIS

There are many creative financial tools that can help blended family couples provide for one another and their children. You don't have to choose between your spouse and your children. For a thorough examination of the dynamics related to money and blended families, read my book *The Smart Stepfamily Guide to Financial Planning* (co-authored with Greg Pettys and David Edwards). In addition, you can consult with a Certified Financial Planner (CFP) or estate attorney. For more, visit https://edwardsgroupllc.lpages.co/blended-family-finances.

10

TILL DEATH DO US PART

As I write this chapter, the world is in a pandemic. It's May 2021 and we're beginning to see a little light at the end of the tunnel, but we're still not sure if it's a train barreling down upon us.

In case you missed it, the coronavirus pandemic was a global pandemic of coronavirus disease 2019 (COVID-19). The outbreak was first identified in December 2019 in Wuhan, China. The World Health Organization declared the outbreak a public health emergency in January 2020 and a pandemic in March.[1] As of May 2021, more than 165 million cases of COVID-19 were confirmed worldwide, with 3.4 million people dying from the virus.[2]

I remember when I first heard about the pandemic. I must admit, I didn't think it would travel from China to the U.S. so quickly, and even then, I didn't think it would last long. And no one I spoke to thought it would either. But it did. The pandemic's impact was far-reaching, touching not just the health of millions, but the economy, political climate, work environment, travel, educational system, religious practice—our complete way of life.

A lot of us experienced a kind of shock initially once work and school began to shut down. And a kind of denial. "It can't be that bad," we said. "This will pass soon." But before long, the reality of the situation settled in and we began to adjust.

The experts told us we needed to socially distance. Work from home. Do school from home. And don't go out unless you absolutely need to. Essentially, we were told to pull back to the safety of home and be around the people we trusted most.

Social distancing and staying close to home required many adjustments on our part. Single people quickly found themselves working at home, eating at home, and existing alone. (Thank God for video calls and conferencing that kept us connected at least in some way with others.) Couples and families quickly found themselves schooling from home, working from home, and confined at home, while some children found themselves unable to be with a parent who lived in another home. (Again, thank God for video conferencing!) Parents had to figure out how to help their children do school online and work a full day, and children had to cope with not seeing their friends or having a social life. My youngest son, Brennan, had to come home from college mid-semester and do online school from our home. Boy, was he depressed! My wife and I had to deal with an angry son who invaded our pleasant little empty nest. Boy, were we depressed! Adjustments like this were happening by the thousands in real time while people were getting sick and losing their jobs. At first, it was sort of like a staycation, but then it got old . . . fast!

Couples had to regroup and figure out how they would manage their jobs, the kids, and school. Families had to learn how to share the computer, the Wi-Fi bandwidth, and the living room (I mean, the office/school room). Businesses adapted to employees working at home almost overnight. And professional sports creatively found solutions to allow the game to go on. Did this bring about frustration, irritation, inefficiency, confusion, and discouragement? You bet! And as a result, some people didn't cope well and crashed. Just a few months into the pandemic, news reports suggested that liquor sales, online gambling, and child abuse and domestic violence were up while online dating activity went down. Websites designed to facilitate affairs had increased views, and porn sites saw double-digit growth.[3]

On the other hand, others did cope well. Despite the anxiety and ambiguity caused by the pandemic, communication, flexibility, and the willingness to negotiate the new normal were the skills of the resilient. *We took a breath. Held God's hand. Faced reality. Pressed in. Managed to cope. And most of us made it through.*

The next challenge was about reopening (returning to work, restaurants, and social gatherings). Some said it should come sooner, others later, some slowly, others quickly. Social media wars and political posturing exacerbated this debate. Despite the bluster, one message was clearly communicated: To open wisely, wear a mask and remain six feet away. But putting that into action turned out to be challenging. What, exactly, is the definition of "six feet"? To some it meant an arm's length and behind a Plexiglass window. To others, it meant ten feet apart with you wearing a double-mask and they a hazmat suit. Still to others it meant "back to normal" with no distance and no mask. Clearly the process for reopening wasn't clear at all.

Again, there was public debate, irritating exchanges in the grocery store, and family arguments over if, when, and where into society people might go. I was asked to write an article for *U.S. News and World Report* on co-parenting in the midst of what I called the COVID Crazies. The central question they wanted me to discuss was what co-parents should do if they disagreed about releasing children into social situations. What one household decided would certainly impact everyone in both homes, but what if you disagreed on the definition of "six feet"?[4]

While all of this was going on, the medical community feverishly sought to create a vaccine. The world watched and waited. Reports of their progress carried hope forward even though we were cautioned there would not be a quick fix. Again, *we took a breath. Held God's hand. Faced reality. Pressed in. Managed to cope. And we made it through.*

Today, we have been forever changed by the pandemic. You or someone close to you may have been impacted by a death. Before the pandemic, my father was fairly healthy and living in an assisted living environment, but months of little physical activity and isolation (we could only visit him through video chat) escalated his decline and hid a blood cancer no one knew anything about. He never recovered. Others have been recalibrated for the better, but all of us have been recalibrated, likely in many ways. For example, you may be more aware of how fragile life can be or find yourself slightly cautious about physical spacing when in public. It could be said that we haven't fully "recovered" to life as it was—or as we thought it was going to be. But I do think we've adapted. Grown. And can enjoy life as we've come to know it.

On Pandemics and Blended Families

What does all of this have to do with your plans to form a blended family? The journey of coping with the pandemic is metaphorical to the journey the average blended family travels in becoming family. There are several parallels in the narrative— and in the coping—that you can apply and hang on to.

Have you heard? Right now, you are just starting your family journey. After reading from this book the "early reports" of what may be ahead, you might be like some who reacted with great fear to China's initial reports of COVID-19 while others thought news stories were greatly exaggerated. Either way, I suspect as reality gets closer to home, you'll want to revisit some of the principles of this book or perhaps dive into one of the other books in the SMART STEPFAMILY SERIES (see the list in the front of this book for more titles) so you know how to cope.

Social distancing. If and when stepfamily realities affect your home (in the form of predictable stepfamily dynamics), perhaps you will be like some COVID-19 patients who were asymptomatic: The effects just weren't that difficult, and they barely felt a thing. Others, however, had significant symptoms and needed serious medical attention. Most blended families fall somewhere in the middle; they do experience some distress and "growing pains" as they begin the journey to bond, discover love, and build a family identity. And when they do, most will also experience "social distancing," that is, the natural drift of biological family members (insiders) back toward the people and places that are most safe. Every stepfamily has togetherness forces and distancing forces that create a push/pull effect. As the stress of merging increases, distancing forces become stronger.

Now hear this: Just as in the pandemic, while it makes sense on some level to stop pushing people together if the virus of ambiguity wants to pull them apart, you shouldn't stop altogether. As I said in chapter 8, during times of stress, biological parents should spend more exclusive time with their children in order to reassure them of their love and presence, but that doesn't mean total lockdown from the "outsiders" in the home. Rather, become more strategic—as we did in the pandemic—about when and how to spend time around others. Yes, you may feel strangely vulnerable when doing so, but that's necessary to overcome fear of the unknown and to form trust. Social distancing is not fun, and it doesn't represent the ultimate goal (you want togetherness in your family, not separateness), but when used for strategic purposes for a season, it can serve your family quite well.

Navigating the new normal. Just as the "stay at home" mandate required parents and children to figure out how to live, work, school, and play in the same space—without outside breaks, no less—you will have to navigate the new normal for your family. The Growth Activity of chapter 8 tried to help you anticipate new routines, schedules, and how you will share physical and emotional spaces once you combine every aspect of your lives, but no one can fully anticipate this. Reality will teach you what you really must figure out.

I can imagine, just as we did in the pandemic, that you will step on each other's toes a little. Not intentionally, of course, but you will. And each of those relational missteps will give you a chance to further define your expectations of each other, what you need, and the logistics of life. This is the live-and-learn aspect of stepfamily living that cannot be avoided. But more than that, I believe, it's a necessary evil that ultimately helps bring definition to ambiguous relationships and over time helps to create rituals and traditions that form family identity. The Activities of this book have already opened the door to important conversations between family members. Continue to walk through that conversation door when life invites you to, and together, you'll co-create a familyness filled with reward.

Reopening and "six feet away." Just as not everyone during the pandemic had the same definition of "six feet away," individual members of your family may have different expectations and definitions of emotional closeness and distance. Some are comfortable being two feet away with no masks, while others want a lot of distance and hazmat suits on. Navigating each person's level of comfort and willingness to close the gap over time takes intentional communication. When you connected with a co-worker or friend at church during the pandemic, you may have greeted them with a question meant to bring definition to how you would interact: "Are you shaking hands? I'd prefer we just bump elbows." Likewise, be proactive in your family communication in order to gauge the level of openness of one family member to another. Once you get a baseline understanding, periodically check in with them to see if anything has changed. Imagine a stepdad saying, "It's okay that there's some things you want to talk to your mom about and not me. I get that. Just know I'm cool with it when you are." Proactively defining the boundaries of your relationships lets everyone know where they stand and what to expect, and gives some clarity in the midst of much ambiguity as to how they will interact.

As in the pandemic, *remember to take a breath. Hold God's hand. Face reality. Press in. Learn to cope. And you'll make it through.*

Forever changed. The pandemic changed all of us (at least a little). The journey into familyness will also change you and your family forever. (Relationships—both a vertical one with God and horizontal ones with each other—tend to do that to us.) The pain of your past has changed you and the children as well. Those recalibrations come with you into this new recalibration. The trick is embracing all of it, learning from it, and being changed into who Love would have you become in order to thrive. I doubt you will fully recover the fantasies of blended family life you began with or had before picking up this book. But I do think, in the end, you will have adapted. Grown. And can enjoy life as you will come to know it.

Turning Points

Looking back at the pandemic, we can see how individuals and our society as a whole crossed various turning points in coping with the virus. Again and again, uncertainty and stress rose, and we learned to deal with them. Some turning points we managed pretty well; some we didn't. But I'm sure in both cases we didn't have any idea we were crossing a turning point. It's only in looking back that we can see that the moment mattered and things got better.

You too will one day look back at your journey to family-ness and notice turning points—moments whose significance was hidden from you while going through them, but which you can clearly see now. For example, the moment you persevered through family conflict. You resolved the argument, but what you didn't realize is that your perseverance and communication helped engender trust between family members. A child, for example, saw how committed you were to them, and their hearts softened. Or the time you realized you were trying too hard to get your children to love your spouse, so you took a half-step back; you didn't give up, you just stopped pushing them together and controlling their relationship and gave them a little space. Years later you discovered that "grace space" allowed them to relax around each other and figure out how to take one another, in their own time, into their hearts. Or the time you were totally surprised by your stepchild. You had come to accept that your stepchildren just didn't think of you as someone they could trust deeply; they liked you, even could say they loved you, but they really didn't interact with you as a mom or dad. That's why you were caught so off-guard when you realized one day that they trusted you far more than you knew. "When did that happen?" you asked yourself. "Why did that happen?"

Most of the time you will cross these turning points that quietly and gently move your family forward without noticing. Only time will reveal how significant they were. So trust that doing the best you can with God's guidance is more than enough to bring about good things for your family. But sometimes you will notice the turning point and rejoice.

Cody noticed one and just had to share it with me. He called this turning point his "miracle weekend." Cody and his wife, Kimberly, had been married for five years. She brought four children to the marriage, ages thirty-five, twenty-nine, twenty-three, and twenty-one, and five grandchildren. Not having any children of his own, he explained in his email, led him to settle into the idea that as a stepparent, he would not get to experience many of the special parental moments that most biological parents do.

Kimberly's two oldest were married with families of their own. When Cody came into their life, they were adults and working on starting their careers and families; they didn't have much time for him. The youngest and he got along well, but the third child, a girl, kept her distance from him. Audrey was a daddy's girl. She was generally respectful toward Cody, he explained, but never really let him in. Until the miracle weekend, that is.

"This past weekend," he said, "Audrey got married. She asked me to walk her from the bridal suite to the aisle, where her father and grandfather would give her away. I never thought in a million years that I would be able to walk a bride down the aisle and was so honored to be asked. This was enough of a miracle for me, but God was not through.

"I was also asked to pick up the cake on the day of the wedding. It was about an hour drive each way, so my wife's grandson asked if he could come. I wasn't sure what his dad—my stepson— would say, but he agreed without hesitation. My grandson and I had a great time, and he later told his dad how we had wonderful bonding time.

"Then, seconds before the walk down the aisle, my wife's youngest realized she forgot her earrings and asked me to put them in for her. She actually allowed me to touch her! That trust meant the world to me.

"And then, to cap it all off, a few hours after the reception, I looked at my phone for the first time all night and there was a text from the bride thanking me for being there, because when she saw me, she said, all her anxiety and fear went away. I had choked back tears all night, but now I wept happy tears at the miracles that God put in my life that day."

Now, listen to the next part. "I never tried to be their father and never will; I just show them love and support. But I will always call them my children."

He experienced the wedding weekend as a miracle, but it was his gentle and patient approach for years leading up to the wedding that allowed that moment to occur. His stepdaughter's wedding revealed the turning points that had been happening all along.

You usually won't know you crossed a turning point until many years later, but remember, it's faithful love in the midst of the ambiguity that makes the turning point happen in the first place.

Till Death Do Us Part

Hanging on to the pandemic metaphor will give you perspective and perhaps a framework for understanding where you are in the journey. It's helpful to bring a little clarity to the unknown. But your commitment "till death do us part" is even more important. If and when the going gets tough, it will be your promise that keeps your eyes looking up, not down at the mud through which you walk. Discouragement and disillusionment may enter your peripheral vision at some point, but keep your eyes focused on your promise, your goal of traveling this life together as husband and wife.

In jest I've often said that God's little joke on us is that we make a vow at the beginning of our marriage, and then life teaches us what we committed ourselves to. You have no idea what you're really saying when you declare "Till death do us part." You don't know what sacrifices you'll have to make on behalf of your marriage, what accommodations you'll have to adopt as a stepparent, what suffering you'll have to endure as parents, or what monumental joys you'll experience as leaders of your family. But if you *take a breath. Hold God's hand. Face reality. Press in. Learn to cope. And remain committed to your vow,* you'll make it through.

May God bless your journey together.

TRY THIS

Every journey needs a map and good friends that offer support. After your wedding:

1. Pick up a map: Read my book *The Smart Stepfamily: 7 Steps to a Healthy Family,* the most comprehensive faith-based resource on stepfamily living available, and my book coauthored with Dr. Gary Chapman, *Building Love Together in Blended Families: The 5 Love Languages and Becoming Stepfamily Smart,* a book that focuses on family bonding.

2. Find some friends: Join a small group or start one yourself. Multiple video curriculum, conferences, and virtual classes for individual couples or groups, including *The Smart Stepfamily,* can be found online at SmartStepfamilies.com.

Notes

1. Most couples forming blended families don't seek premarital preparation. Fewer than 25 percent of couples in a series of studies sought relationship or educational opportunities to discuss their upcoming blended family marriage. Less than half even read a book or magazine article about remarriage or stepparenting. See Lawrence Ganong and Marilyn Coleman, *Stepfamily Relationships: Development, Dynamics, and Interventions* (New York: Kluwer Academic, 2004), 68.

Chapter 1 Not Just a Couple

1. S. M. Stanley, P. R. Amato, C. A. Johnson, and H. J. Markman, "Premarital education, marital quality, and marital stability: Findings from a large, random household survey," *Journal of Family Psychology*, 20, 1 (2006): 117–26.

2. J. S. Carroll and W. J. Doherty, "Evaluating the effectiveness of premarital prevention programs: A meta-analytic review of outcome research," *Family Relations*, 52 (2003): 105–118.

3. Brian Higginbotham, Linda Skogrand, and Eliza Torres, "Stepfamily education: Perceived benefits for children," *Journal of Divorce and Remarriage*, 51 (2010): 36–49.

4. Leslie Baxter et al., "Empty ritual: Young-adult stepchildren's perceptions of the remarriage ceremony," *Journal of Social and Personal Relationships* 26, no. 4 (2009): 467–487.

5. Patricia Papernow, *Surviving and Thriving in Stepfamily Relationships: What Works and What Doesn't* (New York: Routledge, 2013), 67.

Chapter 2 Seeing Is Eye-Opening

1. Ron L. Deal, *Dating and the Single Parent* (Bloomington, MN: Bethany House Publishers, 2012), 20, 41.

2. Ron L. Deal, *Dating and the Single Parent*, 102.

Chapter 3 Helpful Expectations

1. Ron L. Deal, *The Smart Stepfamily: 7 Steps to a Healthy Family* (Bloomington, MN: Bethany House, 2014), 99.

2. Lauren Reitsema, *In Their Shoes: Helping Parents Better Understand and Connect with Children of Divorce* (Bloomington, MN: Bethany House, 2019), 146–147.

3. For more on this, see Ron L. Deal, *Placing Your Spouse in the Front Seat of Your Heart*, 2014, www.familylife.com/articles/topics/blended-family/remarriage/staying-married-remarriage/placing-your-spouse-in-the-front-seat-of-your-heart.

4. Ron L. Deal, *The Smart Stepfamily: 7 Steps to a Healthy Family*, 93.

5. S. M. Stanley, G. K. Rhoades, and F. D. Fincham, "Understanding romantic relationships among emerging adults: The significant roles of cohabitation and ambiguity," in F. D. Fincham and M. Cui (eds.), *Romantic Relationships in Emerging Adulthood* (Cambridge, England: Cambridge University Press, 2010), 234–251.

Chapter 4 Planning Your Wedding

1. Leslie Baxter et al., "Empty ritual," 467–487.

2. Leslie Baxter, et. al, "Empty ritual," 478.

3. Leslie Baxter, et al., "Empty ritual," 477.

4. Leslie Baxter, et al., "Empty ritual," 484.

Chapter 5 Co-Creating Familyness

1. Ron Deal, "The Name Game," www.smartstepfamilies.com/smart-help/learn/parenting-stepparenting/the-name-game-dissecting-the-emotional-significance-of-names.

2. Ron L. Deal, *Dating and the Single Parent*, 212.

3. You can learn more about the "no-threat message" in the books *The Smart Stepmom: Practical Steps to Help You Thrive* by Ron L. Deal and Laura Petherbridge, and *The Smart Stepdad: Steps to Help You Succeed* by Ron L. Deal.

4. For more, read "The Name Game: Dissecting the Emotional Significance of Names" by Ron Deal, found here: www.smartstepfamilies.com/name-game.

Chapter 6 Parenting Together

1. Ron L. Deal and David H. Olson, *The Smart Stepfamily Marriage: Keys to Success in the Blended Family* (Bloomington, MN: Bethany House, 2015), 102.

2. As reported in Lawrence Ganong and Marilyn Coleman, *Stepfamily Relationships: Development, Dynamics, and Interventions*, 2nd ed. (New York: Springer, 2017), 83.

3. Ron L. Deal and David H. Olson, *The Smart Stepfamily Marriage*, 106.

4. Adapted from Ron L. Deal, *The Smart Stepfamily: 7 Steps to a Healthy Family*, 145–148. Used by permission of Bethany House Publishers, a division of Baker Publishing Group.

5. Key 1 is adapted from *The Smart Stepfamily: 7 Steps to a Healthy Family* by Ron L. Deal, 176. Used by permission of Bethany House Publishers, a division of Baker Publishing Group.

6. Dr. Susan Gamach, "Parental status: A new construct describing adolescent perceptions of stepfathers" (PhD diss., University of British Columbia, 2000).

7. John and Emily Visher, *How to Win as a Stepfamily, 2nd ed.* (New York: Brunner/Mazel, 1982).

8. Personal communication, July 27, 2020.

9. James Bray, *Stepfamilies: Love, Marriage, and Parenting in the First Decade* (New York: Broadway Books, 1998).

10. Emily and John Visher, *How to Win as a Stepfamily*, 110–112.

11. Keys 2–4 are adapted from *The Smart Stepfamily Marriage* by Ron L. Deal and David H. Olson, 106–110. Used by permission of Bethany House Publishers, a division of Baker Publishing Group.

12. Ron L. Deal and David H. Olson, *The Smart Stepfamily Marriage*, 106.

13. Adapted from Ron L. Deal and David H. Olson, *The Smart Stepfamily Marriage*, 111–113.

14. You can learn more about this parenting strategy in *The Smart Stepdad: Steps to Help You Succeed* by Ron L. Deal, 128–130, and online at www.smartstepfamilies.com/catch-them.

Chapter 7 Creating a Shared Grief Journey

1. John Gottman with Joan Declaire, *Raising an Emotionally Intelligent Child: The Heart of Parenting* (New York: Simon & Schuster, 1998), 24.

2. Adapted from Ron L. Deal and Laura Petherbridge, *The Smart Stepmom: Practical Steps to Help You Thrive* (Bloomington, MN: Bethany House, 2011), 76–78.

3. Ron L. Deal, *The Smart Stepfamily: 7 Steps to a Healthy Family*, 244–245.

4. Ron L. Deal, *Dating and the Single Parent*, 216.

Chapter 8 Anticipating What Will Change

1. Karen S. Bonnell and Patricia L. Papernow, *The Stepfamily Handbook: From Dating, to Getting Serious, to Forming a "Blended Family"* (Kirkland, WA: KDP, 2019), 50–51.

Chapter 9 Merging Money and Your Family

1. As reported in Lawrence Ganong and Marilyn Coleman, *Stepfamily Relationships*, 83.

2. Ron L. Deal and David H. Olson, *The Smart Stepfamily Marriage: Keys to Success in the Blended Family*, 192.

3. Adapted from *The Smart Stepfamily Guide to Financial Planning: Money Management Before and After You Blend a Family* by Ron L. Deal, Greg S. Pettys, and David O. Edwards (2019, 23). Used by permission of Bethany House Publishers, a division of Baker Publishing Group.

4. Ron L. Deal, Greg S. Pettys, and David O. Edwards, *The Smart Stepfamily Guide to Financial Planning*, 52.

5. Adapted from *The Smart Stepfamily Guide to Financial Planning* by Ron L. Deal, Greg S. Pettys, and David O. Edwards, 33–34, 45.

6. Ron L. Deal, Greg S. Pettys, and David O. Edwards, *Setting Financial Boundaries in Blended Families*, www.familylife.com/articles/topics/blended -family/remarriage/staying-married-remarriage/setting-financial-boundaries -in-blended-families.

7. Adapted from "How to Discuss Money with an Ex," *Money*, November 19, 2013, http://time.com/money/2794912/how-to-discuss-money-with-an-ex.

8. Ron L. Deal, Greg S. Pettys, and David O. Edwards, "Guidelines for Discussing Finances With an Ex-spouse," FamilyLife, https://www.family-life.com/articles/topics/blended-family/stepparents/multiple-home-realities /guidelines-for-discussing-finances-with-an-ex-spouse.

Chapter 10 Till Death Do Us Part

1. "Statement on the second meeting of the International Health Regulations (2005) Emergency Committee regarding the outbreak of novel coronavirus (2019-nCoV)," World Health Organization (WHO), January 30, 2020, www.who.int/news/item/30-01-2020-statement-on-the-second-meeting-of -the-international-health-regulations-(2005)-emergency-committee-regarding-the-outbreak-of-novel-coronavirus-(2019-ncov).

2. "COVID-19 Dashboard by the Center for Systems Science and Engineering (CSSE) at Johns Hopkins University (JHU)," Johns Hopkins University & Medicine Coronavirus Resource Center, accessed May 20, 2021, https://coronavirus.jhu.edu/map.html.

3. See the following articles: Robby Berman, "How do people cope with the pandemic? Survey reveals worrying trends," Medical News Today, May 6, 2020, www.medicalnewstoday.com/articles/how-do-people-cope-with-the -pandemic-survey-reveals-worrying-trends; Kaye Quek and Meagan Tyler, "When staying home isn't safe: COVID-19, pornography and the pandemic of violence against women," ABC Religion and Ethics, April 7, 2020, www .abc.net.au/religion/coronavirus-pornography-and-the-pandemic-of-violence -against-wo/12131020; Newsdesk, "Studies show dramatic rise in online gambling during COVID-19 lockdowns," Inside Asian Gaming, April 9, 2020, www.asgam.com/index.php/2020/04/09/studies-show-dramatic-rise-in-online -gambling-during-covid-19-lockdowns.

4. See Ron L. Deal, "Better Safe Than Sorry: Co-Parenting in the Age of Social Distancing," *U.S. News and World Report*, April 24, 2020, https:// health.usnews.com/wellness/for-parents/articles/co-parenting-during-the -coronavirus-pandemic.

About the Author

Ron L. Deal is a marriage and family author, speaker, and therapist. He is founder of Smart Stepfamilies™, the director of FamilyLife Blended® (a division of FamilyLife®), and the author/co-author of numerous books, including *The Smart Stepfamily Marriage, The Smart Stepmom, The Smart Stepdad, Dating and the Single Parent, The Smart Stepfamily Guide to Financial Planning, Daily Encouragement for the Smart Stepfamily,* and the bestselling *The Smart Stepfamily* and *Building Love Together in Blended Families* with Dr. Gary Chapman. In addition, he is the consulting editor of the SMART STEPFAMILY SERIES and has published over a dozen videos and study resources and hundreds of magazine and online articles. His work has been quoted or referenced by many news outlets such as the *New York Times,* the *Wall Street Journal, Good Morning America, U.S. News & World Report,* and *USA Today.* Ron's popular books, podcast (*FamilyLife Blended*), conference events, social media presence, online classes, and one-minute radio feature (heard daily on hundreds of stations nationwide and online) make him the leading voice on blended families in the U.S. He is a licensed marriage and family therapist who frequently appears in the national media, and he conducts marriage and family seminars around the country and internationally. He and his wife, Nan, have three boys. To connect to all of Ron's resources, go to SmartStepfamilies.com.

More Resources for the Smart Stepfamily

Visit smartstepfamilies.com and familylife.com/blended for additional information.

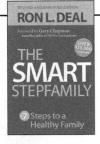

Providing practical, realistic solutions to the unique issues that stepfamilies face, Ron L. Deal helps remarried couples solve the everyday challenges of stepparenting and shares seven steps to raising a healthy family.

The Smart Stepfamily

This guide to financial planning for blended families offers help and encouragement as you plan your combined financial future while protecting your marriage in the process. You'll find tips on handling debt, bills, and child support from previous relationships and advice on planning for college expenses, retirement, and an inheritance.

The Smart Stepfamily Guide to Financial Planning

BETHANYHOUSE

 Stay up to date on your favorite books and authors with our free e-newsletters. Sign up today at bethanyhouse.com.

 facebook.com/BHPnonfiction

@bethany_house

 @bethany_house_nonfiction

You May Also Like . . .

Stepfamily experts Ron L. Deal and Laura Petherbridge show you how to survive and thrive as a stepmom, including how to be a positive influence on the children and how to deal with conflict, as well as practical issues like dealing with holidays and between-home communication.

The Smart Stepmom

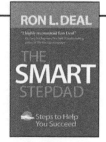

Here is the survival guide every stepfather needs to succeed. Ron L. Deal equips stepdads everywhere with advice on everything—from how to connect with your stepchildren to handling tricky issues such as discipline and dealing with your wife's ex.

The Smart Stepdad

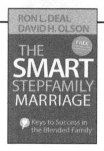

Leading blended family authority Ron Deal and marriage and family expert David Olson show you how to build on your relationship strengths and improve your weaknesses. Whether you're dating, engaged, a young stepfamily, or an empty-nest couple, *The Smart Stepfamily Marriage* gives you the tools you need at any stage to create a remarriage that will last.

The Smart Stepfamily Marriage

CPSIA information can be obtained
at www.ICGtesting.com
Printed in the USA
LVHW081742160322
713622LV00004B/171